The Exceptional Child
in the Family

HELPING PARENTS OF EXCEPTIONAL CHILDREN

By

Alan O. Ross, Ph.D.

Chief Psychologist,
Pittsburgh Child Guidance Center;
Adjunct Professor of Psychology,
University of Pittsburgh

Grune & Stratton   New York · London

By the same author:

The Practice of Clinical Child Psychology

Contents

iii

Preface

THE FAMILY in its varied and changing interactions is the training ground where the child develops his personality and learns to relate to his environment. Family relationships provide the model for his relations to the world and the attitudes the family holds toward him form the basis for the child's attitudes toward himself. In all this parents play a crucial role whether the child is *normal* or *exceptional*. The principles of family interaction are the same in both instances, the conditions differ. In the case of the exceptional child, whose physical or mental state is in some way different from the expected norm, an extra factor is introduced into the parent-child relationship which may disrupt family interaction and be detrimental to the personality development of the child.

Parents of exceptional children have exceptional demands placed upon them. All parents must deal with developmental and interpersonal crises but parents of an exceptional child must deal not only with these but also with the complications introduced by the reality of the child's exceptional condition. The anticipations parents bring to the task of child rearing are largely based on the image of the "normal" child because that is the model most widely encountered and the condition most parents themselves experienced during their childhood. When the child does not conform to this image, the task of child rearing is made more difficult because the parents must adapt their expectations and behavior to the exceptional state of their child.

Just as the parents' reality includes the child's condition, so does the child's reality include his own exceptional state. The difficulty for the parents stems from the fact that at the same time as they themselves are learning to adapt their expectations in order to cope with an exceptional reality, they must also be able to help the child cope with his condition.

Parents of exceptional children must thus learn to deal with situations and conditions which parents of other children never encounter and this learning is not easy. The necessary adaptations can, however, be learned, particularly if the parents are helped by all those whose special skills and training bring them into professional contact with the family. Where parents fail to learn to cope with their child's exceptional condition and where professional people fail to give them the help to which they are entitled, the result is often unhappiness, conflict and emotional disturbance for parents and child alike.

This book is based on the conviction that this unhappiness, conflict

vii

and emotional disturbance can be avoided if every professional person who interacts with the parents around their child helps them adapt to their special situation. It is the responsibility of the helping professions, from the clinician who makes the original diagnosis to the teacher who has the child in class, to assist the parents in their task of helping their child; to enable them to avoid distorting and complicating the child's reality so that he can solve the developmental tasks, including their exceptional aspects, in the most adaptive manner possible within the society in which he lives.

Helping parents of exceptional children is largely a matter of understanding and professional skill. No book can teach professional skill; this can only be acquired through supervised training and experience. A book can, however, contribute to better understanding of family interaction around an exceptional child and it is to that end that the present work addresses itself.

The reader is warned that he will be disappointed if he turns to this book in search of answers to such questions as: Should a mentally ill child be kept at home? Should a physically handicapped child go to a regular or a special school? Should a gifted child be given double promotion? Should parents whose first-born is mentally retarded plan to have additional children? A family is a dynamic system of interacting individual personalities who live together in a complex and changing society. This makes each situation different from the next and while it is possible to outline some general principles, it is impossible to give specific prescriptions which would be suitable for every case. What might be the best plan for one family could be the worst possible solution for another, even though their situations appear to be the same on the surface. While specific answers to specific questions will thus not be found in these pages, they do contain guidelines to the understanding of families which, when applied, should help in working out the appropriate answers with and for each family in each situation.

A glance at the table of contents will reveal that this book does not contain separate discussions of each exceptional state one might encounter in a child. There are no chapters on the blind, the deaf, the epileptic, or the speech defective child because the book is based on the premise that there are certain general principles which apply to understanding and helping a family, no matter what the unusual condition of the child. Once the principles of personality dynamics, family interaction, and interviewing and of the roles of such reactions as anxiety, hostility, or guilt have been presented, little is gained by reiterating these principles in discussions of the various conditions to which they might be applied.

This text was written for the advanced student and practitioner in such professions as special education, counseling, psychology, social work, guidance, neurology, pediatrics, orthopedics, ophthalmology, general medicine, nursing, and psychiatry. Because these many different professions come into contact with parents of exceptional children and are thus in a position to help, no specialized terms of any one profession has been used unless its meaning was first defined or made clear by the context. Thus, while it was not specifically written for them, the parents of exceptional children themselves might find this book a useful supplement to their contacts with the helping professions.

Although this work carries no prefatory inscription in the place usually reserved for the author's personal sentiments, it is nonetheless gratefully dedicated to my parents who succeeded—for many years against heavy odds—to create and maintain a family environment which gave their children a solid basis for satisfied and productive lives.

Much of what I know about working with parents of exceptional children I have learned from social workers. To them, collectively, I owe a debt of gratitude but to one in particular who has contributed not only knowledge, thoughts, and ideas but also stimulation, support, and intrinsic rewards to the development of this book—my wife, Ilse Wallis Ross—I owe far more than I need here express.

Others who helped make this book possible and whom I wish to thank are Mr. S. F. Kurzer, who suggested the topic, Mrs. Katharine Zimmerman, whose diligent and devoted secretarial services made life so much easier for me, and Miss Janet Taksa, who with studious and mature judgment, assisted in the preparation of Chapter 10.

Permission to quote from their publications was graciously granted by the following:

American Association on Mental Deficiency
American Medical Association
American Journal of Orthopsychiatry
American Psychological Association
Basic Books, Inc.
Child Development Publications
Child Study Association of America
Children's Bureau
Council for Exceptional Children
Virginia C. Crandall
Bernice T. Eiduson
Family Service Association of America

Bernard Farber
Free Press of Glencoe
Genetic Psychology Monographs
William Goldfarb
Dr. Ernest Harms
Harper & Row, Inc.
Holt, Rinehart & Winston, Inc.
International Universities Press
Journal of Child Psychiatry
Samuel R. Laycock
Marriage and Family Living
Elsa A. Miller
National Society for Crippled Children and Adults
Harold Plotsky
Prentice-Hall
Psychiatry
M. D. Schechter
William H. Sewell
Emily A. Smith
Social Casework
Charles C Thomas
University of Chicago Press
John Wiley & Sons, Inc.
The Woods School
Marvin Zuckerman

I.

The Dynamics of Family Interaction

INTRODUCTION

THE TERM *exceptional child* has implications of semantic, historical, and social nature which we shall later want to explore but for the present it is necessary to state a working definition of the term so that a discussion of the exceptional child in his family can be placed in the proper perspective.

For our purposes the exceptional child is the child whose intellectual, physical, or social condition is seen by his environment as deviating from that of the average or expected child to such an extent as to call for modifications in the usual child-rearing or educational practices because they are necessary or thought to be necessary. This definition thus includes those children whose condition differs in some critical fashion from the condition his parents expected before the child was born. It is immaterial whether the condition realistically calls for modifications in child rearing or educational practices as long as the parents' perception of the condition affects their attitudes and behavior.

As we shall see, the parent-child unit is so closely interrelated that anything that affects the child affects the parents and anything that affects the parents affects the child. For this reason it does not matter whether an exceptional state exists in the child's condition or in the parents' perception. In either case the child's experiences will be affected. We are then, in a sense, not talking about exceptional children but about exceptional families and hope to show how these families can be helped by competent parent counseling.

Before one can hope to understand and through such understanding help the family of the exceptional child it is necessary to gain some insight into the dynamics of family interaction. Just as it has been said that the exceptional child is, first of all, a child, so the family of the exceptional child is, first of all, a family. For this reason we shall need to review some of the relevant recent literature on parent-child relationship and family interaction. We shall try to outline some of the principles of family interaction and parent-child relations, for these principles are the same whether the child in the family is "normal" or "exceptional," it is only the conditions which differ. In the case of the

1

exceptional child an extra factor is introduced into the family interaction and this factor is the particular exceptional condition of the child. Parents in general must cope with a series of developmental crises; parents of an exceptional child must deal not only with these, but also with the complications introduced by the child's exceptional condition. Children in general must learn to cope with reality in a manner considered adaptive by their social environment; exceptional children must learn this coping but their reality includes the exceptional aspects of their own condition. The parents of an exceptional child must thus help the child cope with these aspects at the same time as they themselves must learn to cope with the reality presented by the exceptional features they perceive in their child.

Every society, if it is to continue to function, must have built into its organization a way to socialize its young. McCandless (1961) has suggested that adequate socialization may well be man's most important single accomplishment. In most, if not all societies, the task of socialization is assigned to the family so that it can be said that one of the most important functions the family renders for society is the socialization of its young. Whiting and Child (1953) have postulated that there are five areas in which socialization takes place. These are the areas of feeding and weaning, elimination training, sex training, aggression training, and dependency training. In each of these five areas of socialization the outcome is a function of the interaction between the child and his social environment. The child brings to this interaction his own physiologic needs and constitutional reaction potential. The individuals in his social environment who, in the early stages, are primarily his parents and more especially the mother, contribute to the interaction not only their own physiologic needs and reaction patterns but also a complex array of attitudes and behavior which they themselves have acquired through learning in the course of their development and experience.

We know from studies such as those of Irwin (1930) and Shirley (1933) that neonates differ in general activity level and responsiveness to emotional stimulation. As this writer has pointed out elsewhere (Ross, 1959) any particular mother will react in a different manner to a child with a high activity level than to a child with a low activity level. The mother's reaction must be viewed as the product of her own personality development which, in turn, resulted from an interaction of constitutional and environmental factors. Keeping this formulation in mind should help clarify that a mother who reacts to her child in a manner which is not conducive to the child's healthy emotional development cannot be blamed for the end result of her interaction with the child. Her contribution to this interaction may, at least in part, have caused the child's emotional state but being a causal agent is not the same as being morally responsible.

In discussing mother-child interaction one must always keep in mind that this interaction takes place in the social matrix of the family of which mother and child are only one unit. If, as Brim (1957) has suggested, the mother-child relation is conceived as a separate social system embedded in the more general system of the family, then whatever happens within any one of these sub-systems will affect not only the other sub-systems but also the system as a whole. Conversely, whatever affects the system of the family as a whole will in turn result in repercussions in any one of the sub-systems. From this point of view, the individual child cannot be viewed in isolation; he must be seen in the context of the family system. Even though it is necessary for purposes of exposition to speak of one sub-system at a time, it should be remembered that this is an artificial isolation. When the child acts and the mother reacts, the child will at the same time react to the mother's reaction and this reverberating interaction will have its influence on the father who will, on his part, react and thus influence the mother-child relations. Only an animated cartoon or a moving model could adequately represent the dynamic interaction of a complex system like a family. On the printed page we must be satisfied with viewing one frame of the motion picture at a time, constantly recalling that we are looking at an artificially isolated part of a moving whole.

Vogel and Bell (1960) recently phrased this issue succinctly when they wrote,

> The notion that the family is in large part responsible for the emotional health of the child is a compelling one in contemporary behavioral science. By and large, however, the research has focused largely on the mother-child relationship, and the independent variable by which the mother-child relationship and the child-rearing practices are usually explained is the personality and developmental history of the mother. While in clinical practice there is some awareness of family dynamics, in the literature, the family has largely been treated simply as a collection of personalities, and the child's personality development has been seen almost exclusively as a direct result of the separate personalities of his parents. Rarely is the interaction of parents treated as a signicant independent variable influencing childhood development. Even when broader cultural patterns have been considered, childhood development has been related to child-rearing practices and socialization into the culture, with little consideration of the family as a mediating unit. (p. 382 f.).

Because of the recognized importance of the parents in the socialization experiences of the child and because it is thought that these experiences will have major import for the development of the child's personality, a great many investigators have addressed themselves to questions in the area of parent-child relationships. The parents' contribution to this interaction should, ideally, be studied by direct observations of parental child-rearing behavior. A less direct method of study involves the use of the parents' verbal description of their own behavior and still another approach deals with the assessment of parental attitudes.

In the following pages the dynamics of family interaction are presented in an organization which roughly follows these major approaches to family study. Beginning with a discussion of the family as a social system, a view which is largely the contribution of sociology, we turn to a presentation of some of the relations of childhood experiences and personality formation. Inasmuch as childhood experiences are to a great extent dependent on parental attitudes and these, in turn, are related to parental behavior, these parent variables and their effect on child adjustment will be discussed before a presentation of the dynamic interaction between parental and child behavior concludes the chapter.

THE FAMILY AS A SOCIAL SYSTEM

Social psychologists have for some time been interested in the study of small group interaction (e.g. Lewin, 1943) and the family can readily be seen as a small group whose processes should be accessible to study by the techniques of social psychologists and sociologists. Parsons and Bales (1955) have analyzed family interaction from such a point of view and more recently Bell and Vogel (1960) spoke of the family as an interdependent social system which may be treated either as a whole, undifferentiated system or as a system composed of several sub-systems, examples of which are the husband-wife, parent-child, and sibling systems.

The interdependence of family members is particularly great in the modern urban environment where the nuclear family is isolated from other sectors of the kinship system (Parsons & Fox, 1960), resulting in a situation where anything that affects one member has either a direct or an indirect effect on every other member. The perceived condition of the exceptional child, be he deficient or superior, affects not only the mother, the father and the siblings, but the reactions of each of these will, in turn, have their effect on each of the others, including the child himself.

The family as a social system is thus an organization of individuals who stand in a dynamic interchange with one another and who, as a system, stand in similar interchange with the environment. That is to say that the family is not a closed system, existing in isolation, but an open system which maintains relationships with other such systems in the total transactional field (Bell & Vogel, 1960).

The family plays a crucial role in the personality formation, status conferral, and tension management of its members; Bell and Vogel (1960) believe that this is one of the functions of the family.

> Because of the strengths of family ties, there are very strong pressures operating to prevent group disintegration . . . The family appears to have a certain level of tension tolerance. When tensions become so severe as to threaten the group with disintegration, there is often a sudden rallying of forces to unite the family by dealing with the threat to the family's solidarity. These family "coping mechanisms" operate in ways very similar to individual personality mechanisms. The same phenomenon occurs not only in response to crises such as illness or disaster or separation by war, but to all action by people outside the family that threatens to disrupt the family system (*ibid.*, p. 26).

The personality of the child develops to a considerable extent within the matrix of the family system and is maintained by this family system. Personality can, in turn, be viewed as a system in its own right; a system of activities, perceptions, motivations, etc., which has some internal cohesion as well as a tendency to have and maintain boundaries (*ibid.*). There would seem to be some relationship between personality, as a system, and the family, as a system, and it is heuristically useful to conceive of the personality of the child as a system in interchange with the family system whereby whatever happens to one invariably has its effects upon the equilibrium of the other.

The dynamic interaction between a child's exceptional condition, the family system and the child's personality system was clearly illustrated in a paper by Freedman *et al.* (1957) which shows how the family's failure to establish role expectations for the child appropriate to his limitations can complicate a physical disorder by superimposing a psychological disorder.

The condition described by Freedman and his co-workers (1957) is a relatively rare chronic disease, *familial dysautonomia*. Careful and extensive study of fourteen children with this disease revealed that emotional disturbance was evident in every case. The investigators interpreted the dynamics of the emotional disturbance in terms of a vicious circle, taking its point of departure in a congenital brain abnormality which gives rise to an instability in the autonomic nervous system. The behavior of the child is thus characterized by impulsivity and overreaction to emotional stimuli and his restlessness, anxiety and frequent explosive outbursts arouse anxiety and consequent resentment and guilt in his parents (p. 101). In order to cope with their own emotional responses to the situation, the parents, in turn, make concessions and compromises in their dealings with the child, attempting to appease him by excessive permissiveness and giving in to his wishes and whims. Reacting to this behavior on the part of his parents, the child in turn, continues to manipulate them but becomes distressed when confronted with the inconsistencies and instabilities in the external world, particularly his parents' manifest helplessness in the situation. He frantically strives to attain equilibrium by further manipulating his parents, only to increase his own anxiety and insecurity (p. 102). The child's reactive anxiety further upsets his autonomic balance so that the cycle may be repeated indefinitely until it is temporarily interrupted by some physical crisis such as vomiting.

Freedman and his colleagues speculate about the role of the parents in this interaction. They write,

> Many parents but not all, showed reactions that could not wholly be ascribed to the illness of the child. In studies of brain damaged children it has been a general impression that where parents are integrated, realistic and accepting, the behavioral distress is minimal. We cannot say at the present moment how much of the disturbance seen in the parents of dysautonomia victims preceded the birth of the patient, although this seems to have occurred fairly frequently. One can pose a very important question as to how sick these children would be if their parents were less anxious and more stable. (*ibid., p.* 102).

The child afflicted with this disorder develops a self-image that is characterized by doubts about his own goodness, worth, and acceptance by others.

> This arises through perceiving three negative qualities about his difference from normal children: 1) that his disabilities are unique, 2) that his disabilities cause his parents trouble and disappointment, and 3) that he does not have adequate control of his own body. As a result the dysautonomic patient develops a relationship to people and things about him which reflects his negative self-image and his need to establish a secure place and static order in his world. (*ibid.,* p. 102 f.).

Freedman and his collaborators go on to discuss various therapeutic approaches. The therapist can try to minimize disturbing stimuli by striving for a stable, supporting home situation. This, however, is difficult because of the seriousness of the child's illness and the resulting distress of the parents. Parent groups can be used to encourage stability through the sharing of experiences and the consequent reduction of anxiety. One can set up rigid routines in which the child's entire day is scheduled, thus developing a useful and constructive pattern which minimizes unpredictable change. Since such a routine is established by an outsider, the parents experience less anxiety and guilt about enforcing it. It seems desirable to follow the same routinization in school and other settings where the child spends his days and in particularly difficult situations the child may have to be removed from the conflict of the home situation by placing him in a structured, patterned and impersonal but supportive hospital setting. In one case reported by these investigators the child who had previously suffered fainting spells in connection with repeated crises completely lost this symptom by hospitalization alone. It thus appears that any method which will disrupt the vicious cycle of interaction tends to have salutory effects on the child's personality integration.

Roles, role complementarity and role discrepancy. When the nuclear family is seen as a social system within which the initial and crucial phases of the child's socialization take place, the interaction of family members can be fruitfully analyzed in terms of the sociologic concept of social role (Ackerman, 1958; Parsons & Bales, 1955). From this point of view the family is a system of roles. In a highly perceptive discussion of role conflict within the family Spiegel (1957) uses this frame of reference to describe the behavior of any one family member in terms of his role in transaction with a role partner or partners.

The definition of a role, as formulated by Spiegel (1957, p. 3), is a goal-directed pattern or sequence of acts tailored by the cultural process for the transactions a person may carry out in his social group or situation. The interrelation of roles is crucial for no role exists in isolation; it is always patterned to fit the complementary or reciprocal role of a role partner. As long as the role each family member occupies is complementary with and conforms to the role expectations other members have for him, the family lives in a dynamic equilibrium. As soon as a discrepancy occurs, however—that is, when two or more family members have conflicting or incompatible notions on how to play their reciprocal roles—complementarity fails and the role system moves toward disequilibrium. Such disequilibrium is experienced by the family members in the form of tension, anxiety, hostility, or self-consciousness and individuals will try to deal with these reactions in a variety of ways.

Usually these individual coping mechanisms result in further role discrepancies and if the process continues without improvement it will end in the disruption of the system. Spiegel *(ibid.)* lists five causes for failure of complementarity in role systems within the family but only three of these (cognitive, allocative and goal discrepancy) are of relevance to our discussion.

Cognitive discrepancy describes the situation where one or more individuals involved in the role system do not know, or are not sufficiently familiar with, the roles required of them by the others' expectations. Cognitive discrepancy would characterize a situation where a child who has acquired a physical handicap has not yet learned his new role in the family system.

There are four principal ways in which an individual can acquire his social role and in each case he can accept the role thus allocated to him, or he can refuse it. Some roles are *ascribed,* that is, universally expected, such as age and sex roles. Other roles, such as occupation, have to be *achieved;* others are *adopted.* Adopted roles are chiefly informal in character as when, for example, the mother of a handicapped child adopts the role of martyr. Complementarity of roles requires, however, that in doing so, she has to *assign* to some other family member the role of "torturer," and if the other refuses to play this role, a state of disequilibrium will result. Still another mode of role allocation is *assumption,* where the role has playful qualities. Such roles are taken in make-believe but it is important that all concerned are aware of the playful character of the assumed role.

Allocative discrepancy will result when the individual refuses the role allocated to him or when others fail to complement his role. When the mother of a handicapped child adopts the role of protector, but the child fails to fall into the assigned role of the protected, the resulting allocative discrepancy will create tension and anxiety throughout the family role system.

Goal discrepancy is a closely related phenomenon. It exists when the goal of one family member is to obtain some form of gratification from another but the other fails to meet the demand because his goal is related to withholding or because he is for some reason unable to gratify the demand. Goals may also be related to an individual's defenses, as in the case of the child who, because he needs to test the mother's continuing love after the birth of a sibling, increases his demands for concrete demonstrations of maternal affection.

For those interested in the handicapped child and his effect on family interaction, goal discrepancy is particularly relevant. Spiegel (1957)

points out that one source of discrepancy in goals is biologically determined, rather than of motivational origin. Illness, lack of maturation or
intellectual deficiency are accompanied by a *restricted capacity for goal
attainment*. Such biological limitations may produce disequilibrium when
the parent is unable to change his level of expectancy regarding goals
to be attained by the child. Spiegel *(ibid.)* gives the example of the
parent who cannot accommodate to and thus accept the limited intelligence of his child. In such a situation, one of the role partners (the
child) has disappointed the parental role expectations for him. He is
biologically unable to meet the need for role complementarity and the
resulting disequilibrium leads to tension, anxiety, hostility, or self-
consciousness on the part of the family members.

Because the equilibrium which is brought about by complementarity
of roles is a rewarding state of affairs, disequilibrium serves to motivate
family members to attempt some form of resolution of the existing role
discrepancies. The rewarding nature of equilibrium stems from the fact
that with roles clearly defined and mutually agreed upon, the individual
is spared the necessity of almost constant decision-making about the acts
he performs. His role tells him the part he is to play, tells him how to
behave and this saves effort for those acts which occur in other role
systems which are less stabilized, particularly those, like the peer group,
which are encountered outside the family.

The attempts at restoring equilibrium, "re-equilibration," have been
analyzed by Spiegel (1957) into eleven steps and again some of these
are of particular relevance to the professional person desirous of helping
the family of an exceptional child.

The first five of these steps are manipulative, that is, the person
involved attempts to get the other or others to comply with his expectations. If the others comply and take the necessary complementary role
or roles, equilibrium is restored. These manipulative steps are termed
role induction and consist of coercing, coaxing, evaluating, masking and
postponing. Coercing is defined as the manipulation of present and
future punishments which may range from overt attack to verbal commands. Coaxing, on the other hand, involves the manipulation of present
and future rewards, including requests, promises, pleading or begging.
Evaluation is a less direct manipulative device and includes such activities as praising, blaming, approving, shaming, and disapproving by the
invocation of verbal symbols associated with value judgments. "Stop
acting like a fool!" is an example of this approach.

Spiegel defines masking as the withholding of correct information or
the substitution of incorrect information pertinent to the settlement of

the conflict. In it he includes such behavior as pretending, evading, censoring, distorting, lying, hoaxing, and deceiving. Masking is intrinsic to re-equilibration processes in the family. It finds manifestation in minor distortions and disguises of motives which take place so automatically that they are scarcely noticeable. Masking may enter the interaction between the parent and the exceptional child and Spiegel's example may serve to clarify this form of manipulation.

> A child bumps himself on a chair, and the mother says, 'Naughty chair!,' assigning the chair a human activity and then evaluating that activity as if it were part of a coercive induction. Why does she do this? Pain produces anger and in order to avoid the potential role conflict which may be precipitated between herself and her child, she involves the child in a make-believe conflict with the chair, with herself in the role of referee. Furthermore, she denies the potential negative evaluation of herself as insufficiently protective of the child, by displacing the carelessness to the chair. This preserves equilibrium between herself and the child and thus is functional for their role system. But one can ask whether what is functional for their role system may not be dysfunctional for the child's ability to test reality. She conceals the important information that pain and accident can occur without motive and need to be endured in the inevitable process of maturation and acquisition of autonomy by the child. Thus her masking ties the child to her in a dependent relation in which she plays the role of protector. She conceals both from herself and her child information about her resentment at the growing independence of the child, . . . If the child does not see through this masking, he will take the complementary dependent role which his mother desires for him. (Spiegel, 1957, p. 12).

Masking may take the minor form just illustrated or it may become a form of a major transaction of temporal continuity. The masking of a physical handicap may become a primary mode of coping with the condition. The equilibrium is threatened because mother's adopted role of adequate mother calls for assigning to the child the role of adequate child but the handicap results in a role discrepancy. Re-equilibration through masking would then lead to a denial of the severity of the handicap, a projection of the cause for the consequences of the handicap onto an external object (e.g., the braces) or an exaggeration of the severity of the handicap, in which case the mother could then adopt the new role of the protector. Clearly, none of these attempts at re-equilibration are conducive to teaching the child to cope with his handicap on a realistic basis.

The fifth mode of role induction listed by Spiegel is postponing. This is the process by which the role conflict to be settled is deferred in the hope that the passage of time will bring about a change of attitude (*e.g.*, the familiar "he'll-grow-out-of-it" position toward a child's problem). These then are the manipulative steps in re-equilibration. In the second group of categories re-equilibration is brought about by a change in roles of both persons in role conflict. While in *role induction*, the child is induced to take the complementary role which will restore the equilibrium with the parent, *role modification* involves a bilateral change in role expectations and the modifications are based on interchanges and mutual identifications of two people.

Transitional between role induction and role modification Spiegel places a re-equilibration device he terms "role reversal" in which ego takes the role of alter, trying to see matters through his eyes. (The sociological use of the term "ego" should not be confused with the psychological definition. Ego and alter are here solely used as convenient substitutes for "one person" and "the other person"; the "party of the first part" and "the party of the second part.")

The effectiveness of role reversal in bringing about a change in relations depends in large part on the intensity of masking procedures in the family interaction. An outsider in a therapeutic role might suggest role reversal ("How do you think this makes him feel?") but if the defenses are too strong, masking too intense, this indirect method is bound to fail.

Joking is the first of five steps in role modification, as discussed by Spiegel. Here, the role partners, having obtained some understanding for the other's feelings and perceptions (usually through prior role reversal), use laughter as a device for achieving some distance from their previously intense involvement in the conflict.

When neither role reversal nor joking create role modification, the individuals involved in the role conflict may take the next step: referral to a third party. If the third party is himself involved in the role conflict or permits himself to become involved in it in the attempt to be helpful, he may well steer the process back to a manipulative procedure. This is an important point for the helping person to remember. If he forms a coalition with ego against alter or vice versa, the attempted solution is bound to fail.

Referral is involved whenever a family comes to a professional person for help. The family in role conflict implicitly or explicitly asks the helper to judge, referee, or take sides. "It seems a good working rule that the more information available to the person taking the role of third party, the easier it is for him to avoid getting entangled in a coalition . . . [and] the easier it is for him to help the role partners to a novel solution and to avoid a manipulated solution of the conflict" (*ibid.*, p. 15).

The next step in role modification is exploring. Here the role partners probe and test each other's capacity to establish a new solution. If the helping person has been able to avoid becoming enmeshed in a coalition, he can be of great help in encouraging and supporting exploration or, as it has traditionally been called, working through. The role partners try out a variety of possible solutions, rejecting some and accepting others, a process which often involves temporary relapse to more primitive procedures; but since actual behavior in new roles tends to be rewarding, the step more often leads forward than back.

While the third person may need to take a fairly active part in helping with exploring, he should not have to be involved in the next step, compromising. Here, after adequate exploration, ego and alter come to terms with somewhat different complementary roles than those which originally involved them in the role conflict. With compromise accomplished, the final step to be taken is consolidation, which involves the eventual internalization of the new roles by ego and alter.

If modification is successful the new solution for the role conflict becomes a part of the normal routine of the family. The problem which had caused disequilibrium has disappeared and complementarity has been restored. Modification differs from induction which is primarily defensive. With induction the disequilibrium is warded off but is always likely to reappear because it is an unsettled problem and the resolution of the strain more apparent than real. When induction is used, the role conflict becomes internalized by the members of the family and as an internalized conflict the disequilibrium is likely to produce neurotic symptoms or difficulties in interpersonal relations.

CHILD-REARING PRACTICES AND PERSONALITY DEVELOPMENT

The influence of infantile and childhood experiences on personality formation has become generally accepted by personality theorists despite the fact that this relationship has never been established by unequivocal and generally accepted studies. The dearth of such studies is particularly striking in the area of maternal influences on child personality. Orlansky (1949) conducted a much cited review of research in this area and concluded that the evidence for a relationship between maternal practices and personality development is meagre, contradictory and unconvincing.

When one recognizes the complexity of the diadic interaction between mother and child within the social system in which it is embedded, it is not surprising that a simplistic hypothesis about the causal relationship of one particular child-rearing technique or one specific form of early experience with later personality characteristics fails to find confirmation. A study by Sewell and Mussen (1952), which appeared after the Orlansky review, is a case in point. These investigators were interested in the effects of feeding and weaning experiences on later childhood adjustment and tested the hypotheses that fewer oral symptoms and better adjustment would be found in (1) breast-fed children as compared to bottle-fed children; (2) children on self-demand schedules as compared to those on a regular schedule; and (3) gradually-weaned as compared to abruptly-weaned children. The subjects were 162 five and six-year-olds and the data on feeding behavior and general personality adjustment were obtained in interviews with the mothers. In addition, behavior ratings on the children were collected from teachers and a paper and pencil test of personality was administered to each child. The investigators concluded that the study gave

> no support to psychoanalytic thinking which maintains that breastfeeding, demand schedules, and gradual weaning promote better adjustment than bottle-feeding, regular scheduling, or abrupt weaning. Analysis of the data provides no evidence that one method of feeding, scheduling,or weaning is superior to other methods. In fact, there is no evidence from this study of any relationship between gratification and and non-gratification in any of these three aspects of the feeding process and personal and social adjustment (p. 190 f.).

Aside from the fact that this study singled out a specific form of early experience without reference to the atmosphere in which this experience took place, it also has the shortcoming of basing the evaluation of feeding experiences on retrospective reports of the mother which, as Wenar (1961) and also Mednick and Shaffer (1963) have recently pointed out, may be of questionable validity.

Watson (1959) makes the point that the interrelationships reviewed by Orlansky and investigated by Sewell and Mussen are probably more complex in nature than allowed for in the designs of the studies. He points out that "specific techniques of infant care and training do not have an invariant relationship with specific consequent personality variables. Some techniques may produce more unfortunate consequences than others. However, it appears likely that the specific discipline is not ordinarily of critical significance in and for itself. More plausibly a specific practice may be regarded as part of a larger pattern in which it is embedded" (p. 230).

It does not require a great deal of psychological sophistication to recognize that two mothers who engage in a form of child-rearing behavior which is manifestly identical and is therefore tabulated in the same rubric in a study, may be exposing their children to two entirely different phenomenological experiences. Two mothers may use bottle feeding, one reluctantly and with much guilt, the other spontaneously and in a relaxed manner. One may hold, cuddle and talk to her child while giving him the bottle while the other may resort to a mechanical device to hold the bottle and go about her chores while the child is feeding. If a study on childrearing practices interests itself solely in the dichotomy of breast-feeding vs. bottle-feeding, many crucial variables in the child's experience will obviously not be considered. Martin (1957) has pointed out that "to ask a question—what is the effect of breast-feeding upon the personality development—is to ask the wrong, the unanswerable question. Rather we should ask: 'What is the effect of breast-feeding as performed by a particular mother in a particular way as perceived and received by a particular child under particular circumstances, with regard to both time and space?'" (p. 40). Frankiel (1959) carries this reasoning one step further and asserts that the assumption of a simple one-to-one relationship between any single type of experience and later behavior is untenable. She maintains that it would seem far more reasonable to take the position that personality is formed through the dynamic interaction between the developing organism and the physical and social environment. Not only must we ask how the specific child responds to parental handling in terms of his own constitutional receptor system but, as Burchinal, Hawkes and Gardner (1957) have stressed, one must also take the child's perceptions of his parental relationships into consideration. Chance (1958) makes a similar point when she speaks of the complex interdependence of parental self-experience, child perception and the child's self-experience. This interdependence may well be one of the reasons why, as Hess and Handel (1956) have demonstrated, siblings in the same family are differentially affected by the personality patterns of their parents.

A study designed to test the hypothesis that the mother's character structure is more closely related to child adjustment than are the specific rearing practices and techniques is reported by Behrens (1954), who studied twenty-five mothers and their children at a mental health clinic. The children ranged in age from two to six years with a mean of thirty-six months and Behrens studied their responses to socialization both in terms of their interaction with what she calls "the total mother person" and then with respect to the mother's specific rearing techniques.

The "total mother person" is a construct composed of the mother's attitudes and conduct. It was derived from ratings of the mother's character structure, her integration of character traits to meet maternal role requirements, and her observed and overt conduct in the care of the child. The data were derived from a clinical, interdisciplinary study of the family based on interviews, psychological tests, individual and group therapy sessions, nursery teacher evaluations, and visits to the homes of nineteen of the twenty-five families.

In confirmation of her hypothesis, Behrens found no correlation between the adjustment of the children and such specific infant-rearing practices as feeding, weaning, and toilet-training. On the other hand, there were highly significant correlations between child adjustment and the ratings of the "total mother person." Although Behrens' subjects represent a small and highly-selected sample it is interesting to note that a particular mother would show wide variation and inconsistency in her specific socialization techniques. She might thus be very permissive in her feeding practices but extremely coercive and rigid in her toilet-training. This is a finding which is different from those of Sears, Maccoby and Levin (1957), who saw permissiveness as a general factor running through a great variety of child-rearing practices. The explanation of this apparent incompatibility of findings may well rest with the fact that the parents in the Harvard study of Sears and his associates were representatives of the normal population while those in the Behrens study had been selected from the lists of a psychiatric facility. The inconsistency of the mothers in the Behrens study may well be a reflection of the emotional difficulties which led them and their children to the clinic in the first place. Indeed, Behrens traces these variations and inconsistencies to the mother's own emotional needs and conflicts. She states in her summary:

> In the mother's social interaction with the child as she takes on the maternal role, she both consciously and unconsciously expresses her emotional needs and attempts to satisfy them. Her integration into the maternal role will depend on her perception of self and role and will influence the child's perception of her. It is also evident that the child is both sensitive and responsive to the unconscious attitudes of the mother as well as to her overt conduct. The quality of his adjustment is more dependent on his total interaction with his mother than on any specific aspects of social discipline (Behrens, 1954, p. 237).

Maternal overprotection. One of the earliest attempts to study parental influences from a point of view other than that of specific practices is the classical investigation by David Levy (1943), who concerned himself with the pattern of attitudes and behavior which can be subsumed under the general heading of overprotection. Overprotection is the manifestation of maternal attitudes which may have their dynamic bases in a variety of factors. As with many other typological classifications overprotection by no means describes a homogenous group of mothers. One thing, however, all mothers in this group have in common and that is that they are giving their children more protection than the reality of the situation demands. A child who is in reality frail or infirm realistically requires more protection than a healthy child but when he receives more protection than his condition and situation demand we can speak of overprotection, which, thus defined, is always pathologic.

Because overprotection is based on a distortion of the reality needs of the child we must look for the antecedents of this form of maternal behavior to the mother's reaction pattern and her personality. A mother's need to control through overprotection may be based on her own insecurity and her need to establish herself as a "good" mother in her self-perception and in the eyes of significant persons around her. Over-protection may also be the manifestation of reaction formation to un-conscious hostile-destructive impulses. Features in the mother's person-ality, including her acceptance of the feminine role, her maternal role satisfaction, her marital adjustment, and her perception of the specific child, may have engendered repressed hostile-destructive impulses toward this child which she defends against by their dynamic opposite of overprotection. Related to this may be the mother's guilt for real or imagined damage to the child and in attempting to assuage this guilt she assumes the role of the overprotective mother who, through her overprotection, tries to keep the child from further harm which her unconscious rejection might cause him.

The guilt, disappointment, anger and frustration which parents ex-perience when they produce a handicapped or defective child makes overprotection a particularly relevant issue in a discussion of exceptional children. We are here dealing not only with the parents' reaction to a crisis but also with a situation where the reality of how much protection the child realistically requires is often difficult to determine and easy to distort. Since we shall return to a discussion of parental reactions to the birth of a handicapped child in the next chapter, we shall here ex-plore only the general aspects of overprotection.

Levy (1943) examined twenty cases of maternal overprotection and identified two fundamental types. The first type includes mothers whose overprotection has a controlling, dominating quality while the second type manifests overprotection through excessive indulgence. Both types of mothers are highly permissive with their young children and tend to infantilize them by failing to reward the child's independence strivings. As the child matures his growing independence is seen as a threat to the mother's domination and possession of him so that she attempts to restrict independent activities such as exploration and experimentation. As long as the child is an infant, his natural state of helplessness is congruent with the mother's need to overprotect. As soon as he becomes physically able to do some things on his own, however, his needs and those of his mother become incongruent and the mother may become increasingly threatened in her self-perception of an adequate mother. The conflict between the mother's needs and the needs of the child is resolved differently, depending on whether the mother is of the indulgent or the controlling type. The indulgent mother, whom Symonds (1939) has called "submissive," will consistently yield to the desire of the child and submit to his demands. Levy (1943) reports that such children generally become disobedient, impudent, excessively demanding and tyrannical in their relationship to their mother. In school these children were rated as disobedient, careless, irresponsible, stubborn, rebellious against authority, antagonistic, forward and independent, but self-confident and spontaneous in establishing friendships outside the family (Symonds, 1939).

The overcontrolling, dominating mothers, on the other hand, who would reward submission and compliance produced children who were generally shy, submissive and somewhat withdrawn in interactions with their mothers. These reactions generalized to social interaction outside the home and in school they were reported as obedient, accepting of authority and dependent on others. Despite their difficulties in interpersonal relations based largely on the fact that other people are not as accepting of the behavior patterns which their mothers had rewarded, children from overprotecting mothers did not seem to be particularly impaired in their academic progress. In the case of the overprotective-controlling mothers, Levy (1943) attributes this to the fact that a child's submissive conformity stands him in good stead in most school situations. The overprotective-indulgent mother, on the other hand, tends to find much satisfaction in interacting with her child around schoolwork so that, at least in the early years of school, this becomes reflected in the child's school performance.

Maternal overprotection can have its beginnings at the birth of the child if the child is born prematurely. This was pointed out by Mussen, Conger and Kagan (1963) in a discussion of data reported by Shirley (1939). Shirley had studied ninety-five prematurely-born children and found what she described as a "prematurity syndrome" which was characterized by such features as infantile speech, poor motor coordination, difficulties in sphincter control, shyness and dependence upon mother. Mussen, Conger and Kagan (1963) believe that many of these characteristics might be explained by the parents' reaction to having a premature child. "Early in his life the premature child may be overprotected and isolated. Since his parents may be afraid of harming the extremely delicate organism, they may become overstimulating in their attempts to help the child overcome the discrepancies between him and his contemporaries. Understimulation followed by pressure may lead to various kinds of maladjustment" (p. 79). Mussen and Conger agree with Shirley's (1939) conclusion that the premature child's family environment during his early years may account for most of the social and emotional difficulties he exhibits. Inasmuch as the initial delay in development of premature children eventually becomes obliterated as they catch up with their birth age, while children born with a defect or handicap usually remain exceptional throughout life, Shirley's findings would lead one to expect that exceptional children are highly vulnerable from a social and emotional point of view.

PARENTAL ATTITUDES

The evaluation of parental attitudes. With the recognition of the shortcomings of studies based on specific maternal practices many investigators have in recent years turned their interest to maternal attitudes on the assumption that attitudes have a more pervasive influence on the child's experiences than do specific practices.

One of the first steps in studying parental attitudes in order to relate them to consequent child adjustment is to develop valid instruments for the measurement of such attitudes. This in itself presents a major research challenge to which a number of investigators have recently addressed themselves.

One of the best known of these recent attempts to develop a measure of parental attitudes is the work of Schaefer and Bell (1958) on the Parental Attitude Research Instrument (PARI). This is a paper and pencil inventory on which the respondent indicates his agreement or disagreement with 115 statements about family life and children. A few examples of items from this inventory will serve to give an impression of the task: "The home is the only thing that matters to a good mother"; "Strict discipline develops a fine, strong character"; "A wise parent will teach a child early just who is boss"; "Raising children is a nerve-wrecking job"; "Sex is one of the greatest problems to be contended with in children"; "Few men realize that a mother needs some fun in life too."

Various studies conducted with the PARI suggest that the factorial structure of these scales is dependent upon the roles a woman has had in parent-child relationships. Factor analysis of responses of 100 unmarried nursing students (Schaefer & Bell, 1957), for example, isolated five relatively independent factors which were named Suppression and Interpersonal Distance, Hostile Rejection of the Homemaking Role, Excessive Demand for Striving, Overpossessiveness, and Harsh Punitive Control. A subsequent factor analysis on a sample of 100 mothers with more than one child (multiparae), cited by Schaefer (1961), revealed only three factors: Approval of Maternal Control, Approval of Expression of Hostility, and Approval of Positive Attitudes toward Childrearing. A similar factorial structure was reported by Zuckerman, Ribback, Monashkin, and Norton (1958); but when 100 mothers with only one child (primiparae) were studied, the factorial pattern differed from that of the other two groups.

It will be recalled that a factor analysis is a statistical technique which permits the interpretation of scores and correlations of scores from a number of tests or scales. The PARI, for example, is composed of 115 discrete items which in turn break down into twenty-three scales of five items each. When these scales are administered to a sample of subjects the scores can be correlated with one another resulting in a correlation matrix which reflects the correlation of each score with every other score. A factor analysis permits one to isolate factors or correlation clusters representing scores which have more in common with one another than with the other scores in the matrix. Having thus isolated a number of factors, the analysis enables one to state which scales contributed to its measurement, and by examining the content of these scales one can draw inferences as to underlying traits which seem to be represented by these factors. These traits can then be named; but one should not lose sight of the essentially arbitrary naming which is involved. Although trait and factor are not synonomous, one being a theoretical inference and the other a statistical phenomenon, the two terms are often used interchangeably.

One of the PARI factors which seems to be quite stable, having been isolated in the original study by Schaefer and Bell (1958) and again by Zuckerman, Ribback, Monashkin, and Norton (1958), is that identified as the Authoritarian-Control factor. Mothers who score high on this factor tend to hold attitudes which are authoritarian, suppressive, punitive, and restricting. Zuckerman and Oltean (1959) had predicted that the Authoritarian-Control factor would relate to personality traits char-

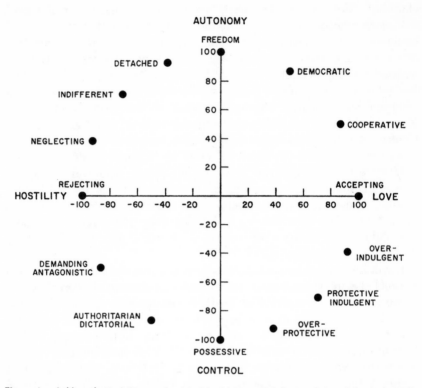

Figure I.—A Hypothetical Circumplex Model of Maternal Behavior (after Schaefer, 1959).

acteristic of the "Authoritarian Personality." Using the California F Scale of Authoritarianism (Adorno, Frenkel-Brunswick, Levinson & Sanford, 1950) with thirty-two female psychiatric in-patients (most of whom were mothers) and eighty-eight unmarried student nurses, they found significant correlations in the predicted directions and concluded that authoritarianism in social attitudes is an expression of personality tendencies which affect attitudes about child-rearing (Zuckerman & Oltean, 1959). The established relationship held even when response sets were *partialled* out in a separate analysis of the data (Zuckerman, Norton & Sprague, 1958). Response set is the tendency of some people to agree with any positively worded statement, a tendency which frequently plagues investigators devising or using questionnaires with unidirectional items.

Schaefer (1959) had found that the factors or traits isolated by a number of different and independent studies could be ordered on a circumplex model in terms of two bi-polar dimensions which he labeled Autonomy vs. Control and Love vs. Hostility. Generalizing from this circumplex model he suggests that other concepts which have been used to describe maternal behavior can be ordered in this fashion. This hypothetical model is shown in Fig. 1 which Schaefer (*ibid.*) described as follows:

> Freedom is placed on the *Autonomy* vs. *Control* dimension with its polar opposite, possessiveness. Democratic behavior and cooperative behavior are placed in the quadrant which indicates both loving acceptance and autonomy. Acceptance and its polar opposite, rejection, are placed on the *Love* vs. *Hostility* dimension. Excessive love, overindulgence, protective indulgence, and overprotectiveness are placed in a quadrant that indicates both love for the child and an inability to treat the child as a differentiated individual who has his own activities and interests apart from the parent. The variables of authoritarian, dictatorial treatment and demanding, antagonistic behavior are placed in the quadrant that indicates both a hostile relationship to the child and control; while neglect, indifference, and detachment are placed in the quadrant that indicates varying combinations of hostility and autonomy for the child (Schaefer, 1959, p. 232).

In terms of Schaefer's hypothesis a mother's social and emotional behavior toward an individual child can be located in one of the four quadrants of his circumplex model. In a later publication Schaefer (1961) presents data in answer to the question whether the behavior of mothers is consistent through time. Behavior ratings based on observations made during the child's first three years of life and ratings based on interviews with the same mothers between the child's age of nine and fourteen years were correlated and it was found that there was a fairly good correlation (r = .68) for the dimension of Love-Hostility, suggesting that a mother's behavior is consistent across this time interval. The consistency correlation for the Autonomy-Control dimension was only .26, however, suggesting that there is greater change over time for this than for the Love-Hostility dimension. Inasmuch as the child's need for love can be assumed to be constant through time, while his need for autonomy changes substantially from infancy to adolescence, this finding of differential consistency appears reasonable. One would assume that in instances where the mother does not shift from relative control to more autonomy, the child's social and emotional development would be handicapped. This inability to give the child more autonomy may well play a role in the personality development of some exceptional children whose mothers have a need to exert continuing control long after it has become realistically unnecessary.

So far, however, the relationship between maternal attitudes and consequent child behavior is largely hypothetical in nature. Schaefer (1961) offers such a hypothesis, holding it possible to demonstrate a relationship between his circumplex model for maternal behavior (as inferred from attitudes) and a similar model for the social and emotional behavior of the child. This particular model was developed for the behavior of boys though Schaefer recognizes that it represents an over-simplification since he speculates in the absence of data relevant to both maternal and paternal behavior.

On the basis of an informal review of the literature, Schaefer (1961) suggests that the Love-Hostility dimension of maternal behavior is related to the Love-Hostility dimension of boys' behavior. That is that the boy who has been hostilely treated will tend to be a maladjusted child who either hostilely withdraws or hostilely attacks. In terms of the Autonomy-Control dimension of maternal behavior Schaefer juxtaposes an Extraversion-Introversion dimension of child behavior and stresses that we must recognize that the child's need for a close relationship with his mother and his ability to seek other relationships vary with age. "If the child's needs vary, the effects of what appears to be similar maternal behaviors at different developmental periods may vary depending upon the appropriateness of the maternal behavior for the child's stage of development" (ibid., p. 144 f.). Where a mother provides little stimulation or contact for an infant and where alternate relationships are not available to the infant he will become reserved, withdrawn, and uncommunicative and thus fail to develop socially. On the other hand, if mothers have emotionally-involved and close relations with their infant sons, the sons may tend to be extroverted at adolescence. Again, mothers who are overprotective and controlling during the ages when the son might be expected to become socially-oriented toward peers tend to have sons who are more inhibited, reserved, shy and less extroverted.

Although Schaefer cites a variety of studies from various fields to support his hypotheses, they are admittedly speculative at this point and represent more of a research program than clearly-established theory. At the same time his models of maternal and child behavior lend themselves to useful application in areas where maternal behavior and its relationship to child personality development need to be categorized.

Parental attitudes and parental behavior. Despite the fact that it is

possible to demonstrate predictable relationships between response patterns on different instruments, one measuring child-rearing attitudes and
the other more general personality variables (Zuckerman et al., 1958,
1959), there remains the question of the extent to which child-rearing
attitudes relate to actual child-rearing behavior. What is needed to
answer this question is to relate observations of parental behavior to
parents' responses on attitude questionnaires. Such studies are difficult to
conduct and the few which have been reported are anything but encouraging.

Crandall and Preston (1955) compared behavior ratings made by an
experienced clinical psychologist during home visit observations of
mother-child interactions with ratings the mothers made of their own
behavior on a similar scale. There turned out to be only moderate agreement between the mothers' self-ratings and the home visitor's ratings of
the mothers' overt behavior. The authors felt that the two methods were
not interchangeable, that one can not rely on self-ratings as a valid reflection of actual behavior. On the other hand, they point out, that the
two sets of data were not entirely unrelated. Depending on the area of
maternal behavior under consideration, the amount of agreement between the two kinds of ratings can be quite high. This was particularly
true of such attitudinal areas as affection, effectiveness of control and
home adjustment. Crandall and Preston conclude that their results

> add a note of caution for maternal behavior research. Studies of maternal
> behavior have employed a variety of data-gathering methods including
> observational ratings, interviews, questionnaires and self-rating. Since
> the results of such research are inextricably bound to their data collection
> methods, results obtained by one method may be considerably different
> from those obtained by other methods. Until more research has been
> done on the comparability of data obtained by various methods, the lack
> of knowledge in this area places obvious limitations on the scope of the
> theoretical generalizations which can be made on the basis of present
> maternal behavior research (ibid., p. 276).

Gordon (1957) reports a study which also bears on the comparability
of data obtained by different methods. In a camp where pre-school deaf
children were together with their mothers, professional staff members
observed the interaction of mothers and children over a period of twelve
days. They then ranked the mothers on the likelihood that the mother's
attitudes and behavior toward the child would result in the child becoming a "problem child." These staff rankings were compared with the
mothers' scores on Shoben's University of Southern California Parent
Attitude Survey (Shoben, 1949), a frequently used instrument which

has formed the basis of a number of other attitude scales, including the PARI. Gordon found no significant agreement between staff rankings and the Shoben scale and concluded that his results are best interpreted as suggesting a lack of validity of the attitude survey. One might question whether this conclusion is warranted on the basis of Gordon's study. The staff members who made the rankings were a supervisor of a speech and hearing clinic, an audiologist, two teachers of deaf children, two nursery school teachers, three psychologists, and six graduate students in speech therapy. While these people might have been able to make valid observations of maternal behavior, the rankings actually expected them to draw inferences from these observations as to whether or not the observed behavior might lead to the child becoming a "problem child." This is a prediction which is extremely difficult for even the most skilled of clinicians to make because so many other, unknown variables enter into the eventual adjustment of a child. The Shoben USC Survey invoked no such inference but merely differentiated in its standardization between mothers whose children were disturbed and mothers of normal children. It identifies Possessive, Dominating, and Ignoring attitudes of mothers so that a crucial test of validity would be whether skilled observers see these attitudes reflected in the mother's behavior, a test which has yet to be made.

There are, in this area, three definite steps which must be held conceptually apart. We can speak of parental attitudes and try to ascertain these by questionnaires, check lists, or interviews. The next step is to observe behavior and to try and relate behavior to attitudes. A mother might express the attitude that a child should eat everything on his plate but when it comes to an actual eating situation she can behave in a great variety of ways. She can threaten, force, cajole, bribe, or plead with the child to eat; she can try and get him to eat and then give in; she can make him eat one day but not the next; make him eat when father is home, but not when she is alone with the child; or she can not care one way or the other, having responded positively on the questionnaire because she thought that this was the socially accepted answer. The third step, after attitude and behavior, is the effect of these on the child's response pattern and personality. The effect on the child is clearly a function of a great many variables, in addition to parental attitudes and behavior, so that this third step poses the most difficult problems from a research point of view. Gordon (1957) confounded all three steps, scoring attitudes, observing behavior and inferring to its effect on the child. His negative findings can thus hardly be considered as invalidating the Shoben instrument *as a measure of attitudes.*

Most attitude scales, including that developed by Shoben (1949) are validated through the use of criterion groups. Two groups of mothers may be selected who differ on a criterion which is considered relevant to the variables measured by the attitude scale. One may be a group of mothers of delinquent children, the others of non-delinquent children. On the theoretical assumption that these two groups of mothers hold different attitudes toward child-rearing the attitude scale is held valid if it differentiates between the two groups. This method of ascertaining concurrent validity makes several asumptions; if any one of these assumptions should be erroneous, the validity measure is spurious. One assumption is that the criterion used is relevant to the attitudes to be measured and that the two groups are actually differentiated by that criterion. In the case of delinquent children, for example, the question of definition immediately raises itself. What is a delinquent child? Are there "delinquent" children in the "normal" group? Are delinquent children a homogenous group or are we dealing with a variety of personalities whose only common denominator is that someone has defined them as delinquent on the basis of a norm-violating act? Another basic assumption of this approach to test validity is that maternal attitudes are a variable in child delinquency. The differences in attitude scale scores would make this appear to be the case, but it must be recalled that these scales were standardized in order to differentiate between two criterion groups because an *a priori* theoretical assumption held that the attitudes must be different.

Leton (1958) studied the validity of Shoben's Parent Attitude Survey (1949) by relating its scores to adjustment ratings made by the children's teacher. Similar to Gordon (1957) he makes the jump from attitude to child adjustment, ignoring the question of the relationship between attitudes and behavior. There are other unsatisfactory aspects to this study. He had fathers and mothers take the questionnaires home from PTA meetings with the request that they respond independently, without discussing or comparing their responses. To what extent this injunction was heeded is unknown and this method of administration differs from that of Shoben, who administered his survey in supervised sessions. Approximately 78 per cent of Leton's parents returned the forms, raising the question whether the attitudes of non-respondents differed in some significant way from those parents who cooperated. One further shortcoming of which Leton was aware is that he had no reliability measure for the teachers' ratings of the children's personal, social, and emotional adjustment. For this resaon he compared only children with "excellent" adjustment with those of "poor or unsatisfactory" adjustment, apparently assuming that the reliability is greatest at these extremes of the continuum; again an assumption which may or may not be tenable. At any rate, he did not find a significant difference between the mean attitude scores of parents of children with good adjustment ratings and of parents of children with poor adjustment ratings.

Zuckerman, Barrett, and Bragiel (1960) concluded from a review of parental attitude studies that "there seems to be a growing suspicion that parents' verbal descriptions of their behavior and attitudes may be somewhat discrepant from their actual behavior and attitudes" (p. 402). Their own study confirmed this suspicion for they found that parental attitudes of fathers and mothers as measured by the PARI were not markedly related to the child's diagnosis or symptom type, nor did they yield marked differences between parents of patients at child guidance clinics and a control group. Attitude scores failed to predict the parents' cooperativeness with the clinics, and they did not distinguish between those who remained in clinic contact and those who terminated prematurely.

All this might lead one to the conclusion that either the attitude scales are not valid, or that attitudes bear no relationship to behavior. Before accepting either of these conclusions, let us consider a third possibility: that attitude scales do have some validity and that attitudes do bear a relationship to overt behavior, but that the relationship between attitudes, behavior, and child adjustment is far more complex than the relatively simplistic hypotheses of the studies so far examined would allow. The child's personality does not develop in direct response to the stimulus pattern provided by his mother's behavior but as a result of a complex interaction between his own constitutional "given" and the dynamic pattern of relationships provided by his environment, of which the mother is only one, albeit a significant, part. Many investigators acknowledge the importance of the father but then, often bowing to practical considerations, proceed to study only the mother's attitudes and behavior in relation to the child's personality development.

The previously cited study by Leton (1958) gives a clue to the complexity of family interaction. It will be recalled that he obtained attitude measures of mothers and fathers and found that they failed to differentiate between children of "excellent" adjustment and children of "poor" adjustment, as rated by their teachers. This was true when attitudes of fathers and attitudes of mothers were separately analyzed. For thirty-nine father-mother pairs Leton was able to obtain discrepancy scores which reflected the difference in attitude between the father and the mother of the same child. With this analysis he found a highly significant difference. There was a greater discrepancy between the attitude scores of parents of poorly adjusted children than between parents of well adjusted children. This would tend to confirm the widely accepted concept that parental harmony has a favorable effect on a child's adjustment and that parental disharmony or disagreement has an unfavorable effect. The emotional atmosphere in a family would thus seem to be far more important for the understanding of the personality development of the child than the specific attitudes held by either father or mother.

This study by Leton (1958) is one of the few purporting to investigate *parent*-child relations which does not actually deal only with *mother*-child relations. Rarely is the father considered in these studies. Reading the scientific literature in this field, a student unfamiliar with our culture might easily get the impression that fathers play no part in the rearing of our children.

There are obvious reality difficulties to including the father in studies of child rearing and only a few investigators have made efforts to cope with these difficulties. One of these was Radke (1946), who was interested in the relation of parental authority to children's behavior and attitudes. Her subjects were forty-three mothers and fathers of pre-school children. These parents completed questionnaires and responded to interviews about their disciplinary practices. From this she evolved patterns of parental authority which permitted her to classify homes as autocratic or democratic. Relating parental authority patterns to data collected about the children, Radke found that children from relatively autocratic homes were less popular with other children, more prone to fighting and quarreling, less considerate, more daring and uninhibited, less sensitive to praise or blame, and more emotionally unstable than children from the more democratic homes.

The classical studies conducted under Baldwin at the Fels Research Institute and first reported by Baldwin, Kalhorn, and Breese (1945) also considered the father's role, although the ratings of parent behavior made by trained home visitors were largely based on observations of mother and child. Watson (1959) has reviewed the effect of the father on the socialization of the child and concludes that the father's major function seems to be to serve as a model, especially for the boy. This is clearly not the father's only function.

> Besides being a father, he is a husband, an economic provider, a source of intellectual and social stimulation, an arbiter, and a friend. Not always does exercise of these functions involve the child directly. As a husband his functional relations are primarily with his wife. Always, however, he is a member of a network of social relations. Affecting one part of that network ultimately affects all parts. So the child in this social complex is ultimately affected by all of the father's functions (Watson, 1959, p. 393).

Maternal attitudes and child adjustment. One recent large scale study investigated the relationship between maternal attitudes and the general adjustment level of her child. To this end Gildea, Glidewell and Kantor (1961) worked with 830 families from a predominantly urban county in Missouri. The adjustment of the children was assessed by asking the teacher to rate each child along a four-point scale which ranged from "well-adjusted" to "clinically disturbed." In addition, child adjustment was assessed on the basis of the number of symptoms reported by the mother on a symptom inventory administered during an interview. The questions on this inventory covered twenty-one areas of potential difficulty: eating, sleeping, digestion, getting along with other children (acting out), getting along with other children (withdrawn), getting along with adults (acting out), getting along with adults (withdrawn), unusual fears, nervousness, thumbsucking, overactivity, lying, stealing, destructiveness, sex, daydreaming, temper tantrums, crying, rejection of school, wetting, speech (Gildea *et al.* 1961).

Previous pilot studies with the teacher ratings and the symptom inventory had shown them to be reliably related to both external criteria and to each other. Maternal attitudes were assessed by means of a questionnaire composed of seventeen items similar to but not identical with the type of statements included in the PARI. Thirteen of these items had previously been found to discriminate mothers of well-adjusted children from mothers with disturbed children. Three of these items related to whether or not the mother considered herself involved in the child's problem. Four items reflected the mother's attitude toward discipline and conformity; three items dealt with the mother's attitude toward matters of sex; one item indicated parental rejection; and two items could not be classified. In addition to these, three more items dealing with maternal rejection and one item derived from clinical experience were added to make up the seventeen-item attitude scale.

A factor analysis of the attitude questionnaire suggests that responses can be related to three factors: the degree of certainty of opinion concerning child-rearing doctrine and practices, the degree of control the mother sees necessary to exert toward her child, and the degree of protection the mother sees the child as needing.

The comparison between the attitude scales and adjustment ratings "revealed no relationship between general adjustment of children and maternal attitudes toward responsibility, discipline, rejection; control of child behavior; or degree to which children try to cope with their environment" (Gildea *et al.*, 1961, p. 71). In view of the fact that the items in the scale had discriminated between mothers of adjusted children and mothers of disturbed children in the pilot study, this failure to replicate throws some doubt on the validity of either the adjustment ratings or the attitude scale. One would certainly want to consider this hypothesis before deciding that maternal attitudes are unrelated to child adjustment.

A different aspect of the same study produced more promising findings. In addition to the administration of the attitude scales the mothers in the sample were interviewed to examine their concepts of causation of behavior problems, their feelings of potency, that is, whether the mother felt that she had an influence on the outcome of the problem, and their feeling of responsibility in the sense of whether the mother felt responsible for influencing her child's problem behavior. Possibly because an interview is a more sensitive tool than a seventeen-item attitude scale, it was found that while there had been little relationship between specific attitudes and adjustment of children there was a significant relationship between patterns of attitude combinations and child adjustment. That is "the mothers who can perceive the multiple influences on child behavior and, *at the same time* can see their own role as one of potent influence, are relatively *less* likely to have disturbed children. On the other hand, the mothers who cannot see themselves as either responsible or potent are *more* likely to have disturbed children" (*ibid.*, p. 86).

The investigators point out that their correlational data in no way permit one to speculate that a set of attitudes *causes* a certain level of adjustment and the interpretation of their results are further complicated by the fact that social class differences were related to both maternal attitudes and to teachers' adjustment ratings. Teachers had seen middle class children as better adjusted than either lower or upper class children and the data had to be corrected for this effect. In addition, however, there were significant relationships between social class and attitudes of the mothers toward child-rearing.

Upper class mothers most often felt confident of their methods, saw the child as in need of limited parental control, felt responsible for the behavior of their children, and potent to influence the outcome of problems of child-rearing. Middle class mothers were the 'in-between' group: they felt reasonably confident of their methods, saw the child as in need of moderate parental control, felt generally responsible for the behavior of their children, and moderately potent to influence the outcome of problems. The lower class mothers felt least confident of their methods, least responsible for the behavior of their children, saw their children as in need of close parental control, but most often felt impotent to influence the outcome of behavior problems in their children (*ibid.*, p. 87 f.).

At the same time the authors report that

> the lowest disturbance rates found were among the children of the
> *sophisticated* mothers; the next lowest were among the children of the
> *anxious* overresponsible mothers; the third lowest rates appeared in the
> children of the confident, *do-it-yourself* mothers. The highest disturbance
> rates were found among the children of the projecting, impotent, *paranoid*
> mothers; the second highest rates among the children of responsible
> mothers who feel relatively cautious or *reserved* about the success of
> their efforts to deal with behavior problems in children; the third high-
> est rates appeared among the children of *depressed* mothers who felt
> responsible but impotent to influence the outcome of their situations
> *(loc. cit.).*

In view of these findings the conclusions that "mothers with the best
adjusted children could see multiple influences on child behavior, felt
themselves to be one of the influences, and felt potent to exercise influence" (*ibid.*, p. 89) may well be confounded by the fact that mothers
with these attitudes tended to be in the upper social class so that good
child adjustment might be more related to social class than to maternal
attitude.

If the results of the Gildea study are thus so difficult to interpret one
might justifiably ask why we have spent so much time discussing it. The
reason for dwelling so long on this particular investigation was to underscore the many difficulties the investigator meets who attempts to deal
with the relationship between maternal attitudes and child behavior.
Even a team of experienced and skilled social scientists conducting a
well-planned, extensive and long-range study with the resources of a
county health department at their disposal find that with present
techniques this important area of human behavior remains relatively
adamant to definitive investigation.

Social class differences in parental attitudes and behavior have, of
course, been reported by a great many investigators. Sears, Maccoby
and Levin (1957), for example, demonstrated that middle class mothers
compared to working class mothers were more permissive in toilet
training, in allowing dependency, in sex training, toward aggressiveness,
and appeared to impose fewer demands and restrictions on their child.
Bronfenbrenner (1961) states on the basis of a summary of other
studies that "middle class parents, as compared with lower class, are
more permissive of the child's spontaneous desires, express affection
more freely, and prefer 'psychological' techniques of discipline, such as
reasoning or appeals to guilt, to more direct methods like physical punishment, scolding, or threats" (p. 100).

Parents learn child-rearing behavior and their attitudes about child rearing and different social class environments set up different conditions for such learning. The effects of this learning can be seen not only in the gradual shifting of group attitudes over periods of time but also in experimental studies. In 1946 Ericson had reported that middle class families were generally more exacting in their expectations, while by 1952 when Sears *et al.* (1957) conducted their studies they found that middle class mothers were more gentle than working class mothers. Although studies where mothers report on their own child-rearing behavior are always subject to the distortion produced by mothers' possible attempt to report what they consider to be the socially-acceptable behavior, Klatskin's (1952) investigation suggests that learning is indeed capable of modifying child-rearing practices. She found that after one year's exposure to the permissive child-rearing philosophy of the Yale Rooming-In Project mothers of infants born in this setting had shifted in the direction of greater leniency in *all* social classes included in the study, though not in every area of child care.

Before leaving the question of parental attitudes and child adjustment one further and important point needs to be made. Studies relating parental attitude scores to some measure of child adjustment are, no matter what specific statistical technique they employ, essentially correlational studies. Even when the results are positive, they mean only that a certain attitude or set of attitudes of the parents coincides with a certain form of adjustment of the child. As any student of elementary statistics knows, correlation does not prove causation, yet this is an oft-ignored fact in many of the studies cited. Their basic hypotheses often state or imply that "pathogenic" attitudes of the parents bring about pathological adjustment in the children.

Klebanoff (1959) addressed a study to the question whether "pathological" maternal attitudes *cause* child disturbance or whether the experience of having a disturbed child leads, in a reactive fashion, to a mother's "abnormal" responses on an attitude inventory. To test his reactive hypothesis Klebanoff compared PARI responses of mothers of schizophrenic children, mothers of retarded and brain-injured children, and mothers of children who were free of neurological, psychiatric or serious physical disorders. If a child's disturbance, specifically schizophrenia, were the result of pathogenic maternal attitudes, the response patterns of the mothers of schizophrenic children should have been significantly different from the attitudes of the other two groups of mothers. This, however, was not the case. Klebanoff reports that the mothers of schizophrenic children showed fewer, not more pathological attitudes, than did the mothers of brain-damaged and retarded children. A further comparison revealed that the mothers of the two groups of ill children manifested more pathological attitudes than the mothers of normal children, again supporting the over-all hypothesis that mothers react to having seriously disordered children and that this reaction is expressed in "pathological" attitudes. While this study casts doubt upon the notion that mothers' attitudes cause schizophrenia, it does, of course, not negate the theoretical notion that the child's personality develops in response to environmental factors. It seems clear, however, that these environmental factors are far more complex than maternal attitudes reflected on a paper and pencil self-report inventory.

A study by Madoff (1959) revealed that mothers of disturbed children show a different pattern of attitudes from mothers of healthy youngsters, again suggesting that maternal attitudes as revealed on a paper and pencil inventory may reflect the parent's experiences and are probably particularly sensitive to the condition and behavior of the child. This would be in keeping with the hypothesis of Fries and Woolf (1953) who suggested that the infant's behavior is one of the factors which influence the parent's attitudes. Some examples cited by Watson (1959) serve to illustrate this particular aspect of parent-child interaction.

> One infant's early-formed quiet pattern, shown by his rarely crying and by his tendency to sleep more than the usual infant, was welcomed by the parents since it did not disturb their work. Another baby who was very active in her motor achievement was approved by her compulsive intel-lectualizing mother who wanted signs of her child's advanced state and found them in the motor area. Turning to an instance where there was an increasingly poor mother-child relationship, a third very active infant drove her compulsively-overconscientious mother to seek treatment be-cause she could not keep up with a child in his 'all-day' running in the park (p. 235).

We might remind ourselves at this point that a mother's attitudes can also be affected by her perception of the child as in some way differing from her expectations. Indeed, several studies of mothers of exceptional children (Guertin, 1961; Klebanoff, 1959; Margolis, 1961) seem to show that such a relationship does exist. If attitudes affect maternal behavior and if such behavior influences the personality development of the child, maternal attitudes would be an important intervening variable affecting the adjustment of exceptional children. This issue will be pursued in greater detail in later sections.

PARENTAL BEHAVIOR

Maternal behavior and child adjustment. So far we have discussed the possible influence of maternal attitudes on the personality development of the child and found that such attitudes are difficult to define and difficult to measure. As Gildea, Glidewell and Kantor (1961) have pointed out, "the referent of any attitude includes an array of behaviors from unverbalized feelings to verbalized statements of opinion; from vague inner urges to directly observable behavior" (p. 43) so that the measurement of attitudes may focus on any one or on a combination of these interrelated variables. But even if there were no doubt as to what is measured with an attitude questionnaire or interview, there always remains the question of the relationship of an attitude which a parent may express to the behavior in which he engages in a variety of child-rearing situations.

A different approach to the investigation of child-rearing antecedents to personality development lies in the study of maternal behavior. Here the mother is not asked how she would feel about a number of hypothetical situations; instead, she is asked what she did in certain specified periods and situations during the child's early years, or, better still, specially trained observers watch her interactions with the child in carefully sampled child-rearing situations.

One of the most recent major studies on child-rearing behavior is that by Sears, Maccoby, and Levin (1957) who interviewed 379 mothers of five-year-old children, living in two suburbs of a large New England city. Using a standardized, semi-structured interview of which they made a recording for later analysis, these investigators sought to find answers to three major questions: 1) the nature of child-rearing practices in their sample; 2) the effects of these practices on aspects of the personality development of the children; and 3) the relationship of the particular child-rearing practices chosen to the mother's own background and personality.

The Sears, Maccoby, and Levin study represents a major accomplishment in the scientific investigation of child-rearing and as such deserves fairly extensive discussion, provided one does not lose sight of the fact that, with many similar studies, it shares the disadvantage of being based on interviews instead of observations. When a mother reports what she did with her child some years earlier there is no way of knowing whether she actually behaved as she says she did. Similarly, if one is interested in the effect a particular child-rearing method has on the personality development of the child one is dealing with indirect and possibly biased data when the evaluation of the child's personality is based on the mother's own description of her child. A further drawback of this investigation is that it is based entirely on interviews with the mothers so that the father's role in the child-rearing entered only indirectly.

As a study based on a not altogether representative sample from two New England communities, this research is further limited in its generalizability to the American scene at large. Sears, Maccoby, and Levin are well aware of this limitation when they describe their 379 mothers as follows: "Our mothers, then, were from two suburban towns of a large New England metropolitan area. They all had children registered in public school kindergartens. They were all American-born and were living with their American-born husbands. Their husbands were the natural fathers of their kindergarten-age child, and the child was not a twin nor was it handicapped in any way" (p 26). The elimination of children with handicaps is particularly noteworthy from the point of view of the primary focus of our discussion since the Sears survey thus bears only indirectly on ways of bringing up children who are exceptional.

Sears, Maccoby, and Levin (1957) found that only 25 per cent of the mothers in their sample were other than delighted or at least pleased at the prospect of having the child about whom the interview was being conducted. As might be expected, attitudes toward pregnancy were related to the mother's evaluation of her husband. The less her esteem for her spouse, the less positively she would feel toward her pregnancy. A similar relationship was found between the mother's self-esteem and her pregnancy attitudes; the more positively she viewed her life situation in general, the more positively she felt toward pregnancy. On a measure of warmth toward the infant the study showed that those mothers who held their husbands in high esteem were much warmer in their relationship to their children than were those who felt less enthusiasm and respect for their husbands. While, as Sears, Maccoby, and Levin themselves suspect, these relationships may all be correlated with one underlying personality variable of the mother, the data suggest that a mother's attitude and behavior toward her child are intimately related to the interpersonal dynamics in the family.

A similar reflection of family dynamics can be found in the data on feeding practices. The mother's decision about breast-feeding was not related to her feelings of pleasure or displeasure over pregnancy, to the degree of warmth in the mother-child relationship, nor to her feelings of competence or inadequacy concerning child care. On the other hand, the one variable which was significantly related to the decision on breast-feeding was the mother's tolerance about her child's sex behavior which the investigators labeled "sex permissiveness." If a mother was rated low on sex permissiveness she was less likely to breast-feed than if her permissiveness about sex behavior was high. As the authors point out, these attitudes and their resultant behavior are related to the mother's feelings of personal modesty which, in turn, would seem to bear a relationship to her interaction with her husband.

Basing their evaluations on the mother's description of child behavior, Sears, Maccoby, and Levin found that breast-feeding or its lack had no demonstrable effect on aggression, dependency, feeding problems, bed-wetting, disturbances over toilet-training, or the development of conscience. The presence or absence of feeding problems was not related to the mechanics of feeding (breast, bottle, schedule, or self-demand), nor to the child's age at weaning, but were related to the degree of general restrictiveness on the part of the mother. This would suggest that, as in the previously cited Behrens (1954) study, the atmosphere in which feeding and weaning take place has a greater effect on the development of emotional problems than does the specific method or timing which the mother applies.

The study of toilet-training practices also led Sears, Maccoby, and Levin to the conclusion that the mother's personality and the atmosphere of the interaction which this factor presumably produces was a major variable in the nature of the child's reaction to this particular experience. Thus, "severe toilet-training increased the amount of upset in children whose mothers were relatively cold and undemonstrative" (*ibid.*, p. 125). A similar interaction was found in the data on bed-wetting where "the combination of high sex anxiety, a relatively cold and undemonstrative attitude toward the child, and severe toilet-training were most efficient for producing prolonged bed-wetting" (p. 131). On the other hand, warm and affectionate mothers who also had high sex anxiety but used gentle toilet-training methods generally succeeded in achieving night dryness before the child was two years old. McCandless (1961), in discussing these findings, states that "an area of behavior that is extremely important to the mother, but about which she is punitive and cold, may be one in which the child refuses to conform, thus expressing his rebellion and resentment. When the behavior is extremely important to the mother, *but* she is gentle and warm in her insistence on conformity, the child compliments her by taking note of her wishes, and doing as she wants him to" (p. 89).

Maternal anxiety about sex, which Sears, Maccoby, and Levin find to correlate highly with the mother's behavior in both the feeding and toilet training situations, was based on an indirect measure: ratings of the extent to which she was permissive in her control and training of the child with respect to modesty, masturbation, and social sex play. What is called anxiety about sex may thus be merely a manifestation of a more general permissiveness variable, but one might assume that if a mother is non-permissive about her child's behavior relevant to sex her attitude might also play a role in her relationship to her husband. While the Sears data do not lend themselves readily to an analysis of this relationship there is reason to suspect that the interaction between mother and child on sex-relevant behavior should not be viewed in isolation from the spouse system.

Because the general factor of permissiveness, which was an important variable in almost all areas of child-rearing studied by Sears, Maccoby, and Levin, is so closely related to the mother's own personality, the professional person interested in influencing maternal child-rearing practices can here find an important clue. Speaking of toilet-training, Sears, Maccoby, and Levin point out that, by and large, training was more quickly accomplished the later it was begun and that it produced emotional upsets in relatively few children if it was started after the child was twenty months old. This might suggest that mothers should be advised to delay the beginning of toilet-training were it not for the fact that the mother's own emotionally-based needs play an important role. Mothers who chose to begin training early were relatively high in sex anxiety, presumably a personality variable. No amount of exhortation or reasoning on the basis of scientific studies can overcome a mother's sex anxiety and if this is what leads her, at least in part, to early toilet-training professional advice to the contrary will at best make her feel guilty and insecure about her practices, reactions which hardly contribute to making the mother-child relation warm and spontaneous.

In that event, the professional advice may have the effect opposite to that intended. The mother may become tense about what she is doing and "the introduction of pressure, impatience, irritability and punishment into toilet-training produces resentment, recalcitrance, and emotional upset in the child. It does not serve to speed his learning in the slightest, and may, if the mother is rather cold in her relations with him, serve to initiate a prolonged period of bed-wetting" (Sears, Maccoby, & Levin, 1961, p. 136).

The area of child training in which the child's exceptionality may be thought to play a particularly crucial role is that of dependency. Particularly if the child has a handicap, the mother's perception of and reaction to him may come to focus on her ability to permit him to become healthily independent of her. Her greater indulgence toward the child with a handicap added to the realistically frustrating aspects of the disability may lead to difficulties in aggression training. Because this area is thus of particular relevance to the student of exceptional children and their parents we shall want to examine the findings of the Harvard study (Sears, Maccoby, & Levin, 1957) in particular detail.

In weaning and in toilet-training the mother has a definite and concrete goal in mind and her culture gives her a very definite idea of what is to be accomplished. Once the child has learned to drink from a cup and once he is able to take care of his own needs on the toilet there is little else she needs to teach him in these areas. In the realm of dependency, on the other hand, there is no such clear-cut goal nor is the culture specific as to what ideal the training should be aimed. Although all mothers engage in behavior relevant to dependency training, they do not always do so in an explicit and planful way. This diffuse and abstract nature of training makes it a difficult area to study.

It may in fact be necessary to explain just what we mean by training in the area of dependency since the very expression is somewhat ambiguous. The child, who at birth is quite unresponsive to social stimulation, learns to react to and depend on other people during the first six months of life. He passes, as Sears, Maccoby, and Levin (1957) point out, "from the receptive stage to become a social person in his own right, not only responsive to others but actively seeking, controlling and manipulating them" (p. 138). As the child grows older and beginning with the first attempts at locomotion he must learn to become less dependent on his mother who was so necessary for his very survival in the early months of life. It is one of the functions of parenthood to help and enable the child to learn ever-increasing independence and it is this, often implicit, process which has come to be referred to as dependency training.

In the course of having his mother meet his physical dependency, the child learns to form an emotional dependency on the mother, a dependency which becomes a powerful motive, not easily eliminated or ignored.

In fact, the more the child's efforts to satisfy it are frustrated, the more insistent and all-absorbing are his supplications. The socialization task for the mother is one of gradual modification of the form of expression, therefore, rather than one of blunt elimination. She must help the child learn to seek attention and affection from his peers and from other adults, as well as from herself, and she must help him to change from his clinging, engulfing manner of expression to a cooler, perhaps more verbal, one. And withal, she must teach him to 'ask' for signs of love and attention and reassurance in a fashion less demanding, more subtle, more in accord with the propriety and dignity of adult behavior (Sears, Maccoby, & Levin, 1957, p. 141).

Because the child's dependency meets many strong emotional needs in the mother her task of teaching the child to become independent is often difficult and again relates to the dynamics of the family system of which the mother-child sub-system is but a part. When the spouse system lacks emotional responsiveness the mother may have turned to the child to meet her needs for emotional warmth so that increased independence in the child may in effect threaten to deprive the mother of an important source of gratification. Similarly, where the child has a physical defect or deformity the mother's emotional needs may demand that she continue to protect and nurture him as she did when he was an infant so that the task of training the child for independence is again complicated. A further quotation from Sears, Maccoby, and Levin may serve to illustrate this relationship.

> A mother and her child are a *dyad*. That is, each has expectancies about how the other should behave. If these are fulfilled, each is happy and comfortable. If expectations are *not* met, however, there is frustration. Both mother and child learn how to control each other, that is, how to produce in the partner those actions which will make for satisfaction. However, during the child's early life, he no sooner learns one way of behaving than his mother's expectancies change. Then he must learn a new way. For example, he learns to hug and kiss her, to express his affection very openly. But then she begins to view such behavior as changeworthy; she wants him to *talk* his love more and *hug* it less. If she begins to be less responsive to his customary ways of seeking her affection and attention, his first reaction will be to redouble his efforts. That is, he will behave 'more dependently.' Ultimately, if his mother just never responds at all, we would expect these specific forms of supplication to be eliminated (because of non-reward) (*ibid.*, p. 141 f.).

The results of the Harvard study again show how a mother's attitudes and behavior in one area are closely related to her attitudes and behavior in other areas. Thus when a mother had an accepting and tolerant attitude toward the child's dependent behavior, she was also likely to be affectionately warm toward him, gentle in toilet-training, high in sex permissiveness, unlikely to use physical punishments for dependent behaviors, and tolerant when he was angry and aggressive toward his parents. Such a mother would also manifest high esteem both for herself and for her husband. When a mother was irritable, scolding, and wont to pull away from dependent behavior, this would increase the frequency of such behavior, or at least the mother would perceive and report it as such during the interviews. The most dependent children of all belonged to those mothers who handled this behavior in an inconsistent and ambivalent manner. Such mothers would irritably reject dependency demands for awhile but would eventually give in to the demands and thus reinforce this behavior. This form of maternal behavior may not only have acted as an intermittent reinforcement which tends to make behavior highly resistant to extinction, but the conflict involved may also have made the child less secure so that the excessive dependency might well be viewed as symptomatic of such conflict.

The professional person hoping to modify a mother's behavior toward her child would again do well to remember that such behavior almost invariably relates to underlying attitudes, character structure and relationships to significant individuals other than the child. An attempt to change a mother's behavior in the area of dependency training, for example, would thus have to take into account what this particular behavior means to the mother in her whole psychic and interpersonal economy. Advice, admonition, or exhortation will rarely serve to change child-rearing behavior whose roots may lie in the mother's own childhood.

The fact that maternal attitudes are related to the mother's personality and are thus more than transient opinions about child-rearing which might conceivably be changed by superficial educational techniques was demonstrated in a study by Zuckerman and Oltean (1959). Using the Parental Attitude Research Instrument (PARI) developed by Schaefer and Bell (1958), these investigators compared maternal attitudes with a number of personality variables and found several significant relationships. On the basis of the findings of Sears, Maccoby, and Levin (1957) they had hypothesized that the PARI Hostility-Rejection factor would be negatively correlated with a measure of self-acceptance; that is, the lower the woman's self-esteem, the higher her hostility-rejection score. Although the subjects for this part of the study were eighty-eight student nurses, none of whom were married or mothers, the hypothesized expectation was borne out. A person who is not accepting of self would seem not to be accepting of others, in this case the others being husband and children. Zuckerman and Oltean state, "Low self-acceptance can also be related to the role conflict implied in this factor. Since the mothers who score high on Hostility-Rejection are functioning in a role they do not accept, it would be difficult for them to accept themselves. One would also expect a certain amount of guilt, and consequent loss of self-acceptance, to accompany rejection of the homemaking role since the maternal motive is often held up as a cultural ideal" (1959, p. 32).

Another aspect of the same study which included twenty-four subjects who were mothers of college students tested the relationship between PARI responses and manifest personality needs reflected on the Edwards

Personal Preference Schedule (1954). Here it was found that "the mother who tends to be hostile and rejecting in her parental attitudes tends to have a high need for achievement, a low need for nurturance, and a high need for aggression. . . . A woman whose significant rewards tend to lie in achievement outside the nurturing, maternal role is one who is likely to be irritable with her children and her husband because she is functioning in a role which does not fit her needs" (Zuckerman & Oltean, 1959, p. 30 f.).

Observations of maternal behavior. Most of the studies on maternal behavior discussed thus far were either based on responses to questions about how mothers handle or handled their children, or they used attitude scales where the relationship between attitudes expressed and attitudes held and the behavior which might result from these attitudes is largely unknown. Investigations on parent-child relationships are rarely based on systematic, reliable behavior observations, the only way which will ultimately give us the kind of knowledge we need in this field.

A pioneering study where maternal child-rearing behavior was directly observed was that conducted by Merrill (1946) who watched mothers with their children in a standardized play situation. This investigation demonstrated that maternal behavior can be objectively scored and although it was not designed to explore how children react to different forms of maternal behavior it must be considered a major contribution because it used maternal behavior as a dependent variable in an experimental setting. Merrill had two matched groups of mothers who were observed in the same situation at two different times. Before the second session the mothers in the experimental group were told that their child had not shown a full realization of his capacities in the first session. After this relatively mild criticism, mothers in the experimental group manifested changes in their behavior during the second session as compared to the behavior of the mothers in the control group who had not been exposed to this external pressure.

In view of the fact that the criticism implied that there was "something wrong" with the child, it is interesting to study the mothers' reactions for its relevance to how mothers of handicapped or defective children might react to the recognition that there is something wrong with their child. In Merrill's study the mothers of the criticized children tended to become more controlling of their children's behavior and to impose their own standards to a greater extent than they had in the previous session. Almost all of these mothers displayed a significant increase in interfering, criticizing, directing and introducing changes in activities. It would appear from this experiment that when a mother is exposed to someone else's criticism of her child she tends to become more authoritarian and controlling of her child's behavior. Since we know from other investigations, such as those by Radke (1946) or Sears, Maccoby, and Levin (1956), that parental behavior on the dimensions of permissiveness-restriction and autocratic-democratic seem related to child behavior, it may be well to keep this finding in mind for our later discussion of the personality patterns of handicapped and defective children.

One of the most intensive observational studies of maternal influence during infancy is that conducted by Brody (1956) as a part of a larger investigation conducted at The Menninger Foundation under the direction of Escalona and Leitch (1953). Brody selected thirty-two mothers of infants between the ages of four to twenty-eight weeks. Each mother and her infant came to a special observation room for a period of four hours during which she was interviewed and observed by three investigators. These sessions were followed by home visits lasting from three to three and a half hours and in both settings an attempt was made to have the mother carry out her usual infant care practices, such as feeding, diaper changing, and putting the child to sleep.

The investigators were particularly interested in six kinds of maternal activities: feeding, cleaning, moving the child, touching the child, offering objects and speaking to the child. Each of these activities was rated for the sensitivity with which the mother responded to the needs of her infant, using scales which were developed after the behavioral observations had been recorded. Brody (1956) points out that "no objective criteria yet exist for the validity of scales used to evaluate maternal responsiveness to infants, and the scales devised for this research were assumed to be tentative" (p. 245).

In the analysis of the data obtained with these scales Brody used three measures for each of the six kinds of activities. One was a measure of the average amount of sensitivity the mother showed in each kind of activity, another was the frequency with which the particular activity occurred, and the third reflected the consistency of sensitivity which each mother displayed. Brody states that adequately to describe a maternal activity these three criteria must be applied together, and using her three measures she was able to isolate four types of mother-infant interaction. Preferring not to use descriptive typological names for the four groups of mothers, because to her words like "permissive," or "indulgent" are value judgments and not classificatory names of an aggregate of behavioral qualities, Brody designates the four groups as A, B, C, and D, describing these as follows:

The mothers of group A were conspicuous for their ability to accommodate to the needs of their infants. By virtue of the kind of physical and emotional support they provided and the steadiness of their interest in and communicativeness toward their infants, they gave them freedom to move about, to vocalize, feed, rest or play with a minimum of interference. More regularly and with more ease than all the other mothers they recognized and tried to relieve passing discomforts in the infants. The mothers themselves were not without tension, but most of the time that tension appeared to heighten their intimacy with the infants.

The mothers of group B were conspicuous for their conscious willingness to accommodate to their infants. At first glance some of their behavior resembled that of the A mothers, but on the whole they were more tense, less communicative and less steadily attentive. At times they tried more actively to stimulate their infants and at other times they were mildly distant or insensitive to the infants' immediate needs. The quality of satisfaction with the infant and of enjoyment of their mothering tasks, outstanding in the A mothers, was much less evident, although B mothers were generally positive toward their infants.

The mothers of group C were conspicuous for their lack of spontaneity and their intentions to be efficient above all else. Some reduced their attention to the carrying out of a minimum of essential details of infant care, and showed a low degree of interest in any activity with the infant of a non-physical nature.

The mothers of group D were conspicuously active but also erratic in their attentiveness, efficiency and sensitivity. They quite sedulously governed their infants' actions by stimulating, restricting or instructing them, apparently hardly aware of the possible effects of their behavior on the infants' condition. (Brody, 1956, pp. 265–266).

Brody's objections notwithstanding, Watson (1959) suggests that group A might be labeled permissive, group B less permissive, group C restrictive, and group D inconsistent. While such labeling might be considered premature at this stage of our knowledge, it does aid communication and permits one to relate Brody's findings more readily to those of other researchers in the field. At the same time Watson's attempt to label these groups primarily on the dimension of permissiveness tends to obscure the fact that at least one other major dimension of maternal behavior which seems to have been isolated by Sears, Maccoby, and Levin (1957) among others, that of maternal warmth, also seems to differentiate among the four groups. The third major dimension of parental behavior which one encounters again and again in studies of parent-child interaction, that of punitiveness, was probably not significant in Brody's groups partly because of the age of the children toward whom few mothers would display punitive behavior in a situation where they know to be observed.

We have pointed out earlier that there is a dearth of studies which examine the relationship between maternal attitudes and maternal behavior. Brody (1956) reports some data which bear on this issue and although they are not as definitive as one might wish, they bear reporting for their very uniqueness in this badly-neglected field. Based on the mothers' interview responses and a questionnaire in which they had been asked to define what they considered "a good baby," "a fresh baby," "a bad baby," etc. and to explain what they meant by such terms as "being strict," "spoiling," "neglecting," this investigator tried to compare maternal attitudes to maternal behavior. Brody is aware that these data are superficial but in addition it must be kept in mind that they were not independent of the behavior observations so that some of the attitudes a mother expressed might well have influenced the observers in their ratings of sensitivity.

Brody found considerable consistency between the behavioral group in which a mother was categorized and the attitudes she expressed. The permissive mothers in group A expressed more than usual interest in the personalities of their infants, praised their development, and communicated with them socially as a matter of course and with pleasure. Conversely, the restrictive mothers in group C displayed more vulnerable confidence, had attitudes which were explicitly non-indulgent, and seemed a little more inclined to consider the use of corporal punishment in the future. One might wish that Brody had made use of a more standardized and independent measure of maternal attitudes for despite the apparent regularity of attitudes and their correspondence to regularity of behavior patterns convincing research exploring the relationship between these two remains to be done.

The relationship between maternal attitudes and behavior on the one hand and child adjustment on the other is the third area in this general field which calls for investigation. While Brody did not gather data on the adjustment of the infants, she offers some information which bears on the issue. Activity ratings, information on weight gains and results of an examination using the Gesell developmental schedules were compared for the four groups in a cursory attempt to test whether there might be a relationship between the four types of maternal behavior and the kinds of infants contained in each group. The activity patterns of the infants appeared to have no relation to the types of maternal behavior. The data on weight gain showed the highest mean for group C with group A, B, and D following in that order. The results of the developmental schedules revealed differences between the four groups which, though not conclusive, were in the expected direction. The infants in group C, the least stimulated, were the least advanced in the various aspects of performance and development measured by these schedules. The infants in group D which, because of their mothers' inconsistency, were most stimulated, were the most advanced in the areas of *language* and *personal-social.* The infants in group A were the most advanced in the areas *motor* and *adaptive* and the infants in group B fell in between.

Findings as these tend to suggest that specific maternal activity patterns are the antecedents and child behavior the consequences, but such a causal formulation does not take account of the fact that the mother reacts to her child, the child reacts to the mother, the father will react both to the child and to the mother's reaction to the child so that the resulting behavior and adjustment on the part of all members of the family becomes a product of great complexity.

It is this complex dynamic interaction which makes studies in this area so difficult and often inconclusive. Explicitly or implicitly most studies often assume a cause and effect relationship between maternal attitudes or behavior and child adjustment. By thus neglecting the differences in reaction potential of different children the data become confounded and the results inconclusive. More sophisticated techniques should make it possible to evaluate the child's biological reaction potential so that this variable can be controlled in future studies. If, for example, one could select a group of children homogenous as to their reaction potential one could then measure differences in maternal attitudes and test whether or not these differences in attitudes will result in eventual differences in child adjustment and child personality. If one then remembers the father's role in this interaction and tries to consider his attitudes and reaction as a further variable to be controlled, the complexity becomes almost overwhelming and the conclusion suggests itself that at present we do not have the necessary research tools or techniques to investigate the area of parent-child interaction with any degree of thoroughness.

THE DYNAMIC INTERACTION BETWEEN MATERNAL AND CHILD BEHAVIOR

Studies of the development of child personality usually investigate the relationship between the mother's attitudes, emotions and behavior on the child's personality. The child's personality is generally viewed as the dependent variable and it seems commonly assumed that maternal personality is a relatively fixed and unchanging factor and that depending on that factor the child's personality will differ and vary. This approach loses sight of the fact that not only does the mother's behavior affect the child but that the child also influences the mother's behavior.

As Brody (1956) points out, the infant, in acting and reacting to his environment arouses a reciprocal reaction in the mother but the form of this reaction and the intensity of it are functions of the mother's personality. The infant is

> biologically impelled to make demands and to make them imperiously and unreasoningly. He makes them upon an adult who has striven over a lifetime to modify or control her own impulsive demands and who cannot but become disconcerted by having to live two emotional lives, as it were. The infant may re-arouse tensions in her, or may reawaken conflicts or may precipitate the appearance of new ones. But he has not created them. The infant touches off reactions in the mother, but the form and intensity of her reaction are determined by her own history of biological and psychological needs and by her knowledge of infant care. So does she touch off reactions in the infant, but those reactions are in the beginning determined by the intensity of his own biological needs and the strength of his structural reflexes (Brody, 1956, p. 347).

While the statement just quoted goes a long way to make the reciprocal relationship between infant and mother explicit, it ignores the definite possibility that this reciprocity begins prior to the infant's birth. During her period of pregnancy the mother is already responding to the child in emotional and attitudinal ways. We know too little to say whether the child reacts to this already *in utero* but a study by Davids, DeVault, and Talmadge (1961) revealed that women who experienced difficult labor and who gave birth to children with abnormalities tended to have a higher *prepartum* score on a measure of manifest anxiety than mothers who did not have such difficulties and who gave birth to normal children.

Rose (1958) has stressed the interaction between mother and child and pointed out that not only does the mother influence the child's personality but that the child must also be viewed as influencing the personality of the mother.

Viewing human personality development as a process which continues throughout life, a process in which crises such as puberty, pregnancy, and menopause may precipitate major personality changes, Rose (1958) examines the influence of the child on the maturational process of the adult. He points out that "various states of child development not only disturb significant adults, but are actually able to influence the maturational progress of those individuals in constant contact with the child. Much has been discovered with respect to the effect upon the child of parental behavior but relatively little about the counterpart experience with respect to parental maturity" (p. 31).

The mother, Rose (1958) points out, brings to the task of pregnancy and child-care certain assets and liabilities.

> From her past life she will have derived certain ideas as to the value of the roles of women, wife, mother and adult. She would have arrived at some point of experience in the management of past adaptive crises and will bring to bear on the new experience the expectation with respect to failure or success derived from the past. She will have developed patterns of relationship which on the whole make it easy for her to find support from family, husband and friends; or oppositely, to make it difficult. She will have developed certain typical behavior of regression or disorganization in the face of excessive stress. Her educational experience and socio-economic group will have influenced the nature of her values as to what is satisfying and rewarding in life in general as well as her experience in her own family. To this new experience then she will bring a complicated set of needs for satisfaction and happiness and probably a certain predisposition to fail or succeed in such goals. It would appear probable that one combination of assets and liabilities will predispose more to vulnerability and stress than will others (p. 28).

With these predispositions the mother enters upon the task of pregnancy and child-care. An evaluation of the effect of the developing child on the mother's maturational processes is complicated by the fact that parental maturation processes may affect only one aspect of the personality and not the total person. As Rose points out,

> The impact of the child upon that development may affect only the handling of that child or that of other children. There are no doubt radiations of this process into the total machinery of satisfying and dissatisfying aspects of life but the effects are less specific and difficult to distinguish in a unique form. Frustrations in child-care, may, for instance, impose strains on the husband and wife relationship but the manifestation may or may not differ greatly from financial hardship strains, etc. (p. 32).
> From a clinical viewpoint the most impressive evidence of actual increase in maternal maturity may be seen in the differences between experience with first and second children. It has been our impression, for instance, that parents are almost uniformly less tense in the care of second children than of the first ones. They seem to have learned 'how to do it.' As a usual thing, we are accustomed to hearing that the second baby has just been 'allowed to grow' and seems more relaxed and less anxious with respect to developmental tasks.
> The ability of a child to reward and satisfy a mother seems to arise partly from what he is as a real creature and partly from the values engendered by imagination and creative perception. In this sense we may see that the unreward of a mother from a child may arise primarily from her original perceptions; primarily from the difference between what he

is and what he should be, or primarily from a mixture of the two attitudes. In the latter case it is possible to see that if tensions arise from original perception and affect the development of the child, there will be variations between what the child should be (as a satisfying object) and what he really is. This allows for a type of circular interaction in which a mother feels continuously less adequate and a child is really less rewarding (p. 32).

If the mother's reaction to her child is influenced by her perception of what he is, then the reality of a handicap or defect in the child becomes a factor of crucial importance. Rose (1958) discussed the development of the mentally handicapped child from the point of view of parental reaction. He states,

> It has been suggested that what a child 'is' objectively, may be perceived by the mother both realistically and symbolically. Any deviation between the 'is' perceived and that perceived as 'should be' is reacted to with guilt, as if something willfully bad had been done against one's parents or society. Life patterns of management of one's misdeeds are invoked and in the subsequent interaction, it becomes extremely difficult to decide as to whether what the child 'is' is perceived more realistically or more symbolically.
> This tendency in the adult to react with guilt and perceptual distortion not only accounts for the general problem of determining objectively what a child 'is' but, even more importantly, must be handled, if further distortion of the developmental potential is not to occur. The comments most frequently encountered in discussions about the emotional problems of children with relatively simple intellectual deficits are—'the parents expect too much and the child tries too hard and so becomes nervous,'—'the parents have never been able to accept the nature of the handicap—they shop constantly for other medical opinions'—'the mother overprotects this child so much that he is much more infantilized than he should be' (p. 33 f.).

The severity and nature of the child's defect plays an important role in the parents' perception. A defect accompanied by gross physical abnormalities is not only readily diagnosed but also easily apparent so that less room is left for fantasy distortions. Where a definitive diagnosis is more difficult, contradictory medical opinions can be obtained to bolster the parents' attempts to deny the existence of the handicap. Rose (1958) continued his discussion with this factor in mind.

> In past clinical experience, we have been impressed by the impact of uncertainty with respect to damage in a child as a cause of considerable disturbance in both parent and child. This has seemed true whether the uncertainty arose as a parental fear with no significant reality stimulus, or

whether it was derived from contact with a physician and/or the infant himself.

In several instances we have seen cases in which the fear that defect exists in the child has been so strong as to be almost delusional in character. In one case the eventual effect upon the child was breath holding to the point of syncope. In the other, while no gross change had yet appeared in the infant, the intensity of maternal fear was of such character as to lead a pediatric resident to administer an aminophyllin suppository to an infant in whom no objective signs of asthma existed.

The relatively rapid impact of pregnancy and child care on the personality integrative process of the mother seems to increase the probability that such ideas will appear with varying frequency and intensity during these time periods. Fortunately they do not appear with the same intensity as in the cases cited. They are, however, likely to be sufficiently in evidence as to be triggered into activity by apparently slight stimuli. This phenomenon is frequently overlooked by physicians and because of the omission creates immediate and long range complications in care. Some mothers who seem disproportionately anxious when illnes is mild or after symptoms are under control, may actually be perceiving the infant as critically ill or at death's door. A variant of this situation occurs when an inconsequential remark of a physician with respect to a child's condition is construed as having a value referring to gravity of prognosis. Such impressions have led us to stress with pediatricians that care should be exercised in the conduct of neonatal examinations of both well and sick children to avoid burdening the parent with irrelevant professional uncertainties. (Obstetricians should observe similar precautions in prenatal examination.)

We have been impressed with the fact that serious uncertainty and consequent anxiety is rather readily introduced both by objectively appropriate and inappropriate stimuli. Once introduced it seems to acquire a life of its own, continued by all the mechanisms discussed and able to endure despite the passage of time and the pressures of other life events.

It has seemed to us that the parents of premature babies continue with great uncertainty as to ability of the child to survive long after the child is established in a healthy and relatively physically normal existence.

Clinical experience of this nature has led us to speculate that the uncertain complex of feelings and ideas, while most often set in motion by objective events, will exist with an intensity more related to previous life experience than to either the original stimulus experience or the continuing objective problems in a child's performance (p. 35 f.).

Bibring and her collaborators (1961) approach the study of pregnancy and childbirth from a point of view similar to that of Rose (1958) in that they regard pregnancy as a period of crisis, a significant turning point in the life of the woman who must master the crisis if she is to continue her maturational development. While the crisis is inaugurated by and specific to pregnancy, it does not end at the point of delivery but essential maturational changes seem to take place following the arrival of the baby. Since the mother must reorganize her psychic equilibrium following parturition, she is psychologically particularly vulnerable during that period and the frequent problems in early mother-child relationship may be partly due to this disequilibrium (Bibring *et al.*, 1961). The same authors speculate that the continuing process of maturation of the mother may be slow and persistent, keeping pace with the child's developmental steps. They write,

> If we assume that pregnancy involves acutely such profound psychological changes, we may raise the question what effect this could have on the attitude of the mothers toward their infants—especially on that of the primipara who is under the full impact of this new experience. In attempting to answer this question we have to consider whether the reorganization of her psychic equilibrium has not yet taken place adequately in many cases when the woman is confronted with the reality of her newborn and the demands which this reality places on her. This may then be partly responsible for some of the disturbances in the earliest attitudes of the young mother toward her new-born baby and may then lead to the establishment of a vicious cycle of mutually-induced sensitive reactions and frustrations, and finally result in the well-known, frequently-described, early tensions in this relationship (Bibring *et al.* 1961, p. 14).

The maturational steps through which a woman must go in the process of pregnancy leading to childbirth and early motherhood are traced by Bibring, Dwyer, Huntington, and Valenstein (1961), using a psychoanalytic frame of reference.

> An intense object relationship to the sexual partner leads to the event of impregnation, by which a significant representation of the love object becomes part of the self. To accept this intrusion and incorporate it successfully is the first adjustive task of the pregnant woman. Under the impact of the marked physiological and anatomical changes of the first months of pregnancy, the libidinal concentration of the self increases and leads to the integration of, and merging with, this foreign body, turning it into an integral part of herself—until the quickening disrupts this narcissistic process and undeniably introduces the baby as the new object within the self. From here on, to the delivery, the second task of adjustment sets in: within a state of growing self-cathexis, which is due to the pregnant woman's unique situation of extensive body changes and body functions, serving the growth within herself as if it were part of herself, an opposing trend simultaneously develops. This part of herself begins to move on its own, is recognized as the coming baby, begins to be perceived as if it were another object, and thus prepares the woman slowly for the delivery and anatomic separation. This preparedness equals a readiness to establish a relationship to the future offspring, and this in turn represents the new developmental achievement. The relationship, if it fulfills the maturational requirements, will have the distinctive characteristic of a freely-

changeable fusion—varying in degree and intensity—of narcissistic and object-libidinal strivings, so that the child will always remain part of herself, and at the same time will always have to remain an object that is part of the outside world and part of her sexual mate. The variations in this fusion will depend on the inner and outer life circumstances of the woman, the child, and the husband (*ibid.,* p. 15 f.).

The complicated process just described contains many areas of potential conflict. Complications may arise at any point in this line of integration and adjustment:

> Be it from the relation to the husband, or men in general; be it from the modes of receiving, retaining, or releasing which the woman has established as a result of her own infantile development and her leading libidinal positions; be it from the emotional charge of her object relationship which may be prevalently positive or ambivalent or destructively hostile; be it from her relationship to herself as compared or contrasted with that of the external world and its objects. In all these areas the woman will be taxed by the stress of pregnancy, and this in turn will be reflected in the signs of crisis. The solution or partial solution of the different aspects of this stress and the reintegration on a new level toward new experiences represents the maturational step of motherhood and of the attitude toward its functions and toward the child (*ibid.,* p. 17 f.).

Inasmuch as ways of coping with crises and relating to the interpersonal world is learned in childhood, the role of the pregnant woman's early relationship to her own mother takes on major significance. As the daughter moves toward becoming a mother in her own right infantile attitudes toward her mother are often reawakened and the nature of the resolution of this earlier relationship can become central to how the gravida copes with her situation. This clinical hypothesis finds some confirmation in a study by Lakin (1957) who found that compared to mothers of normal infants the mothers of colicky infants had a greater intensity of competitiveness with their own mothers.

Having presented an overview of the general principles of family interaction and parent-child relations, we shall, in the following chapters, explore how these principles apply under the special conditions that arise when one member of the family is an exceptional child.

II.

Parental Reactions to a Child with a Defect

PERSONALITY STRUCTURE

A DISCUSSION of the reactions of parents to the perception that their child has a defect requires a frame of reference based on a personality theory. Since there are a number of such theories it may be well to present a brief review of the personality theory to be employed in this discussion. Of the various theoretical approaches which have been advanced in order to systematize the empirical facts of human behavior, Freudian depth psychology undoubtedly represents the most comprehensive system, particularly if the more recent modifications and additions to this system are taken into consideration (see for example Blum, 1953; Munroe, 1955). For this reason we shall draw on psychoanalytic personality theory to provide a frame of reference in which to view parental reaction patterns.

The following is a simplified review of some of the salient points in Freudian depth psychology. It is in no way intended to be a complete exposition of that complex theory for we shall want to focus on only those aspects of it which are of immediate relevance to the topic under discussion.

The Freudian point of view maintains that personality is composed of three constructs or systems, id, ego and superego. One system, the id, represents the physiological drives and primitive impulses. As the individual becomes socialized through his interaction with the environment, most of these drives and impulses are gradually brought under control. This control is achieved by expressing the impulses selectively, by delaying their gratification, or by giving socially unacceptable impulses socially acceptable outlets. The component of personality responsible for this control, the ego, thus comes to be interposed between the impulses and the outer environment. The ego explores the reality represented by the environment and the perceptual and conceptual operations required for this reality-testing function are important aspects of the ego. In the process of testing and perceiving his environment, the person also perceives the reactions of this environment to him as an individual and out of this perception he forms an image of himself (the self-image) the maintenance of which is yet another function of the ego.

51

In the course of his development, the child comes to identify with the significant adults in his environment (usually and normally the parent of the same sex) and to incorporate that adult's standards and values which form the third system, the superego. These internalized values are composed of positive strivings for ideals of what one wants to be (ego ideal), consciously held and desired standards of goodness and excellence. In addition, the internalized values contain the punitive, stern, and forbidding attitudes of the incorporated parent. An infringement against the demands and strictures of the superego results in guilt which may be viewed as the "weapon" of the superego, the means by which incorporated standards and values are enforced.

The impulsive desires of the id, the stern commands of the superego, and the demands of reality can, and often do, stand in conflict and it is the responsibility of the ego to maintain a balance between these contesting forces. Through the integrating functions of the ego the individual maintains his adjustment, maintains the integrity of his personality. Any threat to this integrity is experienced as anxiety and inasmuch as anxiety is an unpleasant, stress-producing stimulus, the ego tries to deal with the threat so as to reduce anxiety and maintain personality integration,

A threat to ego integrity can emanate from unacceptable impulses about to break forth, from strong guilt or the anticipation of guilt, from realistic dangers in the environment or from fantasied dangers, from discrepancies between the ego ideal and the self-image, or from incompatible, conflicting demands made on the ego by id, superego, and environment.

The demands, impulses, conflicts and fantasies mentioned above need not occur at a level where the individual is conscious of their existence. Many of the psychic functions described occur on an unconscious level; id impulses are, in fact, always unconscious, as are many of the operations of the superego and ego. The unconscious aspect of many conflicts make anxiety and the defenses against anxiety often the only overt manifestation of events taking place below the level of awareness. Anxiety itself, may, in fact, not be consciously experienced when the operation of defenses against anxiety keep this feeling from being experienced.

Defenses against threat. The defense mechanisms to which the ego resorts in coping with anxiety were discussed in some detail by A. Freud (1946) and have recently been reviewed and summarized by Bibring *et al.*, (1961). In keeping with the aims of this discussion we shall briefly sketch those defense mechanisms which are of primary importance to understanding the reactions of parents to the perception of their handicapped or defective child.

Repression is the mechanism through which unacceptable and threatening psychological content is kept from conscious awareness. Repressed activities (including ego activities), impulses and conflicts which are thus excluded from consciousness are not eliminated and they continue to cause stress which may become expressed in various indirect symptoms. Because of the continuing threat posed by repressed material, other defense mechanisms are called into play, making repression the mechanism which is central to many other psychic operations. "In almost every instance of defensive activity, repression plays a part in insuring the effectiveness of the various defenses" (Bibring *et al*, 1961, p. 69 f.). Since much of ego function, and particularly the operation of the defense mechanisms, is in itself unconscious, "repression is the paramount mechanism through which this unconscious ego state is maintained, and the activity of the various defenses kept at an unconscious level" (*ibid.*, p. 70).

Sublimation can serve as an example of a defense mechanism and its relationship to underlying repression. Here, an impulse (usually of an aggressive or sexual nature) is unacceptable to society and thus to the superego. The impulse must be repressed because its expression would lead to guilt, threaten personality integration, and arouse anxiety. With the impulse repressed from conscious awareness and kept from direct expression, the impulse can be given expression in a socially acceptable, constructive manner. Gratification of an impulse with the aim, or aim and object changed from a socially objectionable to a socially valued outlet represents the defense mechanism of sublimation.

While in sublimation the impulse finds expression in a socially acceptable outlet related to the original goal, the expression of the impulse takes the form of the exact opposite of the original goal in the defense mechanism called *reaction formation.*

In *projection* the unacceptable impulse is perceived and treated as if it had its source outside the self. In its most usual form this defense mechanism attributes the impulse to another person and the individual using projection may then react to the other person in terms of the attributes he has projected onto him. The so perceived attributes may then serve as a *rationalization* for attitudes or behavior which would otherwise be unacceptable but can now be justified by the distorted perception.

Intellectualization controls affects and impulses through thinking about them instead of experiencing them. "Intellectualization is a systematic overdoing of thinking, deprived of its affect, in order to defend against anxiety attributable to an unacceptable impulse" (Bibring, 1961, p. 68). This separation of affect from content is also found in *isolation* where the affect may be either repressed or displaced to a different thought or object.

Displacement involves the shifting of an impulse from one object to another in order to solve a conflict and avoid anxiety. Here the nature and aim of the impulse remain the same but the direction of the impulse is deflected. The displacement can be onto one's self, usually involving aggressive impulses which, instead of being expressed against the other person, are given an outlet by *turning against the self.* When turning against the self takes concrete form and the impulse finds expression through bodily symptoms, the mechanism is called *somatization.*

A defense mechanism related to intellectualization and isolation is *ritualization* where, by turning to behavior of a certain repetitious sameness, repression is maintained because the meaning of the behavior eventually becomes obliterated in the preoccupation with the ritual. The stereotyped ritual is usually symbolic of the underlying conflict. A more direct expression of conflict which nevertheless is a defense mechanism is *acting out.* Here the individual lives out the unconscious impulse in behavior and the behavior itself serves to protect him against the conscious recognition of the repressed impulse. "Acting out may occur through the omitting or impulsive exaggeration of a normally adjustive, appropriate behavior, or it may be behavior which is contrary to established modes. Behavior is called acting out if it disrupts social adjustment" (Bibring *et al.,* 1961, p. 64).

So far we have discussed defense mechanisms which largely serve to reduce anxiety stemming from threat originating in internal conflicts. Since external reality can also represent a threat to ego integrity, the ego has at its disposal mechanisms which serve to defend against these. *Controlling* is one such mechanism. This involves excessive attempts to manage or manipulate events or situations in the environment which represent a threat or pose internal conflicts. Such maneuvers as interference with suggestions, excessive compliance, or sabotage of the attempts of others are manifestations of this mechanism.

Denial is a prime example of a defense mechanism designed to deal with external threat. This mechanism prevents threatening perceptions from coming to conscious awareness. "Literally seeing but refusing to acknowledge what one sees or hearing and negating what is actually heard are expressions of denial and exemplify the close relationship of denial to sensory experience" (Bibring *et al.,* 1961, p. 65). Denial must be distinguished from the related defense mechanism of *avoidance* which involves an active turning away from the threatening percept, often literally taking the form of closing the eyes or refusing to look.

Undoing is related to reaction formation but while the latter deals with the threat of unacceptable impulses, undoing provides for the reduction of a threat represented by an action which has already taken place or is fantasied as having taken place. In undoing the individual engages in behavior which is the opposite of the act it is meant to cancel out.

Withdrawal, the last mechanism to be discussed, is a reaction which may occur as a temporary and immediate response to threat and last until such time as the ego marshalls its resources and brings another defense mechanism into play. If other defense mechanisms are not available or inadequate to deal with the threat, withdrawal may become the preferred way of dealing with the conflict. In this defense mechanism interest or affect are removed from an object and invested in preoccupation with the self. In time of crisis such as pregnancy, illness, or personal loss, withdrawal may be a normal and temporary way of coping with the requirements of the situation.

Having briefly outlined the structure and dynamics of personality from the point of view of Freudian depth psychology, we shall now want to discuss some of the sources of anxiety connected with the birth of a handicapped or defective child. Following this, we shall return to the mechanisms of defense and illustrate some of them by showing how they may manifest themselves in parental reactions to a child with a defect, regardless whether this defect is present from birth or develops sometime during childhood.

EXPECTATION AND DISCREPANCY

During the period of pregnancy the parents, and particularly the mother, develop an expectation of what the child will be like. The image of the expected baby, as Solnit and Stark (1961) have pointed out, is an amalgam of perceptions of the self and of significant persons in the parent's past, such as mother, father, spouse, siblings and previous children. "The composite representation includes the image of the expected child which has been conveyed to the expectant mother by her own mother. Each of these kaleidoscopic shifting impressions summons up for recollection and emotional review older issues, conflicts, and fears. This anticipatory process is part of the normal preparation for motherhood. As a preparation it repeats and solves again certain of the basic conflicts and identifications that the expectant mother had with her own mother" (Solnit & Stark, 1961, p. 524). Included in these expectations is the cultural stereotype of the "ideal child," the child with all the attributes of perfection which will enable him to compete successfully and to assume the roles society assigns to him and his parents fantasy for him. While values differ depending on the parents' social class status, their expectations invariably include that the child will be able to surpass, or at least attain, the parents' level of socio-cultural accomplishment. Because of the mother's more immediate biological role in gestation, she has a greater narcissistic investment in these expectations than does the father so that any discrepancy between the expectations and the reality presented by the child, when born, will usually have greater psychological meaning to her.

It is the mother who "produces" the infant, it is she who "gives" it birth. If the "product" turns out to be defective (a term here used to include all defects in the child, whether physical or intellectual) the mother perceives this as a defect in something she has produced. Coughlin (1947) has expressed the view that a defect in the child brings deep-seated feelings of the parents to the surface, feelings which, had the child been normal, would have remained repressed.

By the nature of the reproductive process and the length of time elapsed between insemination and parturition, the father sees himself less immediately involved in the production and, at least on an unconscious level, he is able to fall back on the defensive fantasy that the defective child is not really his own. The difference in the meaning the defective child has to father and to mother is seen by Boles (1959) as related to the difference in parental roles. Since the mother's role is one of nurturance and protection while the father's is that of planning and providing for the future, the father's role does not meet frustration until the child is of school age. The father thus does not encounter the reality of the child's defect until later in the child's life and before that time the mechanisms of rationalization, denial and avoidance can serve him to protect himself against the recognition of reality.

Through the division of labor practiced in our culture with respect to child rearing the mother, on the other hand, is in almost constant contact with the infant and young child. She thus encounters the reality of the defect in everything she does for and with the child, forcing her either to perceive the reality or to call upon mechanisms of defense at an earlier point than father. For this reason, most of the available literature on the subject focuses on the reactions of the mother and we shall here examine her reactions in considerable detail.

In order to understand the mother's reaction to the discrepancy between the expectation for a perfect baby and the reality of the defective child, we must explore the variety of meanings the birth of a child can have to a mother. It should be understood that a child can have a number of meanings at the same time and different meanings at different times and that, moreover, owing to the unconscious qualities of many of these meanings, contradictory meanings may exist side by side.

The meanings of a child. The child may be viewed quite literally as a "product of labor," something the mother has made; a personal achievement. As such it may be equated with archaic productions of childhood and arouse reactions relevant to the new mother's early relationship to her own mother. The infantile aspects of the gravida's relationship to her own mother (Bibring *et al.*, 1961) play a crucial role in how the newborn is viewed. If the infant's maternal grandmother was a critical perfectionist whose love was conditional on the mother's meeting her high demands, expectations based on these internalized values may be for a perfect baby. While there is probably always some discrepancy between the expectations and the real child, the greater and more apparent the discrepancy, the stronger will be the mother's feeling that she has failed to live up to expectations, and the greater will be her emotional reaction which usually takes the form of guilt.

The unverbalized exclamation upon the birth of an infant, "Look what I made!" or "See, how clever of me!" countered by the reality of a defective baby becomes unconsciously interpreted as "I have failed," or "I am no good." Where the infant's mother stands in a rivalry relationship to her own mother, the exclamation, "Look, I'm a big girl now; I can do what you did," is negated by reality and may be taken as proof of inadequacy and incompetence. The internalized values of the demanding mother may invoke reproof and reprimand, resulting in a sense of worthlessness and depreciation.

In certain cases a mother's strongly internalized feelings of worthlessness, inadequacy and incompetence may antedate the birth of the child by many years and in order to maintain her negative self-image of someone who can't do anything right, this mother may need to perceive her infant as defective or, at any rate, as more defective than he realistically is. It is this possibility which has led us to include in our definition of exceptional children that child who is perceived as defective even though this perception is not congruent with reality. Once a parent perceives a child as defective and begins to behave toward that child according to this perception it matters little to the personality development of the child whether the defect exists in reality or in his parent's fantasy. In either case he and his parents need professional help.

Another view of the baby may be that he is a gift and the obstetric term *presentation* may have symbolic value beyond its anatomical meaning. The gift may be the mother's present to her own mother, a situation possibly based on unconscious and long-repressed childhood fantasies about replacing the mother in father's affection and bearing his child (Deutsch, 1944–1945). This unconscious fantasy invokes the threat of mother's retribution and expiation demands that the baby be "presented" to mother to assuage her unconsciously fantasied wrath. One need not invoke depth psychological formulations to understand why the baby may be viewed as a gift to grandmother. The mother-child relationship of the gravida may have been such as to create a feeling that grandmother has been deserted at the time mother got married. To make up for grandmother's fancied loss, mother may wish to present her own baby and in many families it is indeed the grandmother who, under the guise of helpfulness, takes over the care of the infant. The symbolic value of the infant as a gift to grandmother is of course reduced, if not vitiated, if the baby is defective. Society teaches that one does not give an imperfect present; the present is unacceptable if it has a fault. In this case, unconscious needs to appease and assuage grandmother remain unmet and with it, the punishment anticipated for unconscious transgression is meted out by the superego and the outcome is again a sense of worthlessness and guilt.

The intended recipient of the baby as a gift may also be the husband, the infant's father. Rather than seeing the child as the joint product of both marriage partners, the mother may view the infant as something she produced for her husband and the new mother not infrequently awaits with mild trepidation the spouse's verdict upon his first seeing the child. If the baby is defective, the mother may perceive the husband's disappointment as disappointment with her and in her. Unless the marriage is based on a mature and strong relationship, the real or fantasied blame and recriminations can place a tremendous strain on the husband-wife relationship. At times plans for having a child may include explicit or implicit hopes of salvaging an unstable marriage, hopes that a child will bring husband and wife closer together. In other immature marriages the arrival of the first child is symbolic of consummation of the relationship, as external, social proof that the marriage exists and that both partners are capable of producing a child. Having a child is a sign of maturity, of manhood for the husband and of womanhood for the wife. All of these needs are frustrated when the child turns out to be defective. The wife's unverbalized exclamation, "Look what I made for you!" becomes a hollow mockery and it is not surprising that Stone (1948) in a clinical and Farber (1959) and Boles (1959) in experimental studies found a high incidence of marital problems among parents of retarded and cerebral palsied children.

Yet another meaning a child may have to the mother, depending on her religious orientation and values, is that the baby is a gift to her, a divine gift, a sign of grace. The expectation is again for a perfect baby and if the child turns out to be defective, the discrepancy may be viewed as a sign of dis-grace, a punishment for sins, an indication of unworthiness. A mother who is prone to react with guilt and feelings of unworthiness to failure may see the defective child as concrete proof of her own deficiencies but some religious faiths seem to serve as positive support in such a crisis. Religious attitudes may offer rationalizations whereby the defective child comes to be viewed as a special sign of grace for only the most worthy of mothers would be "entrusted" with the care of a handicapped child. Zuk et al. (1961) have shown that Catholic mothers of retarded children tended to verbalize more accepting attitudes toward their child than did non-Catholic mothers. It is, however, not known to what extent these verbalizations correspond to the mothers' true feelings, nor whether the accepting statements were motivated by underlying guilt which this research did not evaluate. This possibility is suggested by a study of mothers of cerebral palsied children conducted by Boles (1959) who found that Catholic mothers expressed more guilt over their child's condition than did Jewish mothers.

In many strata of our society married couples are under considerable social pressure based on the expectation that a marriage should produce children. Out of the need for social conformity, to have a child may thus become "the thing to do" so that couples who might otherwise prefer to remain childless tend to procreate. To be a parent, as Zuk (1962) has pointed out, is a good thing but the expectation also includes that the offspring be normal and thus capable to take his place in our highly competitive, materialistic society. Zuk (ibid.) speaks of a cultural dilemma which results from these expectations, if being a parent of a normal child is a good thing, producing a handicapped child becomes a bad thing. Society disapproves and parents who are motivated by a need for conformity see the defective product as a real disgrace and experience shame which sometimes results in attempts to hide the disgracing object. Baum (1961) expressed parental reaction to a defective child in the form of the syllogism, "If I am a good parent I shall be blessed with a perfect baby." Parents examine the new infant from this premise and when the child turns out to be defective, the conclusion becomes, "The baby is not perfect, therefore I must be bad." This recognition poses a threat to the narcissistic components of the ego and a defense must be found to ward off the anxiety aroused by this threat.

Mourning. Baum (1962) is one of several authors (e.g. Solnit & Stark, 1961; Tisza, 1962) who see parental reaction to the birth of a defective child as one of mourning over the loss of the perfect baby they had anticipated in their fantasies. From this point of view, the psychological preparation for the coming child which takes place during pregnancy includes the anticipation for a perfect child and the fear of a damaged child (Solnit & Stark, 1961). This preparation is abruptly terminated by the birth of a defective child, which represents the sudden "loss" of the expected baby. In depth psychology (Freud, 1949) grief and its behavioral manifestation, mourning, is the normal reaction to the loss of a valued object be it a loved person, a part of the body, or a cherished possession. In mourning the person temporarily withdraws from his involvement with the outside world thereby permitting the ego to concentrate on the work of withdrawing psychic energy (cathexis) from the lost love object in which it had been invested.

> In the mother's mourning reaction to the loss of the healthy child, her wishes for and expectation of the desired child are crushed by the birth of the defective child. Her anxious fears of having a damaged child are realized. These disappointed, highly charged longings for the normal child may be recalled, intensely felt, and gradually discharged in order to reduce the impact of the loss of the expected loved child. This process, which requires time and repetition, can liberate the mother's feelings and interests for a more realistic adaptation. The mourning process makes it possible to progress from the initial phase of numbness and disbelief; to the dawning awareness of the disappointment and feeling of loss with the accompanying affective and physical symptoms; to the last phase of the grief reaction in which intense re-experiencing of the memories and expectations gradually reduce the hypercathexis of the wish for the idealized child (Solnit & Stark, 1961, p. 526).

While Solnit and Stark recognize that the mother's reactions to her defective child are greatly influenced by her past experiences and grant that elements of both denial and guilt are involved in the reactions of parents to the birth of a defective child, their major emphasis remains on the mourning reaction. This view tends to neglect the fact that the recognition of a discrepancy between the anticipated child and the reality of the defective child represents a crisis and that each person has his own mode of coping with crises. This mode is a response learned in earlier crisis situations and thus depends not only on the individual's personality but also on the implicit meaning the defective child's birth has to the parent. It thus seems that the withdrawal taking place during the mourning period is only the first step in the ego's attempt to cope with the crisis. Mechanisms of defense become organized and called upon during this period and the end of mourning will bring with it the reëstablishment of a homeostatic personality balance which is manifested by the appearance of individually suited defensive modes. In the extreme case, where defenses are inadequate to cope with the crisis, the ego may become overwhelmed so that the person remains in an extended state of mourning, a state usually viewed as a postpartum depression.

The healthier personality will recover with the aid of defense mechanisms and, as is the case whenever defense mechanisms are used, the defense is against anxiety which, in turn, is a reaction to a threat to ego integrity. The nature and source of this threat depends on which of the previously mentioned varieties of meanings the birth and defect of the child has for the mother.

One such threat is the threat to the self-image which is presented by the perceived discrepancy. If the child is a product, meant as a gift or intended as a symbol of maturity, womanhood or adequacy, a defect in the product results in a recognition of failure. If failure is incompatible with the self-image it arouses anxiety and calls forth defenses designed to preserve the perception of adequacy.

Guilt. Another threat to ego integrity is guilt and this reaction, like all others, will have its antecedents in the mother's own history. If the values internalized in the superego represent demands which will tolerate nothing short of perfection, the birth of a defective child can in itself arouse guilt which, in this kind of person, was probably never far from the surface. The reason guilt is such a frequently reported phenomenon in parents of defective children (Stone, 1948; Tisza, 1962; Wardell, 1947; Zuk, 1962) may well be due to the fact that in our society child-rearing practices tend to instill guilt in connection with sexual matters and the childbirth is, both consciously and unconsciously, closely related to sex. When the child is healthy and normal, this guilt remains latent but when the child has a defect, the relentless unconscious relates this to the forbidden act and guilt is one of the deep-seated feelings which, according to Coughlin (1947), are brought to the surface upon the birth of a defective child. Ausubel (1955) has pointed out that guilt is one of the most important mechanisms through which an individual becomes socialized and that without the aid rendered by guilt, child rearing would be a difficult matter. With guilt such a pervasive emotion in the general population, it is not surprising that we find it in parents of defective children whose experience should, according to Schmideberg (1956), make them particularly vulnerable to this emotion.

Schmideberg (1956) stresses that guilt may have multiple origins and the archaic sense of sin reawakened by the birth of a defective child need not be its only cause. We turn to Zuk (1961) who points out that the child who does not meet the expectations for a perfect baby his parents entertained before he was born tends to frustrate the parents' anticipations, hopes and needs. The parent does not ask, "What did I do to deserve this?" and unconsciously seek for an answer, but he wonders, "Why did this happen to *me?*" Disappointment and frustration may lead to anger and arouse primitive aggressive-destructive impulses. These impulses, directed as they are against the defective product, are totally unacceptable to the superego and the resulting guilt must now be viewed as directed at the aggression and not, as in the earlier case, against the failure. Baum (1961) has emphasized that parents of normal children also experience negative feelings as a part of their ambivalence about the child. From the moment of conception the child tends to frustrate many elemental needs, evoking at least occasional resentment. Bearing and having children involves countless need frustrations, deferred gratifications and discomforts which must be endured. In the case of the child born with a defect, the strength of these negative feelings is more intense and the resulting guilt proportionately greater.

Yet another source of guilt stems from the threat the birth of a defective child poses to the internalized value system of many parents. If the child is seen as a divine gift and a defective child an expression of divine will, the unexpressed question, "Why did this happen to *me?*" has the correlary, "Why did He do this to me?" and raises the age-old philosophical question, "If God is good He would not have done this." This question is unacceptable to a religious person and the doubt of divine wisdom it implies creates guilt which only an absolute faith in the infinity and inscrutability of divine prescience can preclude.

DEFENSES AGAINST ANXIETY

Having reviewed the variety of sources of anxiety, we can now turn to ways in which different parents cope with anxiety following the initial period of reconstructive mourning.

Denial is one of the more primitive defenses against the threatening recognition of the discrepancy between the hoped-for healthy baby and the reality of the defective child. Parents will try to establish the myth that there is nothing wrong with the child and since this pretense serves to protect them from anxiety, they must try to maintain the myth against great odds. In a discussion of mental retardation Weingold and Hormuth (1953) spoke of the parents' intense resistance to any realistic recognition of the limitations or even capacities of their retarded child. They insist that the child could do all kinds of things if he were only given the chance and project blame on external sources for denying him this chance. It is obvious that as long as denial is maintained, realistic steps which might conceivably be of help to the child are precluded.

Unfortunately, denial is often supported by professional people on whom the parents need to rely. When the professional, through identification with the parents or over-involvement in their situation, experiences anxiety of his own against which he must defend, he may belittle the severity of the problem, hold out unrealistic hopes, or promise unlikely cures. The unsupported prognosis that the child will "grow out of it," is as much a denial as the parents' wishful claim that there is nothing wrong.

It is relatively easy to continue denial as long as the child is young and can be kept away from situations where comparison with normal children might make the reality of his defect too obvious. As the child becomes older and has to enter school this reality may so forcefully intrude itself that further maintenance of denial becomes increasingly difficult. At that point the parents must either add and substitute other defenses or, belatedly, cope with the reality and the anxiety its recognition entails. They often engage in complex psychologic maneuvers in order to maintain their self-deception. More and more denial and other defenses are brought to bear so as to ward off the ever increasing threat represented by reality. In order to prove the normality of their handicapped child, they may overprotect him, keeping him out of competitive situations where his defect might become glaringly obvious. Weingold and Hormuth (1953) point out that intense overprotection often keeps the child from developing capacities even in those areas where he might be capable of achievement simply because the parents are afraid to let him try.

In the reverse, the needs to maintain denial may lead the parents to exert tremendous pressures for achievement on the child. "Since there is nothing wrong with him, why shouldn't he be able to do it?" Such unrealistic pressures inevitably lead to frustration for both child and parents and the resulting emotional instability is often a factor which further complicates the child's condition. Baum (1961) pointed out that aspects of reality often serve the cause of denial. The exceptional child may be the only child of parents who, because of the child's condition, limit their interaction with other families. They thus lack opportunities for comparing the development of their child with that of normal children and, in cases of mental retardation, it is often difficult to arrive at an accurate intellectual evaluation, particularly when the child is very young or afflicted with severe motor and sensory handicaps. Parents, teachers, and even physicians are thus often left able to believe whatever they need to believe about the child's "true" ability and denial continues to serve its anxiety reducing function.

When denial must be maintained but reality ceases to lend the necessary support, parents often call on related defenses to maintain the protecting myth. The professional who tries to point out reality is derogated as inexperienced, disinterested, poorly trained, or downright stupid. A form of projection, this maneuver says, in effect, it is not we who can't see the truth, but he. Acting this out, parents may then begin a long and often desperate search for the professional who will agree with them, the "shopping around" which frequently entails a search for *the* cure.

Projection may also be the primary defense in cases where the defect is not denied but recognized. Here the parent must defend against unconscious guilt by projecting the blame for the child's condition onto something or someone outside the self. As pointed out earlier, guilt over the child's defect need have no basis in reality but may merely represent a focusing of feelings of guilt which antedated the birth of the child. At the same time, the search for an answer to the question, "Why did this happen to *me?*" may unearth a variety of factors which may or may not have contributed to the child's condition. Inadequate prenatal care, neglected complications of pregnancy, failure to heed obstetric advice all of which might conceivably have had something to do with the child's defect; and less realistic omissions or commissions such as alcohol consumption, smoking, or unusual sex practices can become foci for guilt fantasies.

The defense against this guilt may then take the form of the projection, "It is not my fault, it is their fault." The object of the projection is often a physician who did "something" wrong. Not only the blame, but also all the anger resulting from the frustration involved in having a defective child may then be turned against this professional person or, for that matter, against the entire profession he comes to represent. The slightest inadvertent (and unrelated) error is lit upon and becomes enlarged out of all proportion because it serves to support the defensive economy.

Projection can also utilize objects or even abstractions as foci. Anything from heredity to poverty, from a virus to the evil eye, may serve

as an explanatory cause just as long as it is something that is external
to and beyond the control of the person who must defend himself
against his own unconscious and irrational guilt. Where the cause does
not readily present itself, the individual may embark upon an extended
search for something that might be blamed. Doll (1953) has pointed
out that sooner or later most parents ask questions about the cause for
the child's defect. Because of the present state of knowledge this question can not always be answered to the parents' satisfaction (Kanner,
1953); and if the question is motivated not by rational reality testing
but by an irrational need to project blame, an honestly equivocal answer will be unacceptable. Parents will then "shop around" until they
find someone (professional or non-professional) willing to give them a
false but reassuring causal explanation.

When the basic motivation for the search after a cause is not a need
to understand but a need to blame, the child gets little help; but even
the need to understand may be merely the manifestation of defense
mechanisms, those of intellectualization and isolation. These again
serve to reduce parental anxieties but because the resulting behavior is,
on the whole, more constructive and socially useful these mechanisms
might be viewed as more mature than those previously discussed. Here
anxiety is defended against by an intense focus on the defect which has
become abstracted and thus devoid of its anxiety-arousing implication.
The concern is no longer with the deficiency of one's own child but
rather with deficiency *per se*, which can now be intensively studied in
all its aspects. Where the parent has the necessary educational preparation, he may even turn to scientific research into the causes and cures
for the particular deficiency. A related defense mechanism, and again
one with generally positive social consequences, is that of sublimation
where the psychic energy stemming from the initial anxiety is turned
into constructive work related to the child's defect. There exists a great
variety of organizations of parents whose children suffer from some
defect or handicap and the considerable personal energies behind these
organizations undoubtedly represent the aggregate of sublimated anxieties.

Katz (1961) conducted a survey of self-organized parents' groups
which suggests that participation in such groups provides the parents
an outlet for feelings of frustration. The groups do, of course, vary both
in their effectiveness and their activities and the variations express the
different dynamic motivations which lead parents to band together. At
times they may be highly constructive but some professional people
express reservations on the basis of the great emotional involvement the

group members have in the particular problem which serves as the focus. "Because of parent involvement and pressure, the groups are unable to take an objective view of the problems they are dealing with, of proposed solutions, and of limiting factors that necessarily influence the provision of care. The groups are thought to have a tendency to project fantasies in areas about which they are uninformed—i.e., basic medical knowledge—and are consequently unwilling to follow realistic counsel" (Katz, 1961, p. 141). The groups also tend to elevate "lay" opinion over professional judgment and to depreciate the value of professional knowledge and experience. Katz found that 40 per cent of the relatively small number of professionals he interviewed advanced these basic criticisms which were also held by men who were highly sympathetic to the aims and programs of the groups as such. If these opinions are valid they suggest that the groups reflect the psychological mechanisms of the individuals who comprise their membership.

Constructive sublimation can only take place after the parent has worked through and resolved the unconscious conflicts and fantasies around the defect of his child. This also implies that the child's own needs have been and are being met because hyperactive participation in parent organizations may also represent an avoidance of the child's real problems.

Avoidance may also take other forms, such as the parent's desire to have the child placed immediately after birth as if, by not seeing the child, the reality of the defect could be made untrue. The relationship of this defense mechanism to that of undoing ("He's *got* to succeed despite the defect") and the similarity of both to denial suggests that we are once again dealing with reactions which are unrealistic and potentially harmful to both parent and child.

Another defense mechanism with potentially harmful or at least unpleasant consequences for the child is involved in the acting out of hostility toward the child which takes the form of overly rigid adherence to a restrictive diet, a schedule of painful exercises or the administration of unpleasant medications. Since these ministrations are ostensibly for the child's own good they, like the more overt forms of punishment administered by other parents, can be carried out without the guilt which usually accompanies the expression of hostility in well socialized individuals. A parent who has a need to reduce his hostile impulses in this manner may be readily able to accept a therapeutic or habilitative regimen for his child which a parent without this motivation could not possibly tolerate. More often than not a parent settles for the kind of treatment of his child which is most congruent with his own personality needs.

Related to this is the way in which some parents defend against anxiety by ritualization, a mechanism which manifests itself in an over-involvement with the technical or medical aspects of the child's condition. By the preoccupation with the routines and rituals attendant to the care of the child, the compulsive cleaning of his prosthesis, the overconcern with the punctual administration of medications, the punctilious supervision of prescribed exercises permit the parent to shift the focus from feelings attached to the child's condition and thus to isolate his own emotional reactions.

The behavior just described would seem to the casual observer as representing excellent and conscientious care but in its psychological reality it consists of a mechanization of parent-child relations. This aspect makes ritualization similar to the mechanisms of reaction formation and undoing, whose manifestations usually take the form of over-protection or overindulgence. Dynamically undoing is related to parental guilt stemming from the parents' feeling that they themselves are somehow to blame for the child's condition. Having "done" something to cause the defect, they unconsciously attempt to "undo" the damage by taking extra good care of the child or by indulging his every demand. Reaction formation, on the other hand, is related to parental guilt over unacceptable anger at the child for having frustrated their hopes and expectations. The unconscious wish that the child had never been born and the concomitant, equally unconscious desire that he die are countered by the dynamic opposite, overprotection.

Overprotection and overindulgence are forms of maternal behavior which have been recognized for many years (Levy, 1943). Boles (1959) recently reported a significantly greater incidence of overprotection among mothers of cerebral palsied children when compared with a matched group of mothers of normal youngsters. The effect of over-protection on the behavior of the child has been described as increasing dependency and preventing the establishment of healthy independence, while overindulgence is generally associated with fostering aggressive tendencies in the child. Where the child's physical or mental defect itself would normally make him more dependent on parental care or where the normal frustrations of the defect tend to elicit aggression, parental overprotection or overindulgence will greatly exacerbate these overdetermined response patterns.

The parents' unconscious aggressive feelings toward the child may also be warded off by turning these impulses against the self. This, in a sense, is a displacement onto the self and, were it to be verbalized, might find expression in "I'm no good; it is my fault, not his; I deserved no better." With this defense mechanism in the underlying motivational structure, the parent may then proceed to seek punishment in the form of self-sacrifice and martyrdom, atonements which the condition of the child only too readily facilitates. The parent who refuses to institutionalize a severely handicapped child, who carries him around at a point where his weight makes this a tremendous physical hardship, the mother who sleeps sitting next to his bed, who gives up all of her own needs and interests, are all too familiar figures. This behavior serves strong unconscious parental needs and cannot be given up unless and until the parent's underlying feelings become modified. In the extreme case, the guilt attendant upon the parent's aggressive-destructive feelings may lead to withdrawal and depression signifying the failure of the ego to deal with the conflicts by means of more mature and constructive mechanisms of defense. These reactions may also be observed where outside forces abruptly interfere with the carrying out of this adopted self-sacrificing role. The stronger and possibly healthier parent may force placement of the child over the other's weak protests, or the child may die, making the unconscious wish to be rid of the burden become reality. Bereft of the defense and with guilt greatly aggravated, the parent withdraws from the intolerable reality and severe mental illness may result for which the loss of the child is only the manifest precipitating part of the cause.

Before ending this discussion of defenses, one further mechanism bears mentioning though it is usually too impotent to deal with more than very superficial anxiety related to the child's defect. Rationalization requires a realistic appreciation of the child's defect but the threatening impact of this appreciation is softened by focusing on some ameliorating aspect of the situation. The parents of a handicapped boy may thus rationalize that "at least he won't get drafted," as if to say that they are glad that their child is not a healthy, normal boy. It should be readily apparent that this approach is not adequate to deal with the many problems and conflicts which the parents face and other mechanisms may be needed to cope with their more basic feelings. In fact, one often finds that parents resort to more than one mechanism of defense, many of which may coexist and supplement one another so that the point by point listing just completed must be viewed as a somewhat artificial isolation of essentially interrelated psychological processes.

Effects on family equilibrium. Defense mechanisms help restore and retain personality integration after the reactive disruption (mourning) brought on by the birth of a defective child. Yet while the individual's personality may thus remain integrated, this integration is often achieved at the expense of others in the family or the environment. Reaction formation results in overprotection of the child, projection leads to hostility toward those who might be in a position to help, and displacement onto the self may bring about marital disharmony. Marital conflict does, in fact, appear to be very frequent in families with a defective or handicapped child. Boles (1959) reports marital conflict as one of the differentiating characteristics when mothers of cerebral palsied children were compared with mothers of nonhandicapped children. A similar finding is reported by Farber (1959) who investigated the effect of a severe mentally retarded child on marital harmony in 240 families. Though Farber's study did not include a comparison with a control group of parents of nonhandicapped children, his use of a previously validated "marital prediction score" permitted him to state that marital relationships were adversely affected by the presence of a mentally retarded boy in the home. Parents can expect, he concludes "that a retarded boy, especially after the age of 9, will probably have a disruptive effect on marital relations" (Farber, 1959, p. 80 f.).

The presence of a defective child in the family may disrupt marital relations in a variety of ways. Not only can the stress caused by the crisis bring out conflict which might have remained latent under different circumstances, but, as Farber (1959) points out, the difference in parental roles and the disruption of the family life-cycle may also be involved. The mother in her nurturant-protective role may be less threatened by the fact of the child's defect than the father whose role is more focused on planning and providing for the family (Boles, 1959). In addition, the parents may have different and conflicting ways of coping with anxiety. If the father resorts to denial (which is easier for him for he does not have the immediately responsibility for the day-to-day care of the child) while the mother uses reaction formation or ritualization the difference in their resulting behavior will almost certainly lead to conflict. Again, if the mother has turned her hostility against herself and seeks the role of the martyr, the father will find his own life disrupted and his needs unmet. He will become resentful—not against the child, for this is unacceptable—but against his wife, who now becomes the object of his own projections. None of this, as is readily apparent, is conducive to good marital relations.

REALISTIC COPING WITH CRISES

Lest the above discussion lead to the assumption that the birth of a defective or handicapped child will inevitably result in disruptive, maladaptive, or pathologic reactions on the part of the parents, it should be pointed out that many parents succeed in coping with the crisis in a healthy, constructive fashion. Our emphasis on negative reactions has two reasons. One is that the available literature deals almost exclusively with parents who have come to the attention of clinicians because they were unable to cope with some aspect of having a defective child. In fact, the few controlled studies suggest that these parents represent a majority. The other reason is to be found in the basic purpose of this publication: helping parents of exceptional children. It is the parents in need of help, and not those who have been able to cope with the problem successfully, who are of concern. But inasmuch as we wish to help parents to cope successfully, those who have been able to do so can well serve as models for what we hope to accomplish.

The healthy, well-integrated parent can also be expected to go through a reactive period of mourning after the birth of a defective child but he resolves the conflict created by the discrepancy between the anticipated and the actual by facing reality in its totality and dealing with the problems with which he is faced in a constructive fashion. The child can only be helped if the responsible adults around him are able to come to terms with his deficit on the basis of a realistic recognition of his strengths and his handicaps. Neither the exaggeration of the handicap nor its disavowal are helpful in furthering the child's healthy emotional development.

Yet a plea to parents that they adopt realistic attitudes toward a child's defect or handicap is quite useless, since the person with unrealistic attitudes is unaware of holding them. Unconscious mechanisms are exceedingly powerful forces and such defenses as reaction formation or denial do not yield to exhortation. Because of this the understanding, skilled help of the professionals with whom the parents come into contact takes on tremendous importance. The parents themselves do not know that they are distorting reality. It is the professional outsider who must be prepared to help them toward a realistic appreciation of the child's condition. With sensitivity and understanding most parents can be helped to cope with their crisis and its consequences in a realistic manner, especially if professional help is available right from the time when the child's exceptional condition is first discovered.

III.

Counseling Parents of Exceptional Children

ON TERMINOLOGY

TIME WAS when children with a physical defect were called "crippled children" and when a book like the present would probably have had the word "crippled" in its title. Today this word is avoided as if it were an invective, and calling someone a cripple is tantamount to using a most uncomplimentary epithet. For some time one spoke of "handicapped children," but that expression too has come to be frowned upon and seems to be joining "crippled children" on the proscribed list. Nowadays an author writing in this area is hard put to avoid the term "exceptional children," much as he may abhor this non-specific and confusing euphemism. Why has word usage undergone this change?

Our culture makes a fetish of health and tries to maintain the myth that all men are "created equal." Anyone who is not healthy, or who displays manifestations of having been created other than equal, violates the ideal and threatens the myth. Defensive maneuvers on the part of the members of society come into play, the principal one among these being the mechanism of denial. If we can somehow behave as if the unpleasant facts of ill health and handicap did not exist, they need not threaten us and the myth can be preserved. One aspect of this denial is the introduction of euphemisms for words which, because they describe unpleasant conditions, have taken on unpleasant connotations. Thus, "abnormal" becomes "atypical," "consumption" comes to be "tuberculosis" and then the anonymous "TB," the "insane" becomes the "psychotic" and then the "mentally ill," and in the field of intellectual deficit we skip from "idiocy" to "feeble mindedness," to "mental deficiency," to "mental retardation," to "mental subnormality," as if, by changing the label every few years, we could keep the ugly facts from catching up with us. The use of the word "exceptional" would seem to be a reflection of the same, almost frantic attempt to deny reality. All this would be an interesting semantic reflection of social attitudes were it not for the fact that it is more difficult to cope with reality when a reality is denied. If the trend continues, and there is little reason to doubt that it will, the expression "exceptional children" should, before long, find attached to

71

it the same negative connation as "crippled" and "handicapped" and a
new synonym will have to be found. Indeed, one can already observe
the beginnings of this in recent books which carry in their titles such
terms as "unusual child" (Roucek, 1962), "variant child" (Woods School,
1961), and "special child" (Michal-Smith & Kastein, 1962). Little is
gained by all this; cooking, washing, dusting, and ironing do not become more palatable by calling the housewife a homemaker—only the
invention of better techniques reduces the drudgery. The same is true
of handicaps and deficits. New labels do not cure or prevent them, nor
do they make it any easier for the afflicted or their parents to cope with
the condition. This can only be done if the professional person and the
people whom he serves are willing to face an undisguised reality, called
by an unambiguous and truthful name, and learn to deal with this
reality and its consequences in an honest and forthright manner.

In the case of "exceptional children" the cause of denial is further
served by including the gifted child in the category, thus further diluting
the meaning of the term and making it even less noxious. When the
uninitiated first hears the word "exceptional" in relation to a child, he is
most likely to think of it as something good. Indeed, the dictionary definition of the word is "*uncommon; hence, superior*" and it often comes as
a surprise to find that the child referred to has a severe handicap of
physical or psychological nature but that the truly superior child is also
included in the category. One wonders what is to be gained by clas-
sifying the gifted with the handicapped and deficient. Does this inclusion
make exceptionality easier to accept, thus serving the cause of denial?

The need to find a less opproprious label for an undesirable condition
is, understandably, greatest with the afflicted and their families but people in the helping professions greatly contribute to the process of denial
when they use euphemistic terms in their writings. The use of the word
"exceptional" to describe children with handicaps as well as those with
special endowments seems to have had its origin among educators in the
1920s (*e.g.*, Macauley, 1927), a time when just emphasis came to be
placed on equal opportunities in a democratic educational system. It
meant to identify children whose unusual intellectual or physical condition called for special educational facilities and this group included the
"feeble-minded, gifted, psychoneurotic, speech defective, delinquent,
blind, deaf, epileptic, and others" (Scheidemann, 1931, p. 1). From the
point of view of educational planning, this broad definition is indeed
laudable and one could only wish that more than thirty years after its
formulation special educational facilities were indeed readily available for
emotionally disturbed and gifted children. Yet while the specialized and

extended use of the phrase "exceptional children" thus has some merit in an educational context, little is gained when it is indiscriminately used in fields other than education.

All our misgivings notwithstanding, widespread current usage demands that a discussion of handicapped and deficient youngsters take place under the rubric of "exceptional children" and that the gifted child be included in this category. And so we compound the fallacy, hopefully with the understanding that the use of the word "exceptional" is not meant to deny the very real problems which must be faced by parents whose child somehow deviates from the child they had expected to produce.

THE ULTIMATE AIM

A mother of an exceptional child, writing in a professional journal (Murray, 1959), gave expression to what should be the ultimate aim of professional people who hope to help parents like herself when she wrote, "Our greatest need: Constructive professional counseling at various stages in the child's life which will enable us as parents to find the answer to our own individual problems to a reasonably satisfactory degree" (p. 1087).

This simple plea can stand as a basic guideline to the professional worker, yet its very simplicity may be misleading for the kind of help for which Mrs. Murray asks is not easy to provide. It is, in fact, very difficult to provide, for, as Spock (1961) so honestly admits, telling parents that their child has a handicap or defect is one of the tasks most repugnant to the physician.

The professional person's own feelings can easily get in the way of his desire to give parents the help they need. Cohen (1962) speculates that the professional may feel guilty because he is relieved that the misfortune fell upon someone else and adds that few persons can view a small handicapped child without feeling grief. The professional must therefore attempt an honest examination of his own feelings and attitudes before he can expect to be helpful and if he is unable to do so, he will need a consultant, supervisor, or therapist who can help him with this examination. A professional person who is himself anxious and in conflict about the problem with which the parent needs help is likely to exacerbate the parents' difficulties and will contribute most if he refers the case to someone who can approach the problem with objective understanding. "A worker who has mastered his feelings can be more effective in helping the parents face the problems with which they are struggling. He will stand ready to share with them his knowledge of how these problems can be met, but he will not attempt to take over responsibility for meeting the problems" (Cohen, 1962, p. 141 f.).

The ultimate aim of the services we can render is to help parents see the child as a separate human being whose handicap is an unfortunate accident of nature. Parents must be helped to see the issues clearly and to make the necessary decisions in the light of reality. In this way the child can, in turn, be helped to develop his own individual potential to the fullest extent so that, insofar as possible, he can live happily and productively with others. This, as Jensen (1958) has stressed, is the goal for every child, be he handicapped, defective, gifted, or normal.

PROFESSIONAL RESPONSIBILITY

A great many different professions come into contact with parents of handicapped or defective children. They range from the physician who makes the original diagnosis to the speech, occupational, or physical therapist who engages in habilitative work with the child, and the teacher who may have him in his classroom. Psychologists, social workers, nurses, psychiatrists, and school administrators may enter the case at one time or other. With all these professions involved, one might think that the parents are well served, yet the very proliferation of specialists may complicate rather than clarify the issue. Mrs. Murray (1959), in her plea on behalf of parents, asked that the help given be free from petty professional jealousies but interprofessional rivalries, in which one group may attempt to keep another from giving help, are only a part of the problem.

The other source of difficulty is to be found in the anxieties which the handicap of a child may arouse in the professional. They, like the parents themselves, may resort to mechanisms of defense which reduce anxiety by avoiding its source and knowing that other professionals will also be seeing the parents it is all too easy to rationalize that "somebody else" will talk to the parents about their problems. The trouble is that the "somebody else" may have simliar anxieties and similar defenses so that in the end the parents get help from no one. All too often the physician will concentrate on the medical aspects, the therapist on habilitation, and the teacher on education; each carefully avoiding the problem of the family by focusing on the problem of the child. Sarason (1952) points out that despite the fact that parents of exceptional children have seen numerous specialists about their child, they are often amazingly poorly informed about the nature and implications of the child's defect. "In more than a few cases I know," he goes on to say, "the ignorance of the parents is not due to their resistance to facts,

but to the failure of the specialist to inform the parent adequately"
(p. 19).

Who then has the responsibility to help? There is, first of all, no
one professional who can claim the exclusive right to counseling parents
of exceptional children. Every professional who comes into contact with
parents around their child has the responsibility to assume a helping
attitude and to remember that he is dealing not with a spastic limb or
an intellectual deficit but with a whole child and his family. This does
not mean that every professional should therefore enter into a counseling
relationship but that everyone must operate on the basis of the one overriding principle of all healthy interpersonal relations: honesty.

At the same time, and because of the many people who may be involved in a single case, it is important that someone assume the responsibility for over-all coordination of what should be a team effort at
helping the family. Within the team the actual counseling based on a
planned and long-term relationship may become the responsibility of
one particular person, whose personal qualifications are more easily listed
than acquired. They include the human qualities of acceptance, understanding and warmth; the professional attributes of objectivity, confidence, and knowledge; as well as the technical skill of interviewing.
The professional helper must be familiar with available community
resources, he must know when and how to obtain consultation, and he
must have a realistic appraisal of the limits of his competence.

Because the needs of parents range over a wide spectrum, from getting factual information through receiving emotional support to obtaining personal psychotherapy, help may be obtained from a variety of
professions; yet any professional who counsels parents around their child
should possess the qualifications just listed. Some professions, particularly social work, clinical psychology, and psychiatry, place greater emphasis on these qualifications in their student selection and training than
do others, but the need is too great and the available services too limited
to permit a narrowly parochial definition of who shall help.

No textbook can possibly hope to teach such qualities as acceptance,
warmth, and understanding. A student may be able to develop these
in the course of closely supervised experience but some people lack
these qualities in sufficient measure and these should probably not enter
a profession whose central task is helping other people. No amount of
exhortation will make a rejecting person accepting, a frigid person warm,
or a narrow-minded person understanding. Those charged with the
selection, education and training of new members of the helping professions will need to keep in mind that the presence or absence of cer-

tain personality characteristics make the difference between a truly helpful professional and one who leaves a trail of misery and confusion in the wake of his activities.

What we have called the professional attributes of objectivity, confidence and knowledge are largely gained through experience where, with increasing knowledge of the technical material in a specialty, one is able to become more confident and more objective. Again, a general textbook can do little but stress the importance of these attributes, knowing that a statement such as, "Be confident!" is a vain and hollow preachment. Intellectual recognition of the need for objectivity does not make one objective, nor does it instill confidence to read that this is an important quality.

Fortunately, from the point of view of both the student and the textbook writer, something of didactic value can be communicated in written form when we come to speak of the technical skill of interviewing. There are principles which can be learned and knowledge which can be communicated but even here only the practical application of principles and knowledge, initially under skilled supervision, can hope to develop a person who will eventually be able to help others through the use of the interview.

THE INTERVIEW

The first principle: honesty. An interview is a verbal exchange between two or more persons. It is not a conversation. A conversation is a two-way exchange of information in which all parties involved may contribute equally or alternately to the flow of the communication. The implicit rules of a social conversation state that all parties have a responsibility for keeping the exchange from coming to a standstill, periods of silence are avoided, "personal" topics are generally taboo, and the content of the conversation may range widely as the participants introduce new topics in association to something another may have said.

An interview, in the context here under discussion, is a directed communication between a person in a helping role and a person or persons who are seeking his help. This helping relationship determines what transpires during the interview and differs from other interpersonal encounters largely in the degree to which the purpose must be the benefit to be derived by the person in the help-seeking role. The content of the interview may involve the giving or eliciting of specific information, information whose purpose and aim is to help. This help may be concrete and instrumental or abstract and in the realm of feelings and emotions. With the aim of helping personal topics may be discussed, otherwise taboo areas may be entered, silences may be tolerated, and the major responsibility for carrying the interview forward may rest only with the person in the helping role. If there is one overriding principle which guides the relationship and the interview it is the principle of honesty. The helping process is hindered, if not made impossible, unless both parties to the relationship can be completely honest in every respect. This does not only mean that the help-seeking individual must be able to share relevant information without withholding or distorting, it also means that the person in the helping role must be honest both with his patient or client and with himself.

The requirement that the professional be honest with himself is again an exhortation, more easily pronounced than effected. It involves the emotional maturity and personal security which permits a person to be optimally aware of his own feelings and motivations and to have insight into his reactions and behavior. Honesty with oneself is the self-awareness of the helping person which Hamilton (1951) lists as one of the characteristics which differentiate a professional relationship from conventional social intercourse. It is what Rogers (1958) has in mind when he speaks of the need for the helping person to be genuine, to have his words match his own internal feelings. The likelihood of forming a helping relationship toward another person is, according to Rogers (*ibid.*), directly related to the degree to which the professional person can be sensitively aware of and acceptant toward his own feelings. Every normal human being has emotional reactions when he interacts with another person. These emotional reactions may be both positive and negative and the helping person must be able to let himself experience these feelings while, at the same time, not permitting them to interfere with his task of helping the other.

Since it is not unusual for a professional person to have first been drawn into the area of exceptional children because of personal involvement with a handicapped or defective child, the professional's own feelings will also need to be examined from that point of view. He will need to have resolved his own feelings about exceptional children before he can hope to be truly objective in a situation which has such deep emotional meaning to the parents he wishes to help.

Objectivity in a professional relationship does not mean that feelings must be absent. It does mean that feelings must be recognized and kept from distorting interpersonal perceptions. In a mistaken attempt to exclude feelings from the professional relationship some would-be helpers withdraw behind an aloof facade of professionalism, an attitude of "I am the expert" which must surely prevent anything but the most sterile interpersonal contact.

Beck (1959), in discussing counseling parents of retarded children, has pointed out that parents tend to reject unpleasant or painful information that comes to them from a seemingly uninterested or unfeeling source. These sources are usually professional people who try to hide their own feelings behind a mask of objectivity. As long as a professional person has not learned to cope with and face his own feelings he will be unable to be of genuine help to others.

The honesty which the professional person must maintain toward himself is a prerequisite and corollary for his being honest with the people he is trying to help. Honesty with parents of handicapped or defective children is as vital during the interview in which parents are first acquainted with their child's condition as it is during any of the subsequent interviews designed to help them with their situation and feelings. The professional must be honest in disclosing the diagnosis, honest in giving a prognosis, and honest in discussing the etiology. Honesty around these questions not only means that relevant information must not be withheld or distorted; it also means that the areas of ignorance or uncertainty must be frankly shared. Kanner (1953) has pointed out that some of the questions which parents frequently ask cannot be answered unequivocally because in some areas our present state of knowledge is limited. A frank admission of not knowing the answer to a specific question does more to increase parents' confidence in the professional person than an attempt to cover the ignorance with an authoritarian attitude suggesting that the parent has no right to ask.

Sheimo (1951), in an excellent article entitled "Problems in Helping Parents of Mentally Defective and Handicapped Children," discusses the need for honesty and the danger of letting the feelings of the professional distort the communication to parents.

> Opposing attitudes are not infrequently expressed by clinicians: on the one hand, 'feeling sorry,' oversolicitude, and an attempt to 'soft-pedal' the truth; while on the other hand, impatience, and even annoyance, that his position as an authoritative person has been questioned. It is understandable that doctors do appreciate and are sensitive to the unpleasantness of such a situation for the parents. To some it may seem unkind or even brutal to be frank with the parents as to the truth of the situation. Yet perhaps at just such times nothing short of an honest statement is really helpful to any of the members concerned, including the child. If the doctor is able to stand firm and strong in his convictions, while at the same time he allows the parents to react with what sometimes may be even intense rage and denial by stating that they do not and will not believe the doctor, he often proves, in the long run, to be of real, integrative value to these parents. At such moments, the doctor may not even get the satisfaction of having been of help, but in the ensuing months and years the parents may either attain a greater decisiveness or return to that particular clinician for help" (p. 45 f.).

If parents are to be helped they must be given an opportunity to experience simple honesty with another person; a person who neither has to be unsympathetic, impatient and authoritarian, nor oversolicitous and hestitant. "It behooves the clinician to recognize that these parents invariably *know* the degree of a deficiency and that their intense anxiety around the child's defectiveness is the way in which their conflict is manifested. He must therefore not wittingly participate in this manifestation" (*ibid.,* p. 46).

Denial is one of the most common defense mechanisms which parents use to deal with the anxieties aroused by the recognition that their child is handicapped or defective. In trying to support their denial they will seek confirmation from a professional person to the effect that the condition is not really as serious as they fear or that it can be readily corrected or cured. The professional can do no greater disservice to these parents than to fall in with the denial and minimize the situation or hold out false hopes. The only behavior which will be truly helpful is an honest exposure of the reality of the situation even though this reality may be extremely painful and threatening at the time. With every communication he makes the professional person should ask himself "Am I being honest?" and unless the answer is in the affirmative he should know that he is not giving the parents the help they need and seek.

THE TASK OF THE INTERVIEW

The basic task of the helping relationship in which the interview is the principal tool is to render the parent's ego capable of an undistorted perception of reality so that he can make reality oriented decisions. Defense mechanisms tend to distort reality perception in order to protect the integrity of the personality and the task of the interview is to work with or through these defenses without disrupting personality organization. In counseling parents of exceptional children the aim should not be a restructuring of the parent's personality, and the model of the relationship is that of social casework and not that of psychiatry. If a parent is so severely disturbed that intensive reworking of personality structure is indicated, the counselor should refer the parent to a qualified psychotherapist. The techniques of psychotherapy are outside the competence of the counselor and beyond the scope of this book.

The focus of counseling a parent is on the child and on the parent's reactions to the child and his exceptional condition. If this focus is kept clearly in mind in the counseling relationship the counselor is unlikely to be drawn into the intricacies of the parent's basic personality and, fascinating as these may seem, the counselor should remember that the parent has not come to him to have all of his unconscious processes explored. Help can frequently be given by supporting the strengths of the parent, by slight modifications of attitude, and by clarifications in areas of immediate relevance.

Purposes of interviewing. The interview with parents of exceptional children may have one or more of a variety of purposes depending on the stage of the contact. The first stage of the contact is the period of the initial disclosure. Here parents will need an honest statement of the diagnosis, an explanation of its implications, an opportunity to ask questions and to begin making plans for the future. Auerbach (1959) tells us that parents want up-to-date and accurate scientific information, given in language they can understand, about their child's condition and the effect that the disability may have on the usual course of child development. They want to know about the emotional aspects of the condition and the way in which it may affect the child's personality and behavior. Very practically, they want to hear what they can do to help their child best develop to his capacity, and what they may expect this capacity to be. "In other words, they want to know how to manage now and what they have to look forward to" (p. 17).

The interview in which the diagnostic finding is to be interpreted to the parents requires careful preparation on the part of the professional person. In most cases parents anxiously anticipate the confirmation of their fears. Except in the case of a newborn whom they have never seen, it is rare that parents have not themselves suspected what might be wrong with their child, so the professional often walks into well-prepared defenses. For this reason he should know exactly what he is about to say and what the specific situation is. It is irresponsible and unprofessional to enter an interview with parents and to begin thumbing through a chart in order to familiarize oneself with the case. The professional person must know ahead of time just what he want to communicate to the parents and what recommendations he plans to make. The better the factual material is mastered, the easier it will be to handle the interview in such a manner as to avoid having the parents press one into minimizing the problem or holding out false promises.

The interpretation interview should, wherever possible, be held with both parents and never in the presence of the child no matter how young or retarded he may be. After presenting a clear-cut and factual statement of the findings in terms which the parents can understand they must be given an opportunity to react to this information, to ask questions, and to discuss their plans. Such an interview cannot be hurried and should therefore be scheduled in such a way as to leave plenty of time beyond the factual disclosure of the diagnosis. Anticipating strong emotional reactions which they prefer not to handle, professional people sometimes contemplate a hit-and-run technique which would enable them to drop the emotionally-laden information into the parents' lap and then quickly withdraw. It is obvious that such a technique shirks professional responsibility and that any conscientious professional person would shun it. It is unfortunately necessary to stress this point because this practice can still be found in some clinics where the relationship between patients and physicians is impersonal and routinized.

From what we know of the defense mechanisms which serve to protect the personality from threat, we can expect that parents will react to the diagnosis with anger, guilt, denial, or projection. The professional person "must take great care not to let the parents make him say what they want to hear. He must guard against the temptation to alleviate the aroused anxiety by minimizing the problem or by giving false hopes. If he is convinced of the value of a certain recommendation, he should express it with confidence and adhere to it consistently. If treatment is recommended, predictions as to improvement probabilities should be conservatively stated in order to avoid building up unrealistic expectations" (Ross, 1959, p. 55 f.).

A diagnosis is not the end but the beginning of extended professional responsibility. In cases of mental deficiency, in particular, the establishing of a diagnosis has sometimes been viewed as the end of the professional contact. This, as Beck (1959) and others have stressed, is definitely not true. Even the interpretation of findings alone may need to be extended over a number of interviews since parents may need to hear the findings and recommendations several times before they can fully comprehend them. Additional questions may occur to them after the conclusion of the interview and they should be urged to return in order to discuss them. "Frequently, particularly if the interpreted findings were especially threatening, parents will 'shop around' for a more agreeable professional opinion. While it is probably unwise to invite them to do so—unless one is uncertain of one's own conclusions and desires a consultation—one should not openly express displeasure or disapproval at such a plan, but leave the decision up to them" (Ross, 1959, p. 56).

Beyond the initial period which includes the interpretation of a diagnosis, the clarification of the situation and the planning of treatment for the child, the parents need help in working through their feelings and aid in the management of everyday problems and difficulties. This ongoing contact of counseling lasts for an indefinite period and may or may not be with the same professional person who presented the initial diagnosis. Depending on the setting, the counselor may be a person specifically assigned to this task; but it is highly desirable that once such assignment is made, the parents can expect to be seen by the same person over a long period of time.

With an ongoing contact assured, the initial period merges imperceptibly into the second phase in which the focus shifts from the specific deficit of the child and the planning of immediate steps to be taken to the parents' own feelings and long-range plans for the child's future. The parents will need to know more about themselves, their own reactions and their own conflicted but normal feelings. They will want to explore their reactions to the demands which are put upon them, and it is here that they will need someone who will understand them and accept them as they are. "They need to have help in recognizing both where they are weak and where they are strong so that they can turn to appropriate services for help as they are needed. They also want to know and explore the effect of having a handicapped child on the family as a whole—the strain this places on the marriage, the effect on other children as they are growing up" (Auerbach, 1959, p. 17).

Spock, in a perceptive article on being a parent of a handicapped child, writes that

> usually it is the mother who most wants counseling, because the job of managing the child twelve to twenty-four hours a day falls on her shoulders. Women are also more able to ask for assistance when they are in trouble. Men are less natural in this respect. They have been brought up, in America at least, to feel they are confessing inadequacy if they ask for help. . . . They have also been brought up to be ashamed to show their feelings. Even when faced with serious problems they often recommend to their wives that the best course is to muddle along. But we shouldn't be fooled by them. They do have feelings and they need assistance in facing unusual crises too. Once they swallow their pride, once they get over the hump, they will cooperate (Spock, 1961, p. 15).

Counseling parents takes a variety of forms from giving factual information and recommending resources to giving emotional support to parents in stress. All parents of defective or handicapped or gifted children need information and advice while, as Beck (1959) points out, fewer parents require supportive counseling. Beyond this range there will be some parents, however, whose personal reaction is such that they will need personal psychotherapy and the counselor will need to know when and how to refer a parent for such intensive help. Whether counseling takes the form of information and advice or of emotional support, it is carried out through the use of the interview and we shall want to explore some of the principles of good interview technique in the following pages.

Since interviewing is an interpersonal process, a discussion must of necessity introduce artificial separations which may obscure the fact that we are dealing with a dynamic interaction. It is therefore important to keep in mind that in an interview a great many different things are transpiring at any one moment and that it is only for purposes of exposition that we separate these events and discuss them one at a time.

There are certain techniques of interviewing which can be described and learned but as with any technique, the skilled and constructive application depends on an understanding which only experience under the initial supervision of a skilled practitioner can provide.

PRINCIPLES OF INTERVIEWING

Unconscious motivation. Before one can hope to establish a helping relationship in which the interview can be put to constructive use, it is important that one understand certain basic principles of human behavior. One of these principles is the unconscious nature of the motivation to much of what people say and do. All behavior is motivated but the motivation is often not readily apparent either to an outsider or to the person himself. Defense mechanisms have previously been discussed in some detail and it is well to recall here that these mechanisms are instituted on an unconscious level and can thus in no way be viewed as purposive behavior. A parent who uses denial to deal with the threat represented by his child's deficiency, or who displaces his anger and expresses it through hostility toward the professional person, is not doing so "on purpose" and nothing can be gained if the professional person responds to such behavior as if it were intentional.

If one can recognize and accept the fact that much human motivation is unconscious one can be more tolerant, less condemnatory, and thus better able to help a parent effectively. Instead of becoming impatient with denials the interviewer can recognize that the parent needs this defense at this particular time in order to protect himself against anxieties which might otherwise overwhelm him.

The non-judgmental attitude made possible by the recognition of unconscious motivation furthers the relationship because it keeps the interviewer from responding to a parent's behavior on a superficial level. In ordinary, non-professional social intercourse we tend to react to aggression with counter-aggression, to deceit with anger, and to obvious rationalizations with exasperation. It is readily apparent that if the interviewer were to permit himself the luxury of these "normal" reactions he would quickly find the relationship at an end. From everyday relations with other people parents have come to expect arguments, persuasion and judgmental responses. The non-judgmental attitude of the interviewer sets the interview apart from other social relations so that the parent can be in a better position to use the help the professional person has to offer. This distinctly different feature enables the parent to differentiate this contact from a conversation and once this differentiation is established he will cease to expect a response to every statement he makes, an answer to every question he asks, an equal contribution to the flow of the discourse. We are more ready to share our deeper feelings with someone who does not pass judgment, someone who does not disapprove of things we say, someone who accepts us as we are and where we are. From the interviewer's point of view the important thing is to understand the parent and to seek the cause of his behavior; impatience, indignation or annoyance may prevent such understanding.

Just as every behavior has both conscious and unconscious motivations, so does every experience have both objective and subjective qualities. A parent may report a certain activity in which his child has engaged. The objective aspect of this behavior is usually readily understood and in ordinary conversation this is often all that is communicated. In a helping interview, on the other hand, we are intesested not only in what the parent observed but also in how he felt about it. This feeling aspect is the subjective quality of an experience. A handicapped child may have fallen off his tricycle. That is the objective fact. In and of itself it may not tell us much; but when we begin to search for the subjective experience of the parent, we may discover that this event has once again confirmed for the parent that the child will never be able to succeed at anything or that he is once more convinced that he will at all times have to watch over and protect his child. Since we want to help parents with their feelings, it is these we must try to elicit for merely collecting a catalog of reality events will not contribute to an understanding of the parent-child interaction.

Ambivalence. Still another basic factor in the understanding of human behavior is the appreciation for the existence of ambivalence. Any specific situation elicits not only feelings but often feelings which are conflicted and indeed contradictory. The concept of ambivalence is difficult to comprehend for many people. In the material world we are used to clear-cut dichotomies. A thing either is or isn't; an object can be present or absent. This is how the child first learns to perceive the world. As we mature and become cognizant of the world of values we learn that things are not necessarily black or white but that there are many shades of gray between extremes. In the realm of emotions there is yet another dimension for here we can find positive and negative existing at the same time and when we encounter their existence in someone's behavior we often find it difficult to understand.

Instances of ambivalence arise almost continually in interviewing. We find parents who obviously want help but are unable to ask for it; parents who ask for advice but do not follow it when it is given; parents who agree to certain plans but do not carry them out; and parents who tell us one thing but by their behavior manifest its opposite (Garrett, 1942). Here again an appreciation for the unconscious motivation of behavior can help us understand. What the parent says may be what he truly believes on a conscious level but what he does is often motivated by unconscious needs and feelings which only manifest themselves in the ambivalence. If the interviewer is alert to these manifestations, they can aid him in eventually helping the parent resolve his ambivalence through some of the interviewing techniques to be discussed below.

Acceptance. An important basis of a helping relationship is the accepting attitude on the part of the professional person. A parent may be dealing with his exceptional child in a manner which goes counter to the values of the professional person. The parent may be punitive, rejecting, excessively demanding, or overprotecting of the child or hold attitudes which not too long ago were described as "unworthy" in even the professional literature (Thorne & Andrews, 1946). If the interviewer merely condemns these parental attitudes he will not be able to be of help because the parents will be put on the defensive or respond to the criticism with counter-hostility which may lead them to discontinue the contact.

The need to accept a parent's attitudes and behavior is sometimes misinterpreted as requiring approval of whatever the parent says or does. This is not what acceptance implies. The interviewer does not suspend his evaluative judgment of behavior nor does he refrain from bringing his judgment to the attention of the parent. Acceptance means that the interviewer accepts the parent's feelings which underlie his unhealthy or undesirable behavior; it involves the attempt to come to an understanding of these feelings in order to help the parent deal with them in a constructive fashion which will not harm the child.

More concretely, acceptance means that when a parent indicates that he wants to institutionalize a defective child at a time which the interviewer considers premature and in a fashion which he deems precipitous, he neither passively supports this plan in mistaken acceptance nor does he actively oppose it in a peremptory fashion. Instead he points out that the parent wants to get rid of his child and wonders why the parent should have such strong negative feelings. This question, if sensitively pursued, will eventually elicit the underlying feelings of anger, shame, or disappointment, and it is these feelings with which he will have to deal, not with the behavioral manifestations which the plan to institutionalize expresses.

Acceptance then is not to condone undesirable behavior but to understand it in the sense of understanding the feelings which find expression through the behavior. Understanding, however, also means more than the word may suggest. Understanding involves not an intellectual comprehension based on theory but an emotional understanding based on empathy. Such understanding is not gained through one or two interviews but grows out of a continuing professional relationship between interviewer and interviewee. As Garrett has stated it, "To know about emotions and feelings is not enough. One should be able to 'sense' their existence and their degree and quality. Such ability does not come merely from reading a book such as this or merely from classroom study, but requires the constant application of theoretical knowledge in practical day to day contact with human beings and their objective and subjective problems" (1942, p. 25).

Relationship. Despite the fact that the relationship is essential for a helpful interaction between a professional person and a parent, the professional person can neither "build" or "establish" a relationship since this is something which must develop out of the parent's experience in the course of interviews. These experiences are never based solely on the reality of the situation for the parent brings to the interview a set of positive and negative attitudes toward other people and the relationship develops out of this matrix of objective and subjective reactions. Certain features of the interview tend to intensify the positive and negative feelings the parent holds toward the interviewer. Garrett's classical treatise on interviewing (1942), which has been helpful in developing much of this section, explores the nature of this relationship in the context of the interaction between a social worker and his client. She writes:

> For many a client it is a unique experience to talk with someone who, instead of criticizing or admonishing, listens with non-judgmental understanding. This relationship with a person who does not ask anything for

himself personally but focuses his interest entirely on the client and yet refrains from imposing advice or control is a very satisfying one. The discovering of these characteristics in the interviewer accompanied as it is by the absence of closer knowledge of the interviewer's personality with its inevitable personal whims and foibles leads the client to idealize him. The client's feelings are unchecked by personal knowledge of the interviewer which might dilute them. He thus endows the worker with the ideal characteristics one is always searching for, quite independently of whether or not the worker actually is such an ideal person.

These feelings are usually not consciously revealed but indications of them may be recognized in such comments from clients as, 'It's been such a help to talk with you,' 'I see you understand,' 'You're the first person I've ever told this to,' 'What do you think I should do?' Remarks of this sort occur in case after case.

The opposite sort of situation also arises in interviewing. Again quite independently of the interviewer's actual character, the client, because of his own anxieties, insecurity, and deprivations, may endow him with negative characteristics and build up antagonism toward him. Much depends on the client's previous experiences with his parents or with others in authority.

Negative feelings are often even more concealed than positive ones because of social standards of politeness, but they are revealed sometimes by refusals to talk, by the breaking off of an appointment, by refusal to return to the agency, or by trapping the worker into giving advice which can later be proved wrong.

The development of excessive negative or positive feelings by the client is often alarming to the interviewer who may be unaware of having done anything to arouse such feelings. An interviewer tends to want his clients to like him, but sometimes in his eagerness to achieve this end he unwillingly encourages more dependency than he had realized was potentially present. A worker should realize that the development of an emotional rapport, positive or negative, between the client and himself is not abnormal but inevitable, and that he should direct his attention not to eliminating this relationship but to controlling its nature and intensity. He must guard against misleading the client into an overly dependent relationship through appearing too personally friendly or appearing to promise too much, but on the other hand he must not lean over backward in avoiding this danger and make the client feel that he is an unresponsive and unsympathetic listener. It is easy, when one is treated like God, to assume the characteristics of that role, and it is easy to over-correct this tendency.

If an interviewer notices that the relationship with his client seems to be developing negatively, he should not become overly alarmed because this may be due not at all to him but to factors deeply hidden in his client's personality. He should review his own activity in the case and make sure that he has given no objective grounds for the antagonism the client seems to feel for him. He may have given inadequate help, broken an appointment, or himself have developed negative feelings toward the client of which he was not fully aware. If there are no such objective sources for his client's negativism, he can assure the client by a continued attempt to understand the reasons for his difficulties that he is not retaliating with disapproval of his own.

The development of an inter-relationship of this general sort, positive or negative, betwen interviewer and interviewee is not at all a unique phenomenon but a universal one. It is a commonplace that people tend to become dependent upon their doctors, lawyers, and ministers. Toward the end of her pregnancy a woman often relies more on her physician than on her husband. A patient under psychoanalysis develops a strong emotional attachment to the analyst. The analyst has developed methods of making therapeutic use of such a relationship. He calls it technically 'transference.' We are concerned with it here only in some of the less intense forms mentioned above." (Garrett, 1942, pp. 19–20).

Listening. Whether it is the very first contact between a parent and the professional person or a later interview in an ongoing series of contacts, the interviewer should permit the parent to begin with what is uppermost in his mind. Even if the interviewer has planned to ask a specific question or to discuss a specific topic he must permit the parent to set the opening topic, for if the parent comes into the session with a pressing problem he will not be able to attend to anything the interviewer might say which is unrelated to this problem. For the interviewer listening must always come before talking and the skill of the interviewer usually stands in inverse relation to the amount of talking he does during a session.

The comfort and relaxation of interviewer and interviewee are important for a productive session. A tense and uncomfortable interviewer will usually do too much talking while a tense and uncomfortable interviewee often contributes too little to the interview. The first step in any interview must thus be to help the parent relax and feel fairly comfortable. This is not to say that establishing a relaxed relationship is a step distinctly separate from the helping relationship as a whole. Some interviewers feel that they must "establish rapport" before they can engage in an interview, forgetting that rapport is the result of a relationship and not its prerequisite. Wall (1958) has urged that the helping relationship be viewed as a process, suggesting that the best way to expedite the process of developing a relationship is to deal immediately with the problems which bring the client to the interview.

Listening on the part of the interviewer also helps to differentiate the interview from the usual social conversation and thus establishes for the parent that he is now in a situation which is different from most he has encountered in the past. Unless this differentiation is made, old social responses, such as not troubling other people with one's problems, will generalize to the interview and hinder the helping process. Finding someone who can listen understandingly without intruding his own feelings and judgments is often very gratifying to a parent and may in itself be a helpful experience.

Listening to a parent, particularly during the first interview, gives the professional person on opportunity to gauge the parent's intellectual, social and emotional level, and helps him to address his own eventual remarks to that level. Unless one knows the kind of language and vocabulary the parent is likely to understand and the kind of suggestion he is likely to be ready to accept, many interview hours can be wasted and attempts to be of help are likely to be vitiated for lack of communication.

In working with parents of exceptional children in a counseling relationship it is often necessary to make concrete suggestions and to recommend plans for dealing with the reality presented by the exceptional child. While suggestions and recommendations cannot be communicated by merely listening, it is extremely important that before the interviewer engages in directive activity he has given the parent plenty of opportunity to express himself. Sometimes, as Garrett (1942) has pointed out, the parent may even suggest the course of action that the interviewer intended to advise. In such cases the parents own suggestion can simply be confirmed and strengthened. The fact that he regards the plan as coming from himself will make it more likely that the person will carry it out.

Whatever the plan that may be proposed for the child, it must be remembered that it is the parents who have to carry it out. As long as guilt, conflict, or confusion stand in the way even the best plan is doomed to failure. Guilt, conflict, and confusion must be dealt with before the parents can be ready to accept a plan, but the interviewer will never know whether the parents are ready unless he gives them the opportunity to talk and himself a chance to listen.

The "shopping around" which is a frequently-encountered phenomenon with parents of defective or handicapped children is in a large part a manifestation of the fact that they have not received the help they need in a way in which they can use it. Sheimo (1951) worked with parents of defective or handicapped children and found that it

became progressively more evident that the doctor's mere presentation of clinical diagnosis and recommendation was neither sufficient nor perhaps *really* what the parents were seeking. Advice and suggestions seemed to be of no avail and unconsciously impossible for the parents to accept and find useful. In an attempt to help these parents, it is necessary for the doctor to become sympathetically aware of the conflicting attitudes of the parents towards such a child. The parents' denial of the child's deficiency seemed to be an important element in their defense mechanism and very necessary in the maintenance of their self-esteem" (p. 44).

The need to listen is clearly brought out in Sheimo's discussion of the relationship between the physician and the parents. Keeping in mind that the physician is not necessarily the only professional person who can stand in a helping relationship to parents of exceptional children, the following quotation can serve as an excellent exposition of the importance of listening:

> To be aware that the parents usually *know* their child is handicapped and defective and that their anxiety is predominantly an expression of their own internalized conflict, increases the possibility of being of real help to the particular parents. To tell parents that they *should* institutionalize the child, should, in a sense, 'get rid of him,' often tends to increase the guilt and strengthen the defense against this already forbidden impulse. The doctor fulfills his medical responsibility when he quite frankly states his clinical diagnoses—both in regard to mental and physical status of the child—estimates the probable future difficulties, and recognizes the added burden which such children are to parents. He becomes a physician in the true sense of the word, however, when he *recognizes* and *respects* the parents' right to decide what *they* want to do in terms of their total situation, including their own ambivalence and conflict. This implies that the doctor be ready to accept whatever decision the parents make, whether it be to keep the defective child in the home or to place him outside the home. The doctor's offer to discuss some of the parents' difficulties in arriving at a decision, becomes a beginning move in the direction of a possible resolution of the conflict.
>
> If the doctor's efforts at being of help are directed, not toward a decision, but rather toward a resolution of the conflict and consequent relief of anxiety, it begins to liberate the parents from feeling they must come to an immediate decision. Also implicit in this is that an approach on the part of the parents toward a resolution of the conflict need not necessarily mean a decision to place the child outside the home. In the doctor's sympathetic understanding of the realistic aspect of the added burden and emotional drain such children are to parents, as well as the impulse within parents to reject such a child, he actually becomes of help in reducing the intrafamilial tension. The parents may then feel easier and consequently more ready to keep this child in the home indefinitely. In the meantime, the fruitless searching for a 'cure' as a manifestation of the unresolved conflict no longer becomes as necessary (Sheimo, 1951, p. 45).

The emphasis on listening as fundamental to constructive interviewing might give the impression that the interviewer should be silent and unresponsive. This, of course, is not the case. Few people would keep on talking if the person whom they address did not give indications of interest and understanding. Brief comments and relevant questions or even an encouraging nod of the head serve to encourage a parent to continue talking. These comments, of course, must not become mechanical interjections but should be based on careful attention to important details. Honesty is again the basic guideline for the interviewers behavior. He should never say, "I understand" when in reality he has not understood, nor should he announce, "I know just how you feel" if this is not really true. If the interviewer has not understood a point he should say so for this not only enhances his understanding but it also demonstrates to the parent that the interviewer is interested in what he has to say.

Through generalization from behavior in social conversations beginning interviewers are often made uncomfortable and embarrassed when a silence occurs during the interview. They feel impelled to say something in order to break the silence and by doing so they often hinder rather than help the progress of the interview. Tindall and Robinson (1947) have shown that pauses during interview can have a variety of meanings. They usually represent the natural termination of a statement and give the interviewee time to organize his thoughts prior to the next verbalization. If the interviewer interrupts the silence too hastily he may disrupt the parent's thought processes and thus prevent him from making an important communication. This is particularly true since silence often precedes something which is difficult to say because it has important meaning to the parent.

The skilled and sensitive interviewer learns when to be silent and when to be active and there are pauses which require his intervention lest the interviewee become too anxious and uncomfortable. At those times it is well to briefly recapitulate what the parent has just said and to encourage him to continue by a relevant comment or question.

Questions. The interviewer's questions can be extremely useful by helping the parent to talk about his feelings, though they should never become a routinely-used technique. A question which may bring out a flood of material when directed to one individual may elicit nothing of relevance when asked of another. There are, thus, no "good" questions, no list of things one should routinely ask. Garrett (1942) tells us that it is a good general rule to ask questions for only one of two purposes: to obtain information which is specifically needed, or to direct the interview from a fruitless to a fruitful channel. Because their purpose is to help the parent express his feelings, questions should be phrased in such a way that they cannot be easily answered with a brief "yes" or "no." Contrary to the procedure of the courtroom, in an interview the leading question is the best question because it leads to an elaboration and thus contributes to the flow of the interviewer. At the same time the question should not imply a "right" answer and in that sense a leading question must also be a non-directive question. In asking about a child's school performance, for example, the interview should say, "How is he doing in school?" rather than "Is he getting good marks?"

The questions asked of a parent should have an honest purpose. Conversely the answers to a question asked by the parent must also be honest. Because of the role relations in an interview, parents perceive the interviewer as a resource person who is presumed to have more knowledge and information than the parent himself. This naturally leads to the asking of many questions of a factual nature. It is the interviewer's responsibility to answer questions although he must, at the same time, attempt to determine the meaning of the question and why it is being asked. When the answer to a factual question is available it should be given in a straight-forward fashion and phrased in a manner the questioner can understand. If the answer is not available the interviewer should freely admit that he does not know. If the answer can be obtained elsewhere the interviewer should either undertake to obtain it or direct the parent to the person able to supply it. There are questions, particularly those relating to the etiology of the child's handicap, for which no answer is available in the current state of knowledge. Ignorance or uncertainty must be shared with the parents. Frankness and honesty further the development of a helping relationship while evasion and deception alienate and antagonize.

Interviewers are almost invariably asked personal questions and the professional who is never asked such a question might do well to examine the image he presents to the people he is trying to help. It is likely that he is seen as a forbidding authority figure who maintains such distance from his interviewees that they are to cowed to ask personal questions.

Personal questions have a variety of meaning other than their manifest content. While they too should be answered frankly and honestly the interviewer must try and understand why the question is asked. After a brief and factual answer the interview should in each case be turned back to the parent and his problems and concerns for which the personal question often provides a clue. A parent who asks the interviewer, "Do you have any children?" may actually be asking, "Can you really understand my problem?" Depending on the state of the relationship the interviewer may want to give a factual answer to the manifest question and then add a comment which suggests that he also understands the latent content of the question. Parents of handicapped or defective children often wonder whether anyone who has not had the same experience in his own life can possibly understand what they are up against. This concern may find expression in a question about the interviewer's children and it becomes important for the interviewer to assure the parent that he can be of help even though he himself has not lived through similar difficulties. Ultimately, however, the answer to the unspoken question, "Can you really help me?" lies not in anything the interviewer might say but in a demonstration of help which can only come about if the parents' concerns and conflicts are understood and this understanding is communicated by sensitive and relevant remarks.

The converse of the parents' personal question is sometimes found in the interviewer's personal comments about his own interests or experiences. Inexperienced interviewers sometimes hope to establish a relationship by commenting on the attractiveness of a parent's clothes or making a personal statement about a neighborhood which both interviewer and interviewee know. Even if such a statement is genuine and does not represent dishonest and therefore unacceptable flattery, it carries the danger that by an introduction of personal opinions and feelings the interviewer turns what should be a professional relationship into a social conversation and thus loses rather than gains an opportunity to establish a helping relationship. "It is better for the interview to proceed with the client as the focus of attention, for his ideas and opinions rather than the interviewer's are paramount in the professional relationship" (Garrett, 1942, p. 42).

Interpretation. Recalling that the task of the helping relationship is not a restructuring of the parent's basic personality nor a complete exploration of his unconscious motivations but a freeing of the parent's ego to enable him a clear and undistorted perception of reality as it affects his child, we now turn to a discussion of the use of interpretation. It is in the amount and nature of interpretations that counseling and psychotherapy can best be differentiated.

From the point of view of the interviewer the helping relationship is a continuous series of hypothesis formation and hypothesis testing. From the moment of the first contact the interviewer will try to understand the parent and his problems. Initially this understanding is at best an approximation based on theoretical concepts and it is only as the interviewer gets to know the parent better that he can refine these approximations as one hunch after the other is tested, refined, or rejected. What a parent initially says about his child and the feelings he has toward him can rarely be taken at face value, not because the parent purposely falsifies but because his defenses do not permit him to perceive his own feelings in their true light.

A parent may state that he really does not mind the child's handicap at all and then shift the conversation to talk about the recent death of a distance relative. The interviewer, alert to the change of topic, may relate the statements in his own mind and form the hypothesis that the parent is indeed concerned about the handicap, that he may have strong hostile, destructive, yet unconscious, wishes toward the child or that, on the other hand, his concern centers around what will happen to the child when the parent himself is no longer alive. The interviewer thus has at least two hypotheses but he should under no circumstance communicate either to the parent but keep both in mind for further testing. As the contact with the parent continues these tentative hypotheses may need to be modified or discarded but even when the interviewer is entirely confident of the validity of his hypothesis he must not make the interpretation to the parent unless he can be sure that the interpretation will be helpful.

It is an essential function of the interviewer to interpret a parent's behavior to himself but to pass these interpretations on to the parent is usually inadvisable. The very fact that what is interpreted was not communicated in a direct fashion indicates that the parent is defending against a threatening recognition. As long as the defense operates it will also defend against the interpretation which, if made prematurely, will either raise anxiety to the point where the parent might not return for another interview, antagonize him and thus disrupt the relationship, or merely be passed off with strong denial. A parent's recognition of his underlying feelings or motivations is rarely accomplished through a verbal statement made by the interviewer. This recognition or insight must be arrived at by the parent at his own pace and through his own efforts and only when insight can be a meaningful experience can it become an accepted part of conscious ego content.

While the interviewer should not communicate his interpretations to the parent, interpretations he has made to himself can be extremely helpful in enabling him to guide the parent toward the necessary recognition of feelings and motivations. There are many ways in which the parent's ego can be helped to a clearer recognition of internal and external reality. The interviewer may present carefully phrased questions and comments which point out inconsistencies in the parent's statements or between the things he says and the things he does. He can relate statements the parent made in one context to similar statements made in another context. He can underscore recurrent references to a topic which suggests an area of concern. In all this the security the parent has gained from his relationship with the counselor, the counselor's non-judgmental, non-punitive accepting attitude, and the over-all atmosphere of honesty and frankness reduce the need for the defenses and thus permit better reality testing.

At no time should the interviewer become involved in arguing with a parent. There is a difference between holding up reality to a parent and arguing a point. If, for example, a parent denies the severity of his child's handicap the interviewer should juxtapose this denial with a statement of the reality; but if the parent then needs to defend his own distorted perception, counter-argument will be of no avail but may retard the helping process. Remembering that a defense mechanism such as denial serves to protect the parent against becoming overwhelmed by anxiety, the interviewer recognizes that since it serves an important need the defense will be guarded against all onslaught. Only a clear understanding of the dynamics behind a defense mechanism such as denial and gradual reduction of the underlying anxiety can eventually help the parent give up the defense so that he can recognize and deal with reality. Again it should be pointed out that in cases where the underlying anxiety is too great or the defenses too rigid, counseling as here discussed may not be sufficient and referral for psychotherapeutic intervention may be necessary.

GROUP COUNSELING

Parent counseling may take place in individual or in group sessions and in settings where a number of parents with similar problems are in contact with an agency at the same time, the group approach may be a feasible method. As with individual counseling, group counseling is not to be confused with group therapy. The aim of group counseling is to give the individual parent emotional support and help in dealing with the reality he faces.

Despite the fact that the uninitiated may consider group counseling a method which saves professional time by helping a group of parents simultaneously, group counseling should only be used where it is honestly deemed to be the most effective method for helping a particular parent. Some parents are better able to make use of help in individual sessions while others can benefit more from group sessions. Beck (1959) has pointed out that group sessions are not more economical in terms of time or professional effort; its economy only lies in the fact that if it is the more appropriate form of treatment it becomes the more effective one.

It is up to the professional person to evaluate which type of approach —individual or group—is the more suitable for a particular parent or parents. The kinds of parents for whom group processes are most helpful have been described by Beck (1959). These are parents who are basically mature and emotionally stable but whose functioning is temporarily impaired by the overwhelming nature of their problem. Others are parents with a tendency to project or intellectualize, to whom an experience with a group of other parents can become emotionally corrective. Still other parents who can benefit from group processes are those with pronounced yet well-controlled feelings of hostility, for these can find relief through some of the limited acting-out made possible in a group setting. Finally, the group identification and group support can be helpful to parents with dependency needs which might come to interfere with the relationship to an individual counselor.

On the other hand, there are parents who can either not benefit from group or who have personality patterns which tend to disrupt groups. These are parents with highly individualized needs which must be dealth with in face-to-face interviews; parents with strong emotional dependency which might result in their monopolizing the attention of the group leader; or parents with intense masochistic tendencies who might too readily make themselves the object of the group's hostilities. A certain type of passive-aggressive individual who tends to disrupt the group process through indirect opposition and subtle sabotage, and finally, the parent with psychotic tendencies will also be among those for whom group counseling is counter-indicated.

Beck (1959) reported the case of a mother who was unable to make effective use of individual counseling because she covered up her intense feelings of hostility and adopted an attitude of submissiveness. When this lady entered the group counseling situation she quickly assumed a certain amount of leadership but the group process managed to keep this tendency within bounds. Once in the group this mother gained a better understanding of her own problems and learned from other parents some of the techniques for handling situations. Because she was permitted some outlet for her need to dominate she did not disrupt the group nor did she have to assume the submissive attitude in reaction formation to her hostility which had earlier disrupted her individual sessions.

Auerbach (1959) has described a group counseling plan in which giving emotional support and factual information takes place in a program which she identifies as parent group education. Through such a program parents gain the factual knowledge they want about their children and about the immediate situations they face in dealing with them.

> Toward this end, the group members share their everyday experiences, encouraged by the leader who helps them to focus the discussion, strengthens their contributions and, where this is necessary, adds information and interpretation which the parents show they do not have. Parents also express some of their expectations, fears and fantasies, and check them against reality; they look at their own emotional reactions and come to know and accept themselves a little better; and finally they begin to think differently about things they can and want to do regarding their children, choosing, each one for himself, what seems best for him and his particular children. Here, with the help of the trained leader, parents can learn at their own pace and can focus on what is most significant for them (Auerbach, 1959, p. 18).

The benefits which parents can derive from participation in group counseling come about through the exchange of ideas and experiences among the members. One mentions a problem and another, reminded of his own similar experience, discusses how he handled this situation. Many suggestions of what to do at a very practical level are thus brought out and through the subtle process of group interaction each member can slowly clarify his or her own ideas. Since the group provides a protection to each of its members, individuals are able to discuss feelings which they may be hesitant to reveal in a one-to-one relationship. As Auerbach has put it, "The parents seem to gain courage from the other group members; the dam bursts and ideas and feelings pour forth. Once they are out, the parents seem better able to look at their situations more realistically" (ibid., p. 19).

To be a leader of a parent group requires preparation and skills which are different from those of the professional engaged in individual counseling. A knowledge of the group process is vital and can best be obtained by working under expert supervision. Like his colleague engaged in individual counseling the group leader should have a good knowledge of the special problems of the children with whose parents he is working as well as an understanding of normal child development, parent-child relations, and personality dynamics. The group leader should have familiarity with the cultural background from which the parents come so that he can understand some of their feelings and fears. He should also have knowledge of other community resources which might need to become involved for additional services. Since group settings, often more so than individual interviews, bring out dependency needs and hostilities of group members the leader must be aware of his own feelings and reactions to these. While he may be able to deal quite comfortably with the hostility of one individual in a face-to-face contact, being confronted by the mutually supported hostility of five or six people can constitute a considerable threat.

The many different things which parents gain from group meetings, including a better understanding of their children and the implications of the disability and how to handle it, a better recognition of their own feelings and attitudes and the ways in which these affect the child as well as the rest of the family, are best illustrated by the following summary of a series of meetings of parents of retarded children:

> The group discussed a broad range of problems that were of concern to them, including discipline, toilet training, eating, how to establish expectations for the child and help him to make the best use of his abilities, the causes of mental retardation, the burdening feeling of disappointment and guilt experienced by the parents, the relationship of the mentally retarded child to normal children in the family and in the community and a review of community resources and what they offer. Some of these were discussed in detail, others were explored only more briefly.
>
> The group brought out many of their basic concerns. They were troubled about the dangers of pushing too hard and expecting more than the child could reasonably accomplish, yet aware, too, of the importance of avoiding overprotection, of the need to help a child to capitalize on his eagerness and readiness to grow up. . . .They drew many parallels between their situations and those regarding normal children and were able to see that the process of determining readiness was somewhat comparable, although they could not anticipate the time table of growth-steps or level of readiness exhibited by their retarded children at different ages as readily as they could for normal children. They began to show a greater willingness to experiment and to try new approaches in helping children to help themselves. More basically, they discussed the importance of their own feelings as an essential of this problem. . . . They shared their feelings of bitter disappointment in having retarded children and told of their deep personal feelings of guilt. They were quick to give strong moral support to one another and to try to convince each 'guilty' parent how unfounded the reasons were for such feelings.
>
> Although this was a brief and limited experience, the program seemed to make some gains toward the following goals: 1) the parents experienced a great sense of relief and support from sharing their mutual heartaches

and successes, they verbalized that they no longer felt so alone in their tribulations; 2) they appeared to some extent to experience less of a sense of overwhelming guilt; 3) they seemed to have a better understanding of how to gauge the readiness of their children to take a forward step in growing up and to be more aware of the many alternative ways of helping them. To this one might add that these parents seemed to have become better able to come to terms with their children's limitations and to be freer to help them function to their optimum (Auerbach, 1959, p. 19 f.).

When counseling, whether in individual or group session, can accomplish all this it has been truly a helping relationship.

IV.

The Mentally Retarded Child in the Family

OF ALL the varieties of exceptional children the mentally retarded child has been most intensively studied and the professional and scientific literature which has grown up around him thus is the most extensive. There are inter-related reasons for this; sheer incidence of mental subnormality is only one of many. As Masland, Sarason, and Gladwin have stated, "It is unlikely that in this country there is any form of disability which equals impairment of mental ability in respect to its toll of economic uselessness and human misery. If one uses as the criterion of disability the inability to obtain gainful employment one can say that, with the possible exception of mental illness, mental subnormality is the most significant handicap of our present society" (1958, p. 3).

The child who is unable to benefit from exposure to the teaching of the public school has long been a puzzle to educators and he was one of the first groups of subjects to come under intensive psychological study. Mentally defective children were the first group for whom society provided special schools and institutions and the parents of mentally retarded children were the first to organize into a national group designed to improve the services available for their children. Aside from these factors, however, there may be still another reason which contributes to making the retarded child an object of greater interest to professional groups than other types of exceptional children. Mental retardation is in many respects more perplexing than other handicaps or deficiencies, particularly when it occurs in the absence of demonstrable physical manifestations. It is far more easy to comprehend why a child with a clubfoot has difficulty walking or why one with retrolental fibroplasia is unable to see than it is to understand why a healthy-looking youngster is unable to learn how to tie his shoes or how to read a first grade primer. Even though the sighted person cannot possibly know what it feels like to be blind he can nevertheless imagine what it might be like by walking blindfolded into a strange room. He can similarly imagine what it is like to be deaf or otherwise physically impaired. On the other hand, it is totally impossible to achieve any degree of empathy for the state of the mental defective for we cannot suspend our higher mental processes or temporarily cancel everything we have learned.

THE PARENTS' REACTIONS

The unimaginable quality of mental retardation not only stirs the scientific interest of many professional groups, it also makes the counseling of parents of mentally retarded children a major challenge since it becomes one of the tasks of a counselor to help the parents understand the nature of their child's condition.

We are in this context using the terms "mental retardation" and "mental deficiency" interchangeably, fully cognizant of the fact that sophisticated usage requires a differentiation in terms of etiology (Sarason, 1953). Such diagnostic refinements are, however, of little use to the parent who needs help around his feelings about having a child with intellectual deficiencies which prevent him from learning things other children his age are capable of mastering (Patterson, 1956).

One must remember that parents of retarded children do no more form one homogeneous group than do the children who have subnormal intelligence. In order to understand the individual parent's reactions and be able to help him it is not enough to know whether his child is mildly or severely defective, whether he is "retarded" or "defective" or whether his condition is "endogenous" or "exogenous." What one also needs to know is what this particular child's specific condition means to this particular parent in his specific situation. For a family with high intellectual standards and expectation, having a mildly retarded, "educable" child can represent a greater crisis than having a severely retarded child may to a family with a different set of values.

The more thoroughly a family partakes of the success-oriented values of our culture the more likely they are to be traumatized by the discovery that they have a defective child. Zuk (1962) speaks of the cultural dilemma in which such a family finds itself. The dilemma stems from the fact that our culture holds it a good thing to be a parent but a bad thing to be a parent of a defective child, since our highly competitive society disapproves of those individuals who are unable to maintain the standards of materialistic success. The expectations which parents hold for their child, usually even before he is born, are in one form or another variations of the basic cultural stereotype of the successful individual. When these expectations are frustrated by a child who is not equipped to fulfill these expectations the ensuing disappointment, anger and guilt complicates the parent-child relationship. Zuk (1962) believes that these reactions are culturally relative and points out that in such societies as the Peruvian and Chinese, or among the Hutterites of the United States, the birth of a defective child does not produce the same reactions, so that those parents are better able to accept a mentally defective child.

Parents are, unfortunately, not the only people who tend to get caught up in the cultural dilemma. The professional people who should be able to help them deal with their problem often tend to become equally involved. Because they are professional they value intellectual capacity and achievement and tend to become personally threatened by individuals who are defective in this area. Both Spock (1961) and Zwerling (1954) have spoken of the anxiety which is provoked in the pediatrician by the diagnosis of mental deficiency. As Spock put it,

> . . . Worst of all I dreaded being the one who would have to tell [the parents] that their fears were justified. I felt guilty in giving them the diagnosis, almost as if I were the creator of the defect. So I would put on my severest professional face and drag out the history and physical examination as long as possible, to put off the painful moment. When I sensed that the parents were searching my face for signs of my conclusions, I bent lower over my desk. Finally, when I had told them the diagnosis I would go on to give them the talk which I knew was theoretically right: that though there was no cure for the retardation, this child, like all children, would need cheerful, loving parents who would appreciate his good qualities (rather than dwell on his limitations) and who would provide him with companionship and suitable playthings and training. But how hollow this talk must have sounded coming out of my grim face. I must have really been convincing them, by my manner, of how tragic I thought their problem was. This could only have the effect of making them more uncomfortable with their child, rather than reconciling them to him.
>
> When I made the diagnosis of Mongolism in a newborn baby, I (like most pediatricians at that time) believed that I was giving the best possible help to the parents by advising them, if they could afford it, to place him at once in a nursing home, preferably without ever seeing him. This was on the theory that then they would not become painfully attached to him, and would be better able to provide a cheerful atmosphere and plenty of attention to their subsequent children. As if anguish and guilt could be solved by trying to forget! (Spock, 1961, p. 5 f.).

The feelings Spock reports from his early days as a young pediatrician are those experienced by most professional people when they have to communicate the unwelcome diagnosis of mental deficiency to parents. Yet the point at which the parents are given the diagnosis of mental deficiency is a point of crisis where constructive professional help has the best chance of succeeding while an unconstructive negative experience can start the parents off on a long series of desperate defensive maneuvers involving blame projection, denial, and "shopping around" for someone willing to hold out false hopes with promises of impossible cures.

Parental awareness. When the child is born with obvious physical defects or motor handicaps accompanying his mental subnormality, the parents know that there is something wrong, yet they may still find it difficult to accept the diagnosis of mental deficiency which, particularly in the pre-school years and where retardation is relatively mild, does not have dramatic manifestations. In these cases the anxiety about the child's condition often becomes focused around the physical defect with parents maintaining the hope that if the physical problem could be alleviated the mental retardation would vanish.

Several studies have addressed themselves to the question whether parents are aware of the nature and severity of the child's intellectual deficit. Schulman and Stern (1959) obtained parents' estimates of the intelligence of their retarded child and compared these estimates with results of psychological testing. There was good correlation between the parents' guess and the tested I.Q., a finding which led these investigators to conclude that there is no basis for the widely held belief that parents are unaware of their child's retardation before they seek professional help.

Interviewing parents whose children were enrolled in classes for trainable children, that is, children who had already been diagnosed and whose parents must have accepted the diagnosis at least to the point where they were willing to enroll the child in these classes, Stoddard (1959) found that there was no correlation between parental awareness and the childs intellectual level. Ewert and Green (1957) also found discrepancies between the mother's estimate and the child's capacity. They report that the estimates were more accurate for younger children and for those who had been younger when the mother first became concerned about the child's condition. The different findings of these studies suggest that it is not only important how and when one asks one's questions as to the mother's estimate of a child's intelligence. It must also be considered, as Mahoney (1958) has stressed, that parents of retarded children differ depending on their own personality, so that it is dangerous to consider them an undifferentiated group and to draw general conclusions on the basis of a few cases.

Parental needs. Whether or not parents have an accurate perception of a child's problem, the manner in which the professional diagnosis is transmitted to them is of tremendous importance, requiring professional skill, sensitivity, and patience.

Sarason, who discusses the emotional needs of parents of mentally retarded children in several of his publications, writes:

> In working with parents of defective children one must never lose sight of the fact that they have experienced keen frustration and hardship, have generally previously been given ambiguous or contradictory advice, and have been given little or no opportunity to unburden their anguish and disappointment. Unfortunately, there are too many professional specialists who give parents the feeling that they have little or limited time in which to discuss the problem with them, conduct the interview in the form of a monologue so that the parents are seldom given an opportunity to ask questions, communicate in a technical jargon which effectively confuses and overwhelms the parents, and in general manifest little or no interest in the personal problems or reactions of the parents. Unless one is able to identify with the problems and feelings of the parents one is likely to conduct the interview in an impersonal, superficial, routine fashion—a fashion which may be considered successful by the specialist but is frustrating and confusing to the parents. In working with the parents of defective children—in fact, in working with the parents of any problem child—one must not only be able to experience vicariously the nature and strength of their frustrations but also to structure the relationships so as to enable one to facilitate change in parental attitude and practice. (Sarason, 1953, p. 334).

The mentally retarded child is more dependent on parental care and remains dependent for a far longer time than the unimpaired normal child. The parent-child interaction is therefore likely to be more intense so that from the point of view of the child's emotional stability it is of particular importance that parental conflicts and anxieties don't disrupt the relationship. The child derives his self-image from the attitudes those around him hold and manifest toward him. Worchel and Worchel (1961) had parents of retarded children rate the personality traits of their own child, their concept of the "ideal" child, and the average child. They concluded that there is greater parental rejection of the retarded child than of the normal child and plead for efforts directed toward developing better attitudes on the part of parents. Since a study by Barsch (1961) suggests that the siblings of the mentally retarded child imitate their parents' attitudes toward him, the environment in which the defective child grows up can be highly conducive to creating emotional complications for him.

For many years the professional people with whom parents of mentally retarded children have come in contact have, by the nature of their profession, been primarily interested in the child and his problems. Pediatricians, neurologists, psychologists and educators have tended to focus on the child and have considered the parents' feelings and attitudes of importance only inasmuch as they affect the child and his development. This orientation on the part of the professional was reflected in an article by Thorne and Andrews (1946) who spoke of "unworthy" parental attitudes and saw "the handling of the parent" as an important problem.

Only lately, and particularly since social workers have entered the field, has the professional attitude shifted to some extent so that there is now a greater recognition of the emotional needs of parents of exceptional children, needs which they have in their own right as people quite apart from the effect they might have on the child.

Sarason (1953), though he also speaks of "the parent problem," writes:

> It is our belief that in every case of mental retardation or mental deficiency our goal should not be only to plan for the child but to assume the responsibility, whenever possible, of aiding the parents to lead more happy and effective lives. If we feel any obligation to the exceptional child, then it is hard to justify the lack of feeling of obligation toward his parents (p. 468).

In recent years an increasing number of centers serving the mentally retarded child are also helping parents in their own right (e.g., Beck, 1959; Cummings & Stock, 1962; Miller, 1958; Sheimo, 1951). While this work with parents is at times referred to as "therapy," the approach is usually based on the assumption that the parents of mentally retarded children are essentially healthy people who are faced with a crisis around which they can use professional help. Cummings and Stock, who experimented with brief group therapy for mothers of retarded children, believe that "appropriate therapeutic goals for these mothers include an increase in awareness and acceptance of the child's condition and the mothers' feelings about themselves, the retarded child, and others with whom they appear to be in conflict as a result of having produced a retarded child. Hopefully, this can lead to an increase in the adequacy and consistency of their own training measures with the child and of the decisions which they make regarding the use of schools and institutions" (1962, p. 742).

Similarly Michaels and Schucman (1962) base their work on the assumption that an appeal to the healthy core of the parent can provide him with a sounder basis on which to continue on his own. They write:

> The optimal solution for the parents of retarded children is, of course, to approach the real tragedy as constructively as possible, channelizing their energies into solving the realistic problems of the child and the family, without exploiting the situation for their own neurotic purposes. This, however, presupposes a degree of mental health which is, unfortunately, too seldom encountered. Some parents are apparently able to make a reasonably successful adaptation without external assistance. Nevertheless, for the majority, it is probably wise to provide some sort of professional help, however minimal, if only as a prophylactic measure to prevent tendencies toward chronic persistence of possible pathological reactions. Without specialized help, defenses may become extremely complicated, and pre-existing neurotic tendencies may combine to form a highly complex superstructure. Regrettably, it is usually only after the neurotic complex has gained ascendence and persistence that the parents seek help.
>
> The chief therapeutic aim . . . is to bring the parents to a more realistic orientation with regard to both themselves and the child, thus providing a reference point from which they can think more constructively about their problems, better judge their own reactions, and guide their own behavior. Given sufficient resourcefulness, we have found that, in time, most of the parents have been able to make constructive use of therapeutic assistance. And with appropriate help, many of them have finally been able, albeit with disappointment and sadness, to confront the reality of the child's status and to take some measure of constructive action (1962, p. 572).

One of the crucial differences between psychotherapy with an emotionally disturbed adult and counseling with a parent of a retarded child is that the latter is focused around a specific problem and includes a great deal of education and clarification. Parents have a great many specific questions to which they need answers. These questions vary with the nature of the child's defect, the child's age, and the level of the parent's sophistication. Sarason (1953) lists some of these typical questions which center around whether, how, and when the parent should teach the child such activities as walking; whether, how and when to discipline the child; how to help him in his social relations with other children; when and where to send him to school; and in what way the retarded child will affect other children in the family.

> One could list a great many more problems for which parents seek guidance. Some of the problems require a detailed knowledge and understanding of the child, parents, and family constellation. Other problems require, in addition, a knowledge of community resources: educational,

recreational, and institutional. But in discussing any problem with parents one must, wherever possible, give specific advice and guidance. For example, if a mother is bothered because the child is frequently teased by neighborhood children, one must attempt to outline concrete steps which might be taken by the mother to cope with the problem. One should, of course, first determine how the mother has previously handled the problem: Has she bawled out the other children? Has she asked their parents to punish them? If the parent has reacted in this way then one must point out why such an approach is likely to be self-defeating. One might then suggest that the mother have a talk with the children and explain to them that her child cannot do some of the things that they can, that he needs a little more consideration and protection, that he is not as able to protect or defend himself as they are, and that she is discussing the matter with them because she knows that if they understood her child better they would not tease him. Another suggestion concerns discussing the matter in a similar vein with the parents of the neighborhood children (Sarason, 1953, p. 342).

Sarason stresses that the parent must not be given the impression that these suggestions are sure to work after one application. They need support in coping with disappointment and encouragement to repeat the approach as many times as necessary. When parents have an excessive emotional involvement in the particular situation they cannot be expected to act upon the recommendation no matter how correct it might be, and it is in these cases that more intensive help of a therapeutic nature might be indicated.

Gardner and Nisonger (1962) who prepared a manual on program development in mental retardation urge that any such program include counseling services for parents. Such services would give parents assistance in understanding the results of the diagnostic evaluation, including information about the etiology of the disorder, the child's present condition, and the prognosis. This covers the four basic questions which Doll (1953) once listed as points that parents of mentally retarded children ask sooner or later.

In addition to a transmission of this fairly concrete information which may need to be repeated and reviewed with the parents at different times and in different contexts, an adequate counseling service also gives parents an opportunity to plan for the immediate and long-term needs of the child including day-to-day care, management and training. Parents further receive help in accepting the child and in dealing with their own personal-emotional reactions and the crises which arise. A counseling service finally, helps implement plans which have been evolved for the child's care and training during the course of the contact with the parents. Such plans cannot be prescribed unilaterally for if they are to work and not leave emotional scars the parents must have had an opportunity to participate in the planning and to integrate the various implications.

THE DIAGNOSIS IS A BEGINNING

One cannot repeat too often that, as in any other form of pathology, the establishment of the diagonsis of mental retardation is only the beginning of professional responsibility. Proper diagnosis of the child's condition is an important step in planning treatment but in no way is the diagnosis identical with treatment. The parents' most crucial need for help occurs at the time when the diagnosis is first presented. Beck (1959) has pointed out that the parents' expectancy and readiness for help is aroused during the diagnostic process and that if the diagnosis is not promptly followed with an actual plan of treatment their readiness to involve themselves in the treatment procedure may be lost.

> The parents' most crucial need for service occurs at the time when they first learn of the diagnosis. It is then that they need support in handling their emotions, help in clearly understanding the diagnosis and its implications, and assistance in planning for the child.
> Considerable anxiety is usually aroused by a diagnosis of mental retardation. If this is not handled promptly, parents may develop rigid defenses which are not easily amenable to change. A caseworker can help parents set up the kind of defenses that will cushion reality adjustment rather than paralyze functioning. Even the most stable parents have to cope with a certain amount of personality disorganization in reaction to severe stress and shock. Professional casework services at this point work as a catalyst for helping parents to recognize their thoughts and reestablish ability to function (Beck, 1959, p. 226).

While Beck discusses help to the parents from the point of view of social casework, the kind of help parents can and should receive can, of course, also be given by skilled and well-trained members of other professions. This help includes the development of some understanding of the meaning of the diagnosis as it applies to their specific child and with it they can arrive at an understanding of the degree of the child's handicap and how it will affect him in the future. They can develop an ability to understand the child's assets and strengths, his needs and his difficulties. With skilled help given over time parents can develop an appreciation of the effect the retarded child has on the family as a whole, including the effect on the other children, on the parents themselves, and on the adjustment of the family within the community. Many parents labor under the misunderstanding that the child's retardation and his behavior are one and the same thing so that they fail to attempt to modify the child's behavior, at least to some degree, through the usual child-rearing approaches. A skilled counselor can help parents to judge whether neighborhood reactions are to the child's behavior, to the parents, or to his mental capacity. Attempts to modify neighborhood reactions, particularly those of the child's peer group, take a different form depending on the basis of these reactions.

It is clear that the variety of help to parents of retarded children cannot possibly be given in one or even two sessions, but that the parents must have the opportunity to maintain an ongoing contact which may, though not on a regular basis, extend over a long period of time.

In some settings parent counseling takes the form of group guidance in which carefully selected parents meet with a trained group leader in order to work on problems related to their retarded children. Cummings and Stock (1962) have experimented with one such group of mothers and they report that during a limited number of sessions the mothers gained much practical advice and new ideas from one another in the matter of training and management of the child. They were able to ventilate about their situation and frequently found reassurance in the recognition that they were not alone in their problems or in their feelings of frustration, inadequacy, and anger. Beyond that, a potential gain in counseling consisted of giving the parents a better recognition of the reality surrounding the mentally retarded child and their relations to him.

> Many mothers are out of touch with their own feelings about their child. Some arrive with the fantasy that their child will someday become normal, or that others will or must change and become more accepting, less curious, more helpful, or more realistic. In some instances such wishful fantasies give way to a more realistic recognition that certain problems and situations are inevitable and recurrent. This paves the way for some mothers to gain a greater sense of mastery over their difficult situation, and in fact find more adequate ways of dealing with their own feelings and problems (Cummings & Stock, 1962, p. 746 f.).

Some writers have addressed themselves to the question of the best setting in which to offer counseling services to parents of retarded children. Cummings and Stock (1962) who experimented with a treatment group in a setting other than that where the retarded children were being seen, came to the conclusion that the treatment opportunities should ideally be offered to the mothers in the setting which also extendeds help to the children. They felt that in such a setting the contact with the family can be more adequately integrated with the program developed for the child. Gardner and Nisonger (1962) are of the opinion that counseling services for a parent should only be associated with a residential facility if the child is a patient in that institution. They feel that parents are reluctant to accept help within an institutional setting for fear that the orientation of the helping person will be to encourage institutionalization. These writers suggest that counseling services should be associated with outpatient clinics, educational settings, or child guidance centers, but they too point out that the services should be an integral part of the program providing service to the retarded child.

THE QUESTION OF PLACEMENT

One of the most crucial decisions that face the parents of a mentally defective child revolves around plans for the child's education and training. This decision is complicated by the fact that few communities have adequate facilities for these children and that professionals are often of different opinions as to the best plan for a mentally defective child. The choice between private or public residential schools, community special schools, or special class placement must depend on a number of factors among which are the specific condition of the child, the parents' economic situation, the family constellation, the community attitudes and the resources available.

Cruickshank (Cruickshank & Johnson, 1958) stressed the importance of selective placement which involves the careful and complete assessment of the child's abilities and limitations and which takes the child's home and community environment into account. Such an assessment is conducted by qualified professional persons from a variety of disciplines. The ultimate joint recommendation of such an evaluation team as to the optimum and most realistic educational plan should result in placing the child into a situation where he can learn to make the best possible use of his limited endowment. The theoretically most desirable placement can, however, be brought to naught if the parents cannot accept it as a solution which is satisfactory to them but parent counseling should not be viewed as the work of "selling" reluctant parents a plan for placement. Indeed, a plan cannot be considered desirable unless the feelings and attitudes of the parents have been considered in making the plan. If it is remembered that one is dealing with a family unit and not with an individual child in isolation it will become clear that planning for the child cannot be conducted apart from a planning for the rest of the family. All too often professional people will make a plan which they consider ideal for the child and then turn to the parents expecting them to accept it because it is deemed best for the child. The inability of parents to accept a plan for their child reflects not on their worth as parents but on the fact that the plan was made without taking the parents' needs into consideration.

The best plans for the future of a child are those which are worked out jointly by the parents and the professional specialists. Once the diagnosis has been established and communicated to the parents the ongoing work with the parents should include a discussion of plans for the child's future. If the parents are involved in planning for their child the eventual decision will be their decision and not the imposed dictate of an authority.

Because of the many factors which must be considered in arriving at a decision about what steps to take for the child and his family it is impossible to present rules or guide lines which a professional person might follow in helping parents arrive at their decision. What is needed is a thorough knowledge of the child's condition, an appreciation for the family situation, and complete familiarity with the various facilities available. Anyone who thinks that he or his institution has a standard plan would do well to consider whether this plan takes individual differences into account. Doll (1953) stresses that the counselor must consider the age, education, economic position and personality of each of the child's parents; the question whether there are other children in the family; their age and sex, and, of course, the degree and nature of the exceptional child's retardation. It must also be stressed that a plan which is suitable and acceptable at one stage in the exceptional child's devlopment may become entirely unsuitable at a later stage. Doll (1953), for example, believes that, depending on the situation, a defective child might be kept at home during the first decade of his life, placed in an institution during the second decade and, if his ability and situation permit, returned home during the third and fourth decade. In considering such a plan one must of course also look ahead to the time when the parents of the retarded individual are no longer able to take care of him either because they are too old or because they are dead. Whether one can expect the siblings to take over the care which the parents were willing to assume depends on the family constellation and relationship. Elderly parents frequently seek help in making provisions for a retarded child they had kept at home when they see themselves becoming less able to carry the burden. This is obviously one of the realities parents must be helped to see when they first decide to keep a retarded child in the home.

Caring for a severely defective child at home creates many problems which must be taken into consideration when the question of institutional placement is discussed with the parents. A study of the problems reported by families who cared for mentally retarded children in their home (Holt, 1958) listed the resulting limitation of family activities as a complaint of 41 per cent of the 201 families questioned. Other problems mentioned with some frequency were the constant supervision, the extra expense, the exhaustion of the mother and the frequent need for attention at night.

One question which is frequently asked deals with the effect a mentally defective child will have on the other children at home. Again, the answer must be relative. It depends on the ages and sex of the other children, the position of the retarded child in the birth order, and on the parental attitudes toward him. We have already alluded to the study by Barsch (1961) which suggests that the siblings will adopt parental attitudes toward the exceptional child. If the parents see him as a source of shame or a burden, so will the other children; if they fully accept him as a member of the family who has a particular problem, his siblings will do likewise. The reactions of teenage siblings were investigated by Graliker, Fishler, and Koch (1962) who found that the presence of a young retarded child did not have an adverse effect, particularly when parent counseling was available to help maintain the family equilibrium.

Institutionalization and family integration. Recent years have seen an increase in the number of studies designed to explore the effect of institutionalization of a child on the rest of the family (Caldwell & Guze, 1960; Farber, 1959; Smith, Ricketts & Smith, 1962). Caldwell and Guze (1960) compared sixteen families whose retarded child lived at home with sixteen families where the child was placed in an institution. Interviews and tests of the mothers and siblings of the retarded children failed to detect impressive differences. The far more extensive study by Farber (1959) arrived at different conclusions, an inconsistency of results which may be due to differences in sampling, sample size, measuring devices, and the difficulty of controlling for differences in the types of families which decide to place their retarded child and those who choose to retain the child in the home.

Farber (1959) studied the effects of a severely mentally retarded child on family integration. He views the long-term changes in family relations as the life cycle of the family and the relations between family members as an interacting system of careers. It is through the interaction of these careers that the family life cycle proceeds from one stage to the next. Farber describes the contemporary American family as roughly passing through the following stages in their life cycle: the married couple; the family whose youngest child is of pre-school age; the family with a pre-adolescent youngest child; the family with an adolescent youngest child; the family in which all children are adults; the family in which all childen are married.

When one of the children is a mentally retarded child Farber believes that the family cycle is arrested. With respect to retarded children parental roles are fairly constant and regardless of the retarded child's position in the birth order he eventually takes on the social position of the youngest child. As a result the family with a severely retarded child in the home does not emerge from the pre-adolescent stage of its family life cycle. Farber's hypothesis is that arrest in the family life cycle results in disruption of family integration because each individual has his anticipated roles frustrated. This disruption of individual role careers is felt differentially by the parents and the siblings of the retarded child. Viewing the family as a series of triads representing a mother-father-child relationship, Farber (1959) believes that "the parents would generally perceive the arrest of the retarded child's life career in the context of the life careers of all the family members and be affected in the marital relationship by gross deficiencies in the development of the child's life career" (p. 10). The retarded child's siblings, on the other hand, view the arrest in his "life career in terms of its immediate effects on their own family roles" (*loc. cit.*).

Viewing family integration as his dependent variable and whether the child lived in the home or in an institution as one of a series of independent variables which also included the age and sex of the retarded child, the sex of his normal siblings, the family's social status, the mother's view of dependence of the retarded child, and the presence or absence of supportive community relations, Farber proceeded with an extensive study of 240 families with a severely (I.Q. fifty or below) mentally deficient child sixteen years of age or under. Of the 240 families in the sample 175 had a retarded child at home while sixty-five had placed their child in a private or state institution. The procedure of the study involved a lengthy (two-and-a-half hour) interview conducted in the home by two members of the research team. The interviewers asked questions which could be answered orally and also presented the parents with a series of scales and questionnaires which were completed in writing. Marital integration was evaluated by an index which had been independently validated.

Farber's results lend strong support to the caution that parents of mentally retarded children must under no circumstances be viewed as a homogeneous group for whom one standard set of recommendations would be valid. A variety of interacting factors must be taken into consideration before even the most tentative formulation of a plan can be advanced. The effect on family integration of whether the retarded child was kept at home or lived in an institution was found to be a function of the interaction of social class, sex and age of the retarded child, the sex of the siblings, and the religious affiliation of the family. When the retarded child was at home it was found that the marriages of the parents were more often adversely affected if the retarded child was a boy. The differential effect was, however, more pronounced in lower social class families than in middle class families. Farber attributes these differences to the variations in parental expectations for the life careers of boys and girls as well as to the greater stress which lower class families place on sex differences. The older the retarded boy who is kept in the home the greater was the disruptive effect on his parents' marriage. This result follows from Farber's conceptualization of individual career roles and the arrest in the family life cycle.

When the severely retarded child was in an institution Farber found that the marital integration of the parents was higher than that of parents with a retarded boy at home. This was true whether the institutionalized child was a boy or a girl. Farber thus concluded that "in general, placing a retarded boy in an institution had a beneficial effect on the parents' marital relationship" (*ibid.*, p. 78). Whereas the retarded child's sex and the family's social status interacted in their effect on the parents' marital integration, these factors did not markedly influence the adjustment of the normal siblings to their family roles. What was of effect here was the sex of the normal sibling and his age relative to the age of the retarded child.

Farber's data on normal siblings show that normal sisters manifested more personality problems when the retarded sibling was in the home than when he was in an institution. Normal brothers, on the other hand, were adversely affected by the institutionalization of the retarded sibling. Farber seeks to explain this differential effect on normal siblings by pointing out that with the placement of the retarded child in an institution the normal brother faces demands from the mother which he had previously escaped because of her preoccupation with the retarded child. The normal sister, on the other hand, was probably expected to help care for the retarded child while he was in the home but is relieved of these responsibilities by the removal of the retarded sibling to an institution.

In evaluating these results and the explanations offered by Farber

it must be recalled that his data were not based on comparisons between family integration before and after the placement of the retarded
child in an institution. While the internal consistency of his results tends
to argue against it, there exists the alternative explanation that parents with high marital integration find it easier to decide on the institutionalization of their retarded child because, they are able to give each
other the emotional support needed to make this decision and to work
through its psychological impact. In families with low marital integration, on the other hand, parents may not be able to agree on this
decision and the mother in particular may cling to the retarded child
because her psychic economy demands his presence to assuage her guilt
or to use him as a weapon in the ongoing discord between herself and
her husband. The causal question of better marital integration in families where the retarded child has been institutionalized cannot be considered resolved by the correlation approach of Farber's study.

The emotional support available to the mother in relations outside
the immediate family appears to have a positive effect on marital integration. Where the wife had frequent interaction with her own mother this was found to be conducive to high marital integration, not because grandmother served the role of a helper but rather because she
provided emotional support. On the other hand, high participation with
the wife's mother-in-law was found to have a disturbing influence upon
marriage relationship, suggesting that the husband's mother provides
little emotional support in the handling of the retarded child. Another
result suggestive of the importance of emotional support for the wife
in the maintenance of high family integration will be found in the
fact that the beneficial effect on marriage relationship of placing the
retarded son in an institution was found among non-Catholics but not
among Catholic parents. Farber takes this to suggest that in crisis
Catholics receive a greater amount of emotional support from their
religious affiliation than do non-Catholics. This interpretation is similar
to the conclusion reached by Zuk (1959) who, on the basis of workers' impressions, reported that Catholic mothers were more accepting
of their retarded child than non-Catholic mothers because their religion
gives them emotional support and provides them with a means to ab-
solve themselves from guilt.

Farber's study has been discussed in some detail because it represents the most extensive and sophisticated research effort which is
available in this area. The practical implications which he himself
draws from his results should be kept in mind by anyone in a position
to work with the parents of mentally retarded children.

Taken together, the results concerning the hypotheses in this study present important considerations in deciding upon institutionalization of the retarded child. Effects of age, sex, and dependence of the retarded child in combination with the presence of normal brothers and sisters and the social status and religion of the family determine the impact of the presence of the retarded child on the family. The parents cannot, of course, predict the future effect of the child on family relations precisely. Yet, the results of the study can serve as guideposts: the parent can expect that a retarded boy, especially after the age of nine, will probably have a disruptive effect on marital relations; he can anticipate personality problems for the sister, who is given many responsibilities for the child; the parent must be aware of the degree to which the family has its own resources and supportive interaction in facing crisis situations; and he can expect the degree of helplessness of the retarded to affect the personality of his normal children adversely (Farber, 1959, p. 80 f.).

If one perceives of the family as an interacting system it is readily apparent that the removal of any family member from that system will have an effect not only on the other individuals but also on their interaction and role balance. As stated above, the retarded child may have a psychological meaning of special significance and his presence in the family, though disrupting, may be necessary in order to maintain a delicate interpersonal equilibrium. Smith, Ricketts, and Smith (1962) discussed the effect of placement on the remaining family members and urged that counselor and family carefully explore the possible effects of placement on the family unit. The possibility of upsetting the family equilibrium does not, however, necessarily mean that placement is contraindicated. What is indicated is that here as in all other situations where a family has to cope with the presence of an exceptional child the family receive sensitive, sympathetic professional support in dealing with the feelings created by the crisis situation.

Writing from the vantage point of a psychiatric clinic in which most of the placements involved children with severe emotional disorders, Smith, Ricketts and Smith (1962) report that their experience "seems to indicate that placement is an upsetting experience for the siblings remaining at home. Among the feelings roused in siblings were fear of placement, resentment toward the parents for placement of the brother or sister, guilt over the sibling's being sent away, and envy of the placed child" (p. 45). The case of Mary reported by these writers serves as a dramatic illustration of the possible consequences of a placement when the family situation is not carefully explored and ongoing counseling not available to the family.

Mary, a ten-year-old deaf, brain-damaged, retarded girl, was placed in a state school for retarded children. At the time the placement recommendation was made, the family life had become centered around efforts to calm Mary. Her frequent outbursts of rage, hyperactivity, screaming and constant demands had exhausted the family. The urgency of the need for placement overshadowed all other considerations. Clinic staff paid insufficient attention to the mother's brief description of Mary's jealousy toward an older sister, or to the reported remark by the sister that the mother wanted to get rid of Mary. Neither the family nor the staff anticipated reactions which might occur following Mary's placement. In the follow-up interview one year after Mary was placed, the mother described feelings of relief experienced by all members of the family except the older sister, who had become obsessed with the belief that Mary was mistreated and cruelly placed. The sister's agitation and depression, apparently based on her feelings toward Mary, increased to such an extent that psychiatric treatment was necessary. At the time of the follow-up interview the sister had made slight progress in managing the emotional conflict which flared up when Mary was placed (Smith, Ricketts & Smith, 1962, p. 45).

It was the opinion of Weingold and Hormuth (1953) that families with retarded children seem beset with problems of sibling rivalry and marital conflict much more intensely than other families. While this impression may be based on a biased sample it seems well to recall their statement that the presence of a retarded child in a family seems to accentuate personality difficulties which may exist in other members of the family and if this is so the unplanned and unsupported placement of the retarded child does not necessarily reduce these difficulties. If, for example, the exceptional child has created excessive guilt in one or more of the members of the family, then placing the child in an institution is more likely to exacerbate this guilt than to assuage it.

REALITY FACTORS

A number of interrelated and interdependent reality factors which enter into the counseling of parents of mentally retarded children have been discussed by Begab (1956) who feels that each of these aspects must be carefully considered by the professional counselor if the parents are to receive adequate help with their problems. These factors are related to the environment, the social attitudes, the child's condition and the parents' personality.

The environmental factor is of particular importance when parents are considering placing the child in an institution. The expensive private institution can be viewed as a boarding school and is thus not subject to the unfortunate stigma which is still attached to state institutions for mental defectives. Inasmuch as only a minority of parents are in a position to afford private institutional care for their child, the question of institutionalization in a state school must be faced by the majority. In its relationship to the state and because of the legal aspects of admission and commitment the state institution is easily perceived as representing authority and sending a child to such an institution can be all too readily viewed as a punitive measure.

It is unfortunately true that many state schools for mental defectives have anything but a good "public image" in the communities they are supposed to serve. Many have been in existence for fifty or more years and during that time have acquired the stigma of an isolated, forbidding place, many miles away from the city, where dull children are sent, never to be heard from again. It is, in fact, not at all uncommon to find towns and cities where generations of children have encountered the semi-facetious threat that if they don't do well in school they'll be sent to *That Place.* In many communities the name of the state school serving the area has become synonymous with defective intelligence. "He looks as if he'd come straight out of X" readily communicates the stereotyped image of a mental defective to another inhabitant of a particular area. Little wonder then that parents of a mentally defective child are none too eager to consider institutionalization.

Making the decision to institutionalize and adjusting to the fact of institutionalization is often further complicated for the parents by the attitudes of relatives and friends who, rather than being helpful, may bring added pressure against commitment by making the parents feel that they are not living up to their responsibility by agreeing to placement. Helping these parents again involves an exploration of attitudes and feelings and aid in exploring the various aspects of the reality with which they are faced. One of the realities which they must be helped to explore is the nature of the institution itself. As plans for placement are being made, the parents should have an opportunity to visit the institution or institutions under consideration so that they can become acquainted with both the physical plant and the school's program. The more information available to the parents, the less likely they are to let their anxieties distort or influence their planning. As with all other perceptual processes, the more realistic and unambiguous the information, the more likely it is that the person's ego will be able to cope with the situation.

Closely related to attitudes about the institution are the factors involving social attitudes toward mental deficiency. As Begab (1956) points out, social prejudices and widespread misconceptions about deficiency can have a tremendous impact on the parents' decision regarding placement. The counselor must recognize these attitudes and be prepared to deal with them in helping the parents arrive at a realistic plan. Pressures from the neighborhood based on primitive and often almost superstitious fears of people who are "different" may either serve to precipitate the parents into premature decisions or lead them to react with negativism whereby, in defense against environmental hostility, the family draws closer together against the outside world and makes the decision to keep the child at home.

Neighborhood fears are frequently related to trepidations about potential sexual acting-out on the part of the deficient child. Such fears often have their basis in the anxiety related to strongly repressed unacceptable impulses and can, because of their unconscious motivation, be extremely irrational. Individual parents, even with professional help, are usually unable to change neighborhood attitudes and such change must probably await public education and enlightenment which local, state and national organizations of parents of retarded children have recently begun to initiate. Until a change in social attitude can be brought about the counselor must keep these attitudes in mind as one of the realities which parents face. When this factor is not taken into consideration parents may react to community rejection with hostility, withdrawal, overprotection, or displacement of hostility on the child, thus further complicating an already difficult situation.

Yet another set of factors which enters into the counseling of parents of retarded children are those related to the child and his condition (Begab, 1956). One of the realities which parents of mentally defective children must face is the extreme and prolonged dependency of the child which, in the most severe cases, is of indefinite nature. This dependency, as Forbes (1958) has pointed out, complicates each developmental stage and makes expectations of child development based on the implicit norms of lay persons completely irrelevant. The parents must be aware of and prepared for slow development in every area involving learning. They must, for example, know that their child is unlikely to be toilet-trained by the time normal children achieve control over their eliminative processes. Even when knowledge of retarded development has been accepted on an intellectual level parents frequently don't experience the full impact of the realization until they are faced with the experience in the course of the child's life. This again argues for the need of ongoing counseling and suggests the inadequacy of a series of didactic explanations at the time the diagnosis is first brought to the parents' attention.

Other factors related to the child's condition are the great financial and physical drain which parents of retarded children must encounter as the years go by. Even the most careful and patient of explanations will not serve to make the mother aware of the full impact which the prolonged physical care of a retarded child will have on her and the family in the course of years to come. As the child gets older and physically more mature the discrepancy between his intellectual capacity and his physical size, strength, and ability will become ever more marked and parents who see little to be concerned about when thinking of the physical care required by a two-year-old will find their frustration tolerance tested to the limit ten years later. It is about that time when fears of the child's sexual acting-out also enter the picture.

Nonconformity to the neighborhood sexual mores has frequently been attributed to the high suggestibility of the mentally defective child or adolescent. While it is true that the reduced ability to learn and to recognize implications and consequences make it more difficult for the defective child to adhere to socially accepted standards of behavior, suggestibility is, as Begab (1956) has stressed, only one of many complicating factors in the sexual misdeeds of the retarded. Emotional factors, such as a need for affection, curiosity, or an attempt to escape from an unhappy home environment, may well play a role; these can, of course, be vitiated if, with professional help, the parents are able to give their child the necessary emotional support.

Socially unacceptable behavior of the retarded child may also be the result of the lack of acceptable outlets for physical and emotional drives. The fact that the neighborhood does not furnish the retarded child with clubs, dances, parties, or athletic events, as it does for the normal child and adolescent, not only compounds the social immaturity of the retarded but may also lead him to seek outlets which run afoul of social custom and taboos. The normal adolescent with reduced social activities is able to compensate for these by intellectual achievement, but for the retarded this compensation is impossible. All of this must be taken into consideration when the parents of the retarded child are counseled regarding placement. Good institutions for mental defectives do furnish social and athletic outlets so that in many ways the child's life can be more normal in an institution than it can be in a rejecting neighborhood.

The fourth group of factors in counseling parents of retarded children are those associated with the parents themselves (Begab, 1956).

In order to help parents it is necessary to consider their emotional strengths and weaknesses, their fears, anxieties, guilt, and frustrations, as well as their physical, financial and social resources. "In many instances, the factors which influence parent counseling are basically those related to the personality makeup of the parents themselves rather than external considerations. Crisis situations tend to strengthen the ego and solidify personal relationships or weaken the total personality structure and create further disharmony and disintegration" (Begab, 1956, p. 524). The meaning which the child has for the parents must be considered and the influence of his defective condition on this meaning must be evaluated. Where parents have looked forward to the arrival of the child as the culmination and fulfillment of their marital relationship, a defective child can be an extreme disappointment. Where parents had hoped to express their own aspirations through the child, his defective condition is a serious frustration and where the child was viewed as proof of personal adequacy, his exceptional state will be a major threat to the parents' ego. Guilt, hostility, and fantasies of having been punished for real or imagined wrongdoings are responses frequently encountered in parents of defective children and where these feelings exist parents find it extremely difficult to accept the child and to give him an emotionally supportive environment. "They deny his deficiency or reject him completely as unworthy of their attentions. They are either unable or unwilling to accept outside help because of the social stigma, real or imagined, with which their parenthood is associated" (Begab, 1956, p. 523).

The unconsciously-motivated need to deny mental deficiency frequently receives support if the child in addition to his intellectual impairment also manifests physical handicaps. Where this is the case the parents tend to focus on the physical condition, blaming all manifestations of mental impairment on the physical state. Depending on the nature of the condition, they will desperately seek such corrective measures as braces, speech lessons, physical exercises or surgery, and while these may be necessary to correct the physical defect it is the responsibility of all professional people coming in contact with these parents to help them recognize that the mental deficiency will not thereby be alleviated.

Michaels and Schucman (1962) report that in their experience the vast majority of parents with defective children who come to them for help hold the belief that their child's major, if not his only problem, lies in the area of speech. They cling to the hope that if the child can only be helped to develop adequate speech all of his problems will magically vanish. These authors believe that this hope for a cure is needed by the parents as a defense which permits them to continue to function and feel that it might be dangerous to dispel this belief too abruptly before more realistic expectations have been accepted in exchange. They maintain that premature emphasis on the reality of a situation can lead the parent into feelings of hopelessness and chronic depression (p. 570). From the point of view here represented it seems highly undesirable for the professional person to participate in the parents' defenses by not stressing the reality of the situation and postponing the inevitable communication of the truth no matter how painful this may be. What is important and a definite responsibility of the professional person is to help the parents accept the reality and to assist them in handling the feelings of hopelessness and despair of which Michaels and Schucman speak. It must again be stressed that this cannot be done in one or two interviews but that it involves a continuous contact which may need to last over many years and that the longer the recognition of reality is avoided the more difficult the eventual acceptance of the fact of retardation will be.

In addition to the help which the individual counselor can and should be to the parents of the retarded child many parents find support by joining formal or informal groups of others parents with similar problems. Community pressures and social stigma are difficult to withstand when one feels isolated and alone. They become easier to cope with if one has the support of a group. Organizations of parents of retarded children have been effective on many levels of society, not only in improving available facilities for retarded children and in public education and enlightenment, but also in providing the parents with a better understanding of their problem and in giving them the support of a strong and active group. Working with a parent organization can serve as a constructive form of sublimating frustrations and anxieties. The professional worker can play a constructive role by helping parents get in touch with such a group and, when asked, taking an advisory role in the organization.

V.

The Child with Sensory Defect or Physical Handicap in the Family

THE PARENTS AND THE CHILD

PARENTS WHOSE child has a sensory or physical handicap, whether it be congenital or acquired through accident or illness, have to learn to cope with a problem of which they are almost constantly aware. The deficit is a part of the reality which is present in the parent-child relationship and which complicates the child's relations to his environment and the parents' reactions to the child. Inasmuch as the handicap affects the child's environmental interactions in different ways at different periods during his development parents will need to have professional help available to them for an indefinite period even though they may resort to it only from time to time.

Professional help is important not only because having a handicapped child has a profound effect on the parents but also because their reactions and their way of handling him will have a tremendous influence on the kind of character and personality structure he will develop. Beyond this the presence of the handicapped child in the family has an influence on the siblings who, as at least one study revealed, (Shere, 1956) may be more disturbed than the handicapped child himself.

As with all other exceptional conditions of children the aim of parent counseling is to help them accept the handicap on a realistic basis. Yet often the reality of a physical handicap or sensory defect is such that it may be extremely difficult for a parent not to respond to it in an irrational, unconsciously-determined manner. These reactions may play into the child's fears and fantasies, thus complicating his emotional development.

An excellent publication prepared by the U. S. Children's Bureau and dealing with emotional problems associated with handicapping conditions in children states:

There is hardly a mother who does not respond with deep feelings of guilt and self-accusations to a congenital defect of the child, a birth injury or a chronic disease—even operation or accident leading to invalidism. Parents in addition to their normal worry and compassion for their

123

handicapped or chronically ill child, frequently feel personally injured and attacked by fate, and are inclined to reject the child to some degree. . .

Some mothers can hardly disguise their punishing attitude and act it out, often in the rigidity with which they hold their children to a restricting diet or painful medical schedule. Others, in their attempt to cope with these tendencies, lean over backwards to a point where, with the same rigidity, their lives are sacrificed completely, responding to an unjustifiable degree to the slightest need or demand of the little patient and to the detriment also of other members of the family. Another group expresses this conflict by behaving as if they were cursed and are determined never to have another child. Some parents—without comprehending the meaning of their emotions—feel ashamed of the child as if the fact that they have a defective child reveals a shameful weakness of their own, thus being the counterparts of the neurotically ambitious mothers and fathers who drive their healthy children, and demand from them outstanding success in every area as a token of their own greatness. Other parents cannot bring themselves to see what is apparent to everyone else and they deny that here is a permanent situation they need to learn to live with. Such parents may go from one physician to another, to various healing practitioners and quacks, seeking support in their evasion of the situation and the result is usually a postponement of treatment (Children's Bureau, 1952, p. 2 f.).

While one might expect adjustment problems to be greater the more severe the handicap, a clinical study reported by Miller (1958) suggests that the child with a mild handicap has more severe adjustment problems arising from disturbed parent-child relationships than does the child with a severe handicap. While these findings may be biased by the fact that all of the children had been referred to a psychiatric facility and thus represented a selected population, the difference between the mildly and the severely handicapped children might well be understood in terms of the differential degrees of ambiguity in their conditions. When a child has a severe handicap the obvious and concrete nature of his disability leaves less room for questions about the presence, permanence and consequences of the handicap, thereby reducing the likelihood for unrealistic expectations, ambivalence about getting help, and disagreements between parents regarding the child's condition. It also appears that some parents at least are more comfortable with a concrete defect whose basis is readily communicated to relatives and neighbors than they are with a vague and intermittently noticeable defect which leaves people to wonder what might be wrong with the child (Barsch, 1961).

EXPECTATIONS AND DEMANDS

Setting and maintaining realistic expectations for a handicapped child's performance and accomplishments are among the most difficult aspects with which a parent must learn to cope. Implicit norms for expectations, which in the case of unimpaired children are derived from a composite made up of the parents' own childhood memories, ambitions and accomplishments, comparisons with other children in the family or neighborhood, and society's general notion of what a child of a certain age should be able to do, are inapplicable in the case of the exceptional child. Norms of child development in either the professional or lay literature cannot be applied and, because of the highly individualistic nature of a specific child's handicap or deficiency, meaningful norms for exceptional children cannot be established. Only a detailed professional evaluation of the individual child's strengths and weaknesses can furnish guide lines and these must be interpreted to the parents, taking account of the parents' ability to accept and apply them. Boles (1959) found that mothers of cerebral palsied children are generally realistic about their child's *present* capacity but highly unrealistic in their hopes for improvement and future capacity. Inasmuch as hopes for the future invariably affect present attitudes this finding again underscores the need for wise professional counseling.

Where expectations for achievement are greater than the child's capacity for accomplishment, the pressure which is exerted on the child and the frustrations both he and his parents experience when he is unable to meet the expectations may result in irritability, hyperaggressiveness, and a sense of failure and inadequacy. Expecting more than the child can accomplish is one extreme of unrealistic parental attitudes. The other extreme is represented by overprotection resulting from unrealistically low expectations of what the child can do. Here, instead of helping the child do as much as possible for himself and by himself, the parent anticipates his needs and helps him with tasks which the child would be able to carry out himself.

Boles (1959) reports that when compared with mothers of non-handicapped children mothers of cerebral palsied children are significantly more overprotective. Overprotection not only leads to retarded social and emotional development of the handicapped child but it may also result in adjustment problems for the unimpaired sibling. Comparing the adjustment of thirty pairs of twins where one twin had cerebral palsy and the other was unimpaired, Shere found that ". . . the behavior of the cerebral palsied child was more desirable than that of his non-cerebral palsied twin. He considered himself to be accepted by his parents and exhibited the behavior of a secure, accepted child. His non-cerebral palsied twin, however, contrasting the casual acceptance accorded him by his parents with the excessive attention given to his cerebral palsied twin, considered himself rejected, and exhibited the behavior of the insecure rejected child" (1956, p. 206).

The psychosocial development of all children involves a gradual move from total dependence of the very young infant to the independence of the late adolescent. The handicapped child may have increased needs of physical dependence and these needs may extend over a longer period of time. In case of severe involvement the individual may in fact have to remain dependent on the physical help of others throughout his life. The parents of the handicapped child must be helped to learn to differentiate between realistic physical dependency and the psychologically stunting emotional dependency of their child. In the healthy psychological development of the normal child the emancipation from physical dependency is paralleled by the increasing emotional independence or by a shifting of emotional ties from parents to heterosexual love objects. This parallel achievement of independence in both the physical and emotional areas is disrupted where the child's handicap requires continued physical dependence. This makes it doubly important for the parents to permit the child to develop psychological independence by demonstrating increasing respect for his judgment and ability to make his own decisions. The parents must learn that merely because they have to help their child in certain physical activities they must not also make his decisions and manage his affairs.

By limiting overprotection and expecting the handicapped child to become competent and independent in areas not affected by his physical deficiency, the parents will also reduce the stress the presence of the exceptional child may place on the unimpaired siblings. If the brothers and sisters can see that their handicapped sibling is expected to cope with problems and to help with household tasks within the limitations of his physical defect, they will not only be less likely to resent the extra attention he realistically must have but they are also likely to show greater respect and acceptance toward him.

Compensatory experiences. The ideal balance between unrealistically high expectations on the one hand and overprotection on the other lies in helping the child to maximize his capacities in areas where he is handicapped and to compensate for his inabilities in some areas by achievement in others. The physically handicapped child can be guided to find accomplishment and success in the intellectual area just as the intellectually deficient child may be able to experience accomplishment in some area of physical activity. Needless to say, the prerequisite for helping a child compensate in an area not affected by his handicap is a thorough understanding of his capacities and deficiencies in all areas. Only added pain and frustration can result if one tries to help a child with an obvious motor deficiency compensate in the intellectual area when in that area his capacities are also limited. Careful evaluations by members of different professional specialties, repeated over time, with results sensitively interpreted to the parents are the only way in which one can hope to avoid the unfortunate consequences of unrealistic demands and expectations. All but the most severely impaired children have some area in which they can succeed in reaching a realistically set goal whereby they can achieve a sense of competence.

The significance of this sense of competence in the psychological development of the child has been stressed by White (1960) who sees it as based on an important motivational principle. The ability to effect changes in the environment which the child has intentionally initiated gives him a feeling of efficacy which, according to White, satisfies a major neurogenic motive which he calls effectance. Within this frame of reference it becomes clear that every child must have areas where he can initiate and effect changes in the environment even though his handicap may restrict the areas in which this is possible. If effectance is indeed a basic biological motive, and White (1959) argues very convincingly for this point of view, then a frustration of this motive may result in the failure of certain neurophysiologic patterns to develop. The handicapped child must therefore be given opportunities to satisfy the effectance motive and to acquire a sense of competence, but if his parents meet and anticipate his every need or set goals which are beyond his ability the motive of effectance cannot be satisfied.

Recent re-evaluations of studies dealing with early maternal deprivation (Casler, 1961) and intellectual development (Hunt, 1961) strongly suggest that a reduction in sensory experience and lack of opportunity for motor behavior during the first one or two years of life may result in irreversible sensory-motor and intellectual deficits. Since a handicapped child, whether his handicap is in the sensory or the motor area, may have reduced sensory-motor experience, particularly if he is overprotected and under-stimulated, it is not unlikely that unwise environmental practices can contribute to further deficiencies above and beyond those which are directly determined by the basic handicap. It follows from this that parents of handicapped children must be helped to give the child opportunities for compensatory experiences which must be of motor nature if the handicap is sensory and of a sensory nature if the handicap is in the motor realm. Compensatory experiences leading to a feeling of efficacy can of course also be given in those sensory and motor areas which are not directly affected by the handicap. Thus the visually handicapped child will need more than the normal amount of auditory, tactual, and olfactory experience, just as the child with a handicap involving locomotion must be helped to develop compensations in his unaffected muscular motor apparatus.

The corrolary to the concept that a child needs opportunity for sensory-motor experience in order to develop his neurophysiologic potential to the fullest is the assumption that certain experiences must take place during specific *critical periods* of development and that if the opportunity for such an experience was not available at that time all later development will be affected. These critical periods seem to depend on a match between the environmental circumstances encountered and the internal sensory-motor-intellectual organization already established (Hunt, 1961).

At present the presumed critical periods are poorly understood and we do not know what experiences are crucial at what time during early development. There are suggestions in the literature (*e.g.*, Hunt, 1961) that for optimal development the opportunities for environmental encounters available to the child should neither be less nor substantially greater than his then-existing capacity; that they should represent neither a source of boredom because the tasks are too easy, nor a source of distress because they are too difficult. As long as the task is a challenge which the child is capable of meeting, the process is a source of pleasurable interest or curiosity leading to growth. Details of this which might lend themselves to a rational program unfortunately remain to be spelled out.

When a child is deprived of a major sense modality, such as vision, his need for effective compensatory experiences is often interpreted to mean that his unaffected sense modalities must receive more intensive stimulation. In terms of the concepts just discussed, there is such a thing as overstimulation when the experience does not match the child's developmental state. Norris, Spaulding and Brodie (1957) conducted an intensive five-year study of nearly 300 pre-school blind children on the basis of which they concluded that the young blind child needs opportunities for learning, not stimulation, if by stimulation one understands that something is done *to* the child without an awareness of his own motivational system and an appreciation of what is appropriate at the various levels of his development.

Opportunities for learning imply "an emotional climate in which the child is given both guidance and freedom in judicious proportions relative to his needs as a developing personality" and "a real knowledge of reasonable expectations for the blind child's development" (Norris, Spaulding & Brodie, 1957, p. 71).

Unfortunately, most recommendations to parents have been given in terms of their responsibility to *teach* the young child the needed skills, without reference to the basic principles involved in his learning processes. The conscientious parent, already concerned with fulfilling his responsibilities toward his child, finds that this emphasis only adds to his feelings of confusion and inadequacy. . . .

Actually most of the basic skills that the pre-school blind child requires if he is to function satisfactorily in his home and community cannot be taught directly. Fortunately, the child who has security, freedom to explore, and an environment in which his needs (including those directly related to blindness) are recognized and understood will develop these skills on his own initiative.

Recognition that, for the infant, 'stimulation' comes only by way of another person and that learning takes place within a relationship which is satisfying to both mother and child appears to be basic to understanding the problem. [These investigators] found that it is only within the framework of satisfying relationships that the child is able to move out to broader experience; attempts to force him to develop new skills are utterly self-defeating. The child, in this pre-school period, can best be understood by an awareness of the needs of a developing personality and the circumstances that will promote its optimal growth. If the parents are sensitive to the needs of the child and flexible in meeting them, they need have no anxiety about the child's active interest in an ever widening environment. The child will then be able to make good use of varied learning opportunities.

Freeing the parents from their anticipated responsibility for teaching specific skills unrelated to daily living is often the first step in helping them to think realistically about the blind child and to be comfortable in their relationship with him. If this can be accomplished within the first few months of the child's life, his responsiveness gives assurance to the parents that they are on the right track. Their resulting confidence in their ability to meet the child's needs and their pleasure in his achievement then become primary factors in encouraging his further progress. Major developmental problems are avoided, in contrast to those situations where failure to understand and meet the child's needs in the early period has created difficulties which are discouragingly slow to respond to treatment (*loc. cit.*, p. 71 f.).

It follows from the above that the crucial variable in whether a blind child develops his fullest potential is the comfort with which his parents are able to cope with having a child with a major handicap. The role and responsibility of the professional in all this is obvious.

Discipline and punishment. Related to expectations and demands is the question of discipline and punishment which troubles many parents of exceptional children. Largely because of such inappropriate emotions as guilt and pity toward the handicapped child they feel constrained in enforcing discipline in the same manner in which they would with an unimpaired child. As long as guilt remains unresolved and pity toward the child an overriding emotion the parents will not be able to enforce limits and use appropriate controls. As a result the child may become more and more difficult to handle, the parents' reaction grow more and more irrational, until at some point the parent-child relationship is completely disrupted.

We have previously discussed that parents need professional help in handling their feelings toward and about the exceptional child. What should here be stressed is that the exceptional child must have reasonable limits which are consistently enforced by the appropriate and realistic manipulation of rewards and punishments. The child should obviously not be punished for actions or omissions which are the direct result of his handicap. This point needs to be emphasized because the parents' repressed anger at the handicapped child may at times manifest itself by irrationally punitive attitudes. Punishments which involve or reflect on the child's handicap should never be used. Thus any threat involving a physician, medical procedures, or institutionalization must be just as much avoided as the cruel practice sometimes reported where parents deprive the handicapped child of his crutches because he was "bad."

The professional counselor must remember that punishment and discipline are problems only when the parents' own emotional problems get in the way of handling the child in the rational and realistic manner in which they would handle an unimpaired offspring. When unusual punishments or remarkable lack of discipline are reported, the counselor must explore the underlying emotions before he can hope to deal with the matter of discipline in other than direct authoritarian fashion and authoritarian pronouncements on what to do and what not to do in the area of child rearing are invariably ineffective because the underlying emotional conflicts are not resolved. A parent who is basically hostile to his exceptional child may, upon command, cease depriving him of his crutches but punishment will take some other sadistic form when the next occasion arises.

THE PARENTS' REACTIONS

The difficulties parents may experience in handling handicapped children are discussed in a clinical report by Miller (1958) who studied and compared four groups of patients between the ages of seven and twelve referred to a child guidance clinic with emotional problems. Twenty-six of these were mildly handicapped cerebral palsied children, sixteen were severely handicapped cerebral palsied children, and thirteen physically and neurologically normal child psychiatric patients.

Miller found that the parents of the mildly handicapped children were generally anxious, guilty, and actually frightened about their feelings of ambivalence toward the child and his condition (Miller, 1958).

One of their big problems had to do with recognizing the condition as handicapping since the child was self-sufficient. Actually, their greatest need was to have this 'almost normal' child be normal. There was real confusion as to what to expect of the child since he seemed so variable in his capabilities. This confusion led to inconsistencies in demands and expectations. The parents expressed strong feelings about being unable to meet the needs of the child, and concern about the mounting negative feelings resulting from repeated frustrations in dealing with the child. Further guilt resulted from the negative feelings, aroused greater anxiety, and greater need to prove there was nothing wrong. The child was generally expected to perform beyond his capacity in all ways, possibly as a salve for the wounded parental ego. Individual parents reacted according to their level of maturity, and their own personality patterns. However, they all reacted with some degree of anxiety, confusion, and over-expectation, and with real ambivalence (Miller, 1958, p. 300).

All parents, except those of the severely handicapped children, were fearful about exercising discipline. The parents of the physically normal children were afraid to express their anger for fear they would inflict physical hurt on the child if they lost their self-control.

In the case of the cerebral palsied, the parents were afraid of doing irreparable damage to an already 'delicate' child. If there had been any history of seizures, there was great fear of bringing on seizures by disciplining or even frustrating the child. In any case, the child was left insecure and anxious, not knowing where he stood, and the parents were left feeling helpless and angry at being controlled by the children when they felt the children should, by all rights, be controlled by the parents (Miller, loc. cit.).

Psychotherapy was offered to 12 of the mildly handicapped and the 13 physically normal children and to the parents of both groups. As in any child guidance therapy the work with the parents was at least as important as the treatment of the children. The parents were helped to gain not only intellectual but also emotional understanding of their child and his condition. Without neglecting constructive realistic planning the treatment was geared to a feeling level and aimed at parental acceptance of the child.

The treatment process was a painful one for the parents as they slowly worked with their conflict around their 'different' or 'difficult' child and began to live with the 'difference.' As the child began to respond to them, however, the parents could more easily respond in return and give more freely of themselves and their love to the child. As the parents could become more comfortable they were able to begin to discipline the child as well as love him, without fear of losing the child's love or of hurting him (*ibid.*, p. 301).

Miller has stressed the difference in the parent-child relationship in the case of mildly handicapped children as compared with children who are severely handicapped. The parents of the severely handicapped cerebral palsied children are reported to have been disappointed and discouraged, burdened with realistic worries about the future, but at the same time much more accepting of the children than the other parents who had been studied.

> The most important aspect of parents' feelings was that of not expecting too much of the child; any little thing the child accomplished was held with delight. There were some complaints that the child did not try hard enough to do things, but he was excused on the basis of the severity of the handicap. This complaint was reflected in the feeling that the child was not motivated in some cases. The parents fostered dependence and immaturity, but gained a neurotic satisfaction from the child's dependence upon them. The child remained secure in the comfortable spot the parents created for him. Within themselves these parents were unhappy and troubled, but in most instances the relationship with the child was not troubling. Essentially, these severely handicapped children had many satisfactions in their home life. One might question the basic mental health in some such situations, but there is a workable adjustment of a kind even if it is a neurotic adjustment (*ibid.*, pp. 300–301).

Comparing this report to Shere's (1956) study of cerebral palsied children and their non-handicapped twins one wonders how the siblings of the severely handicapped children studied by Miller fared in their neurotically involved families. To what extent the neurotic adjustment could have been prevented had the parents been able to obtain professional counseling immediately after the birth of the handicapped child is also open to question. It is the basic premise of this book that the earlier professional help is made available, the greater the likelihood that the family interaction involving an exceptional child can be placed on an emotionally healthy basis.

By the time a severely handicapped child has reached the age of seven the neurotic nature of the family interaction appears to be difficult to reverse, for Miller's (1958) study of this group shows that when they were re-evaluated from one to four years after treatment there was little change in the majority and what change there was turned out to be in the direction of greater pathology. Dependency had continued to increase and in the most severe cases the child's motivation had gradually lessened. For two of the children the withdrawal symptoms were so severe that psychiatric care appeared indicated.

Because the children studied by Miller represented a highly selected sample, having been referred to a child guidance clinic because of emotional problems, it is impossible to draw conclusions from them to the emotional adjustment of cerebral palsied children in general. It is therefore helpful to refer to an article by Margolies and Wortis (1956) who examined a less biased sample of families of children with cerebral palsy. These social workers interviewed the parents of sixty-seven children with severe cerebral palsy who were applicants for or enrolled in a special public school facility for non-retarded cerebral palsied children. The families studied were considered representative of families of non-retarded cerebral palsied children in that area. The authors found that the home situations of every family studied reflected problems of more or less severe nature involving the presence of the handicapped child.

In about half of the families studied, the life of the entire family was overshadowed and its pattern determined by the fact that it included a child with cerebral palsy. The mothers were physically exhausted from the gruelling routine of 24 hour service to the child. Several of the fathers had changed to less interesting and less remunerative employment in order to be more available to help care for the child. These parents had no life of their own, never went out together, either because they were too weary, or because the child would not tolerate their leaving him, or because they could not entrust the child's care to someone else even for a few hours. Most of these parents slept with the child in their room, or one or both shared the bed with him. Outings for the family were complicated by the problem of transportation, since few had cars and the use of public transportation was difficult, or in many cases impossible. When there were other children, the needs of the non-handicapped child were pushed into the background in the all-absorbing task of caring for the handicapped one. It was only when her handicapped child went away to camp that one mother felt free for the first time to take her two alert, eager and normal children to museums and places of amusement which she had not visited with them before because she did not want her handicapped child to feel badly. In other situations, the parents laid down careful plans for the future of their handicapped child, arranging that the older siblings would care for the handicapped child in the event of their death. A relatively small number of families—seven—seemed able to absorb the handicapped child without undue stress and could be characterized as 'normal' in their way of life. In these families there were other children in addition to the handicapped one, there were interested relatives, and the child was integrated into the family's social and community activity. There were no great expectations of the child, and there was shared pleasure in caring for him. For these families, the opportunity to send their child to a special school with medical supervision was all that the parents needed at the time they were known to us (Margolies & Wortis, 1956, p. 107 f.).

While in a number of families there were problems unrelated to the presence of a handicapped child these authors conclude that the tensions, anxieties, and personality disturbances of parents of seriously handicapped children are largely the result of reality factors and not of pre-existing neurotic problems. Where neurotic problems do exist the reality factors exacerbate the difficulties, but in either case the parents could benefit greatly from constructive professional counseling.

Margolies and Wortis found a relationship between the age of the handicapped child and the severity of the parental disturbance. They observed that the problem of cerebral palsy changes for the family and becomes more serious as the child grows older. Physical care, for example, presents less of a problem when the child is young but can become a tremendous burden as the child grows older. Very young handicapped children are more acceptable to parents and others in the social environment. In some respect his helplessness makes him appealing, and since not much is expected of a young child the frustrations experienced by the parents are relatively minimal. The older the child becomes, however, the more obvious are the discrepancies between his age and his capacity so that the extent and totality of the problem becomes more and more undeniable.

The problems with which the parents sought help ranged from financial needs and housing to planning for the future care of the child. All of the parents in this study expressed deep anxieties about their child's future. The question about the child's fate in case of the parents' death was raised in almost every instance. Where a parent sees his child totally dependent on him this question arouses much anxiety.

> In view of the great need of the cerebral palsied for specialized facilities and the small number of community resources, this anxiety seemed ... to be based on an accurate recognition of the child's needs, and the real problem of inadequate resources. In relation to the recognition of community need, it is worthy of comment that several parents had assumed leadership positions in the social action group which had fostered many of the existing facilities for the cerebral palsied in our community (*ibid.*, p. 111).

Becoming involved in organizational activities of this type represents a constructive sublimation of anxieties and is a step with which the professional counselor might well help the parents. The feeling of "doing something" in the face of a condition where drastic improvement is unlikely and no cure known, plus the mutual support gathered from association with other people in similar situations, can be a considerable source of strength for parents of exceptional children.

In describing the parent-child relations in the families they studied Margolies and Wortis give a vivid summary which touches on many of the points we have previously discussed.

Most of the parents were overprotective, were controlled by the child, and were afraid to thwart him. Most of them unduly restricted their child's activities and substituted their own services for independence and self care. A few seemed to receive neurotic satisfaction out of this enslavement. Feelings of guilt and inadequacy were demonstrated, but not by all the parents. In some instances these feelings could best be explained by the actual impossibility of meeting all the child's needs and at the same time remaining an adequate spouse and parent to their other children. Most parents had at some point been urged to institutionalize their child by doctors, relatives or friends, and this was, for many, still a source of conflict. The conflict was sharpened by the fact that the only available placement resources were for the mentally deficient, and these children were not mentally deficient.

Many parents expressed ambivalent feelings toward the child who confronted them with so many problems. Feelings of personal guilt and responsibility for the child's condition were expressed by mothers whose family and friends assumed that the disability was inherited or was a punishment for a parental transgression. This feeling was also expressed by mothers who had not wanted the child and who had tried to terminate the pregnancy before the child's birth. In two instances of severely disturbed marital situations the question of 'inheritance' of cerebral palsy played an important role in the difference between husband and wife. However, in the one family where the nature of the handicap did point to inheritance from one parent, this was not a source of conflict.

Many mothers gave a history of miscarriages, or of difficult pregnancy and delivery, and most parents related their child's handicap to a prenatal trauma or to difficulties in the birth situation. This was consistent with recent medical findings.

Every mother expressed deep feelings of unhappiness when describing the time when she had first recognized her child's handicap, either at the time of birth or when the child failed to develop normally. The depth of emotion displayed in reliving this situation was the most palpable evidence of the great personal tragedy which the mother undergoes when she learns that her child is handicapped (*ibid.*, p. 112 f.).

While most of the parents in this group seemed to have moved beyond this first stage of helpless feelings of tragedy, deprivation and inadequacy, having mobilized their resources to the best of their ability, it seems most likely that if professional counseling had been available to them right from the start and continued to be available as the child grew older many of the problems encountered in this study might have been avoided or alleviated.

The clinical studies cited thus far may be subject to bias because they used families who had been referred to a child guidance clinic (Miller, 1958) so that emotional problems were a selecting factor or because the families with a handicapped child were not compared with families with normal children (Margolies & Wortis, 1956) thus not ruling out the—admittedly far-fetched—possibility that the problems found are not unique to families of exceptional children.

Boles (1959) introduced the necessary controls in his study and it too reflects the strain which the presence of a cerebral palsied child places on his parents. He compared a group of sixty mothers of cerebral palsied children with a matched group of controls and found significantly more marital conflict reported by the mothers of cerebral palsied children than by the mothers of the non-handicapped children. Boles explains his finding by pointing to the frequent upheaval of family life brought on by the presence of a cerebral palsied child. Many of the families studied had to move nearer to hospital or school in order to acommodate the child's needs which had become central to the family life, straining the marriage and increasing anxiety and guilt. Difference in attitudes toward the child's problems created further difficulties between the parents, particularly where one perceived the problem more realistically than the other.

Boles further points out that differences in role expectation and role fulfillment may place a strain on marital adjustment. The mother's role, which is essentially nurturant and protective, is met and satisfied by the child's needs, which are and generally remain congruent with the maternal role. The father's role, on the other hand, is structured in our society as involving the planning and providing for the future. In the family life cycle the non-handicapped child moves from a phase of dependency which is congruent with the maternal role to a phase of increasing independence and interaction with social institutions which gradually prepare him for the assumption of the adult role and place a greater demand on the father's contribution to the family's economy. In the case of the handicapped child the father's contribution to the child's life cycle is frustrated. Boles writes, "It may be that the mother, despite handicaps in the child, finds much fulfillment in the tender care for her child; and the father, having few or no such biological reactions to helpless dependency, may view the child only as a frustration to his potential gratifications and a liability" (1959, p. 212). What is more, as the mother turns more and more to continued care of the child, she not only overprotects the child but as a direct reciprocal of this overprotection, she will tend to neglect the father's needs, further contributing to potential marital friction.

The fact of significantly more marital conflict among mothers of cerebral palsied children which Boles presents is impressive even though one might question some aspects of his explanations. It might be pointed out, for example, that having a cerebral palsied child requires considerable planning and providing for the future and if that is, as role theory would postulate, the role of the father, he could certainly find much fulfillment in this role. It is only where the mother takes over so completely as to concern herself not only with the child's physical and emotional protection but also with the planning for the child's future that the father will feel frustrated. It thus becomes the responsibility of the professional counselor to help both parents participate in the care and planning for the child. If one considers overprotection to be an expression of the mother's neurotic needs it would seem that marital conflict can be forestalled if she can be helped early enough to resolve her guilt about having given birth to a defective child.

Since Boles finds that having a cerebral palsied child is associated with increased frequency of marital conflict one might also question to what extent the child's condition actually *caused* the conflict between his parents. A firmly based marriage between healthy partners is not likely to be disrupted by the upheaval brought about by the birth of an exceptional child. It is more likely that this event can precipitate conflict between marital partners whose personalities and interaction have already predisposed them to conflict. One might speculate that marriages which become conflicted upon the birth of an exceptional child would also have become conflicted by any other unusual stress such as economic difficulties or major illness. Regardless of whether the cerebral palsied child is the cause or the precipitating factor of marital conflict, early and ongoing professional counseling should be able to alleviate or forestall the difficulties.

Professional help. The help a professional person can give to parents of handicapped children was summed up by Reid (1958), who stresses that the parent cannot be expected to give up his whole life for his handicapped child. The professional person must help lighten the load of the 24-hour a day schedule which many handicapped children require by giving the parents a chance to be free of guilt, remorse, and resentment. "We can say in effect: 'You do have your own life to lead, and you should be free to lead it. We will help you by sharing the physical burden, by giving you knowledge of why and how this happened so that you won't feel so badly about it, and by finding adequate financial assistance for you so that the cost of medical care will not leave you bankrupt'" (p. 16).

It is obvious that the professional counselor cannot accomplish all this by himself. Sharing the physical burden means giving the parents help in finding appropriate treatment for the child, in locating such resources as schools, camps, and day care programs and, where necessary, to assist in arranging for institutionalization. Finding adequate financial assistance may involve referral to an appropriate public or private agency and while he does all this, the counselor must work to enable the parents to accept, not only the factual knowledge about the causes and consequences of their child's defect, but also the concrete help he tries to make available to them. The most sophisticated and far-reaching program of assistance is of no avail when parents are too conflicted to make use of it.

VI.

The Emotionally Disturbed and Mentally Ill Child in the Family

THEORIES ON THE PARENTS' ROLE IN ETIOLOGY

AMONG PARENTS of exceptional children the parent of the emotionally disturbed or mentally ill child occupies a unique position. The exceptional condition of the retarded, blind, or physically handicapped child is ordinarily the result of factors which are independent of the relationship between child and parent. When the relationship becomes affected, it does so as a consequence of the child's special condition. While disturbed parent-child relationships may thus follow a physical disability, they are usually thought to precede an emotional disorder. Current psychodynamic theory, to some extent supported by research (Rosenthal, Finkelstein & Robertson, 1959), views such disorders as having their origin in often subtle interaction effects involving the relationship between parent and child, effects which were more fully discussed in Chapter I.

The parents' intimate involvement in the development of emotional disorders of children makes work with these parents different from the counseling of exceptional children discussed in previous chapters. The reason for this difference will emerge more clearly as we outline two of the theories on the etiology of emotional disturbance and mental illness in children which stress the contributions of parents to the development of such disorders.

The scapegoat theory of emotional disturbance. On the basis of an intensive clinical study of eighteen families Vogel and Bell (1960) developed the hypothesis that the emotionally disturbed child is a scapegoat for the conflicts between his parents. According to this analysis, the tensions of the parental conflict become focused and discharged in one child, with the family thus achieving a relative equilibrium at the expense of the emotional health of the scapegoat. As Vogel and Bell see it, a number of factors make the child the most appropriate object through which to deal with family tensions. Compared to the parents the child is in a relatively weak and powerless position. He can not effectively counter the parents' superior power because as long as he is

139

dependent on them he is unable to leave the family. Although in comparison to healthy parents the defenses of those studied by Vogel and Bell were fairly brittle, they were still much stronger than those of their children and since the child's personality is still quite flexible, he can be molded to adopt the particular role which the family assigns to him. Finally, when the child takes on any of the characteristics which the parents dislike in themselves and in each other, they have a symbolically appropriate object on which to focus their own anxieties (Vogel & Bell, 1960, p. 385 f.).

Which particular child in a family is selected as the scapegoat is, according to this point of view, closely related to the nature and sources of tensions to be discharged. Position in the birth order, sex, and physical characteristics of the child may play a role but in a number of cases studied the family scapegoat

> either had a serious physical disease when he was young or a striking physical abnormality such as a hare lip, bald spots in the hair, or unusually unattractive facial features. The mere existence of some such abnormality seemed to draw attention to one particular child, so that if there were some sorts of anxieties or problems in the family at all, the child with the physical peculiarities seemed to become the focus of the family problems. Here again, however, it was not the mere existence of a physical defect but its meaning in the life of the family which gave it its significance. For example, in some families there was a feeling that they had committed certain sins by not living up to their ideals . . .The child's physical abnormality became a symbol of the family's sin of not having lived up to some partially-internalized values, and the malformed child was seen as a sinful child who was not living up to the standards of the group. . . . In another case in which a female child's physical illness became a focus of the family's problems, the parents were extremely concerned about her safety, which was again related in part to the potential dangers in social relationships with the outside world. As a result of the girl's illness, the family became much more cautious than was necessary, and on some occasions they were even reluctant to accept medical advice that she could participate in certain activities without danger to her health (*ibid.*, p. 388).

In another family described by Vogel and Bell problems of achievement seemed to be a source of conflict for the parents and the eldest son became the focus of this family's problem. Though this boy was receiving passing grades in school, the parents were very critical of his performance. Both parents themselves had very poor school records. Because of parental pressures the child worked harder and received somewhat better marks on his next report card. But, as if to maintain the boy in his scapegoat role, the mother now maintained that the child did not deserve these grades, assumed that he must have cheated, and continued to criticize his school performance.

Just as Freedman *et al.* (1957) traced the operation of a vicious cycle in the reaction pattern of families with a brain-damaged child (see Chapter I), so Vogel and Bell (1960) perceive a cyclical pattern in the case of the emotionally disturbed child who has been assigned the role of family scapegoat. Parental inconsistencies and conflicting expectations place the child into an emotionally vulnerable position.

> Since these conflicting expectations existed over a long period of time, it is not surprising that the child internalized these conflicts. Once a child was selected as a deviant, there was a circular reaction which tended to perpetuate this role assignment. Once he had responded to his parents' implicit wishes and acted in a somewhat disturbed manner, the parents could treat him as if he really were a problem. The child would respond to these expectations and the vicious cycle was set in motion. Both the child and the parents, then, had complementary expectations. The particular role assigned to the child was appropriately rewarded. It is difficult, if not impossible, to distinguish just at what point the parents began treating the child as if he were a problem and at what point the child actually did have internalized problems. There does not seem to be any sudden development of the child's problems; rather, it is a process occurring over a period of time. By the time the family was seen in the clinic, the vicious cycle was well established, and the child has internalized his disturbed role to such an extent that it was difficult to effect change only by removing external pressures. This was, of course, particularly true for older and more disturbed children. The fact that the child becomes disturbed adds stability to the role system, so that once set in motion, scapegoating did not easily pass from one child to another (Vogel & Bell, 1960, p. 392).

Where a family assigns the role of scapegoat to one of its children and the child adopts this role, family equilibrium can be maintained, although its maintenance requires considerable expenditure of emotional energy. Parents need to maintain rationalizations for the way they treat the child, not because the scapegoating is a conscious process but because at some stages of the vicious cycle it erupts in manifest behavior. The "bad" child needs to be punished and this punishment is then rationalized in terms of the child's "own good." Scapegoating is functional within the family system but as soon as the child manifests his personality difficulties outside the family, the mechanism becomes dysfunctional since outside pressures from the community now threaten to upset the family equilibrium.

While the family gives the child sufficient support to maintain his role in the family, the use of him as a scapegoat is often incompatible with equipping him to maintain an adjustment outside the nuclear family. This problem becomes particularly acute when the child begins important associations outside the nuclear family in relationship with peers and his teachers at school. It is at this time that many referrals to psychiatric clinics are made. While the child's behavior was perfectly tolerable to the parents before, his behavior suddenly becomes intolerable. While he may still be performing the role the family wants him to play in order to be a scapegoat, this comes into conflict with his role as a representative of the family. The family is thus in conflict between using the child as a scapegoat and identifying with the child because of his role as family representative to the outside (Vogel & Bell, 1960, p. 396).

The increasing tensions resulting from the outside pressures either result in ever-increasing demands on the child to serve as a focus for the family tensions or they eventuate in the family seeking outside help with their problems. If they fail to seek help or are unable to obtain it, the pressures on the child may become so great that his personality disintegrates altogether and at that point the family is then justified in withdrawing the child from interaction with the outside community thus facilitating the maintenance of the family equilibrium. It may well be that some psychotic children represent the end point of this cumulative process for, as Lidz and his colleagues (1958) at Yale have shown, the psychodynamic interdependence is particularly close in families of schizophrenics.

An understanding of the interdependent roles in a family system should make the professional person particularly alert to the effects his intervention might have not only on the personality of the child whom he seeks to help, but also on the personalities of the other family members. Major interventions are as drastic a step as major surgery. Just as no surgeon would operate without first considering the effects of the proposed operation on the rest of the patient's system, intervention on behalf of a child requires careful study of the family as a whole.

In a family where a child has become the focus of psychological conflicts and where a certain physical characteristic or handicap is essential to his role, the parents may well resist professional attempts to ameliorate the child's condition or unconsciously distort evidence of improvement in order to maintain family equilibrium. This reaction is one of the factors to consider in deciding whether or not a child should be placed outside of the home. If the disturbed child serves to maintain family equilibrium, removing him from the home will result in a threat of family disequilibrium which will often be reacted against by selecting an alternate scapegoat. Such a reaction was seen in a number of families studied by Rickets (1958) where the placement of a child resulted either in a disruption of the family or in moving another member into the role of scapegoat.

This caution does not mean that no professional intervention should be attempted. The surgeon (to continue the analogy) may postpone an operation until the patient's system has been strengthened to the point where he can tolerate surgery. Similarly, intensive work with the family may be necessary before its members can tolerate the placement of an exceptional child or the removal of his exceptional condition.

The interaction theory of mental illness. Goldfarb's (1961) clinical studies of childhood schizophrenia led him to conclude that the reciprocal and mutual impact of the child on his family and of the family on the child must be studied if the disorders of these children are to be fully understood. He differentiates two general classes of disorder within the classification of childhood schizophrenia. "One class, which may be called organic, includes children with abnormal organic status, especially cerebral dysfunction. The other class, termed non-organic, includes children who do not present such evidence of organicity" (p. 739). In either class the interaction between child and parents contributes to and complicates the condition of the child but in the organic case the cycle begins with the somatic inadequacy while in the case of the somatically intact child the deviant psychosocial environment of the family is thought to be the starting point.

Goldfarb (1961) cites an example of the organic type of childhood schizophrenia, the case of a boy with cerebral dysfunction whose major symptom was sensory hypersensitivity. This condition started, he believes, with the boy's limited capacity for defining form and meaning in his perceptual environment.

> Sensory stimulation was meaninglessly complicated and strange for him —a source of perpetual puzzlement. However, the complexity of his environment was additionally affected by his parents' behavior . . . Largely motivated by guilt, his mother lost objective awareness of his response limitations and kept striving to overcome them by a driven, inappropriate barrage of hyperstimulation. His adaptive response to the increased complexity of his environment resulting from maternal overstimulation was to withdraw from his perceptual environment. He illustrated typically the schizophrenic child who avoids visual and auditory interactions with his environment (*ibid.,* p. 744 f.).

It is important to note in Goldfarb's analysis that the child's schizo-phrenic reaction was an *adaptive* response to environmental demands, made in terms of his somatic inadequacy. The same inadequacy but different environmental demands might have led to a different response pattern. And yet the parents, who are the crucial environment for the child, respond to him in the only way they can: in terms of their own personalities. Without a doubt, the type of child described by Gold-farb is a very special problem to his parents and he and his condition are the stimuli to their responses to him but, "The effect the child has on his parents in their parental role behavior . . . is determined in large measure by the parents' own individual psychodynamics and their rela-tions as marital partners as well" (Goldfarb, 1961, p. 743).

The intimate interaction between the child's initial condition, the parents' reaction, and the child's final state again underscores the need for early and ongoing parent counseling. The organic deficiency is at present poorly understood and though there is hope that this type of defect can eventually be prevented or corrected, there is little we know to do about it now. We do, however, know quite a bit about how to modify parental reactions so that if one could intervene early enough—that is as soon as the child's condition is recognized—it should be pos-sible to prevent the pathogenic cycle of interaction from getting started.

What has just been said about the need for early intervention is of course equally true in cases of childhood schizophrenia where no ab-normal organic state is demonstrable and where parental influences are considered the starting point of the pathogenic cycle. A difference lies in the fact that an organic deficiency in a young child is more readily recognized by pediatricians and others who see the child than are po-tentially pathogenic personality patterns in the parents. It may none-theless be possible to pick up early signs of the child's reaction which might spell psychological difficulties ahead, such as conflicts around eating, slowness in development, poor coordination, delayed language acquisition, sleep disturbances, or allergies—phenomena which are found with unusual frequency in the early histories of children later diag-nosed as childhood schizophrenia.

Whether these children are really physiologically normal to begin with or whether the phenomena just described are signs of subtle or-ganic impairment is still undecided. There are those who maintain that mental illness in children can be caused by psychological factors alone but this contention is as difficult to prove as to disprove because the child's physiology and the parents' psychology are from the very start so closely interrelated as to make an isolation of causal factors almost impossible.

Donnelly (1960), for example, has suggested on the basis of a study that parents maintain a different relationship to their psychotic child than they do to their normal children. Though they have greater emotional involvement with the sick child, he reports that this involvement has many negative qualities. Compared to their relationship to the normal child he found parents to demonstrate less affection toward the psychotic child, to give him less approval and to be generally more rejecting of him as an individual and a member of the family. They showed less ability to understand his capacities and needs, were more emotionally driven and impulsive rather than rational in their behavior toward him, and generally showed more distance and aloofness in the parent-child relationship (p. 353).

That this observed behavior may well reflect the consequence rather than the cause of the child's difficulties is suggested by the fact that mothers, who are in more intensive contact with the sick child, reacted differently to him than father. They were more anxious, more infantilizing and more impulsive in their behavior toward the child while the fathers were able to satisfy the child's curiosities more readily and were more willing to explain the rationale of the parents' behavior to him.

Evaluations of parental behavior or attitudes toward a sick child, obtained once the child has been diagnosed as sick, cannot be used to substantiate the hypothesis that these were what made the child sick. Living with a psychotic child day after day and year after year can easily affect parental attitudes and behavior. The question of cause and effect thus remains unanswered.

The author has suggested (Ross, 1955) that the most conservative hypothesis on the genesis of childhood psychosis must be phrased in terms of an interaction between biologic and psychologic factors. Relationship factors may or may not precede a child's mental illness, but in either case they do not cease to exert their pathologic influence once the child is identified as disturbed. Thus, regardless of whether childhood mental illness begins in factors intrinsic or extrinsic to the child, professional intervention on the level of the psychology of parent-child relationship cannot help but have at least an ameliorating effect.

WORK WITH PARENTS OF THE EMOTIONALLY DISTURBED CHILD

Counseling parents of an emotionally disturbed child differs from work with parents of other exceptional children not only because of the parents' contribution to the development of the disorder, which must be understood and neutralized if the child's disturbance is to be relieved and its recurrence prevented. With parents of a physically handicapped or mentally retarded child the focus of counseling was on helping the parents cope with the fact that their child had a condition which, though often amenable to modification through educational, medical, or habilitative efforts, was largely a permanent state, potentially affecting the entire life cycle of the family.

Work with parents of an emotionally disturbed child has quite a different focus. Emotional disturbances, particularly in young children, can be treated and often cured so that work with the parents is aimed not at helping them live with a chronic problem but at aiding them to contribute to the child's treatment by making modifications in their own response patterns.

Early in the development of child psychiatry men like Healy, Allen and Stevenson came to recognize that parents, and particularly mothers, play a crucial role in the development of emotional disturbances of children. In attempting to treat these children psychiatrically, it had become apparent that this role must not only be understood but that treatment can best be carried out if the parents—or at least one of them—are also seen in therapy. This recognition led to the development of child guidance clinics which generally base their operation on the principle of concurrent treatment of both parent and child (Ross, 1959).

If the child is to be helped, the parent must not only be interested in obtaining therapy for the child, he must also be willing to involve himself in the treatment process.

> The very act of coming to the clinic for regularly scheduled appointments requires a degree of motivation stronger than the anxieties which contribute to resistance and which make an excuse, such as transportation difficulties, only too attractive. Since the child is brought to the clinic by the parent, the child's motivation may be somewhat less than that of his parent; his resistance can be worked with in therapy while the mother's resistance can prevent and interrupt the treatment altogether (Ross, 1959, p. 26 f.).

Emotional disorders, particularly in children, are often difficult for parents to understand, recognize, and accept. Disturbed behavior is frequently rationalized as attention-getting, restlessness, tiredness, dietary deficiencies, or "nerves." Parents—and all too often the professional advisors to whom they first turn—expect that the child will "grow out of it," that punishment, diversion, bribes, or a sibling's good example will do away with the disturbed and disturbing behavior. To receive psychotherapeutic help, at least one of the child's parents should be able to accept the emotional basis of the difficulty. As long as a parent is unable to accept a psychogenic explanation of the child's symptoms, he will continue to seek solutions in other areas and fail to involve himself in the psychotherapeutic plan.

"The parent—usually the father—who is not actively involved in treatment need not be as highly motivated as the parent—usually the mother—who comes to the clinic, but a definitely negative attitude or open discouragement on the part of the other parent can become a major obstacle to therapy and should, if possible, be handled by involving him, too, in active treatment" (Ross, 1959, *ibid.*)

The author has elsewhere (Ross, *loc. cit.*) attempted to explicate the "ideal" case for child guidance treatment. What was said there about the role of parents can be profitably repeated in the present context since counseling parents of emotionally disturbed children is, with few exceptions, feasible only in a setting where the child is treated concurrently and in coordination with the treatment of his parents.

The parent in concurrent treatment should be able to accept his role in the treatment process and be willing to contribute actively to the child's improvement by recognizing that he himself needs therapy (Wickman & Langford, 1944). The parent's role in child guidance treatment is not merely one of giving the worker information which the child's therapist may find helpful in his efforts. Though the focus in child guidance treatment is largely on the child, one should never lose sight of the fact that his difficulty is to a great extent a symptom of disturbed parent-child, child-parent relations and that all of these interacting individuals must be helped if the underlying pathogenic condition is to be alleviated.

In accepting this principle, one does not "blame" the parents for the child's emotional problems. Each individual child is born with a unique constitutional potential which may be affected by prenatal hazards, birth injuries, physical illness, or injury. A child's personality seems to develop largely in response to attitudes, behavior, and reactions of his immediate environment, but organic factors may affect these reactions and the manner in which the child responds to them. This interaction must never be lost sight of. It is no more realistic to hold a mother responsible for her attitudes and reactions toward her child than it is to censure an adult neurotic for his emotions and symptoms.

While it is thus both meaningless and harmful to blame the parent for the child's illness, treatment of the child is frequently next to impossible unless one can help the parents understand their relations with the child and aid at least one of them to modify his reactions. This places at least as much therapeutic responsibility on the parent's worker as on the child's therapist and it is an unfortunate fallacy to assume that there is a hierarchy within the clinic team which makes the child therapist a more important member and the parent a second-class patient. This point is frequently misunderstood by parents, probably because their workers are unable to interpret it to them correctly as the result of their own failure to accept this principle. Except in the unusual case, such as that of a relatively mature adolescent whom one hopes to help accept his parents' personality problems as a part of reality, treatment of the child should always be paralleled by treatment of at least one of his parents. A mother who merely delivers her child to the clinic so that he can be "fixed up," viewing her time with her worker as incidental, often manifests her attitude by cancelling her own appointments when something "more important" (like a date with her hairdresser) comes up, or by trying to send the child alone or with someone else. Because of the importance of the parent's role, many clinics refuse to see the child unless the parent comes along, thereby underscoring the importance of concurrent treatment and making it clear that parent and child are a unit in the eyes of the clinic (Green, 1948).

The parent in concurrent treatment with the child should be able to progress in therapy at a pace equal to or greater than that of the child. Though in most instances it will not be possible to gauge this factor in advance, the requirement is an important one and should be kept in mind during treatment whenever continuation of therapy is under discussion. One of the major reasons for concurrent treatment of child and parent is that the parent must be prepared to accept the child's reactions to treatment which, in both positive and negative form, may be acted out in the home. When the mother is not ready for the child's improvement or regression, treatment will not only be ineffective but may actually result in an exacerbation of the difficulties it is meant to relieve. Blanchard (1940) has pointed out that a mother, finding her child becoming (in her eyes) worse instead of better or to behave in a manner unacceptable to her, may withdraw herself and the child from treatment at a time when the child most needs to continue (Ross, 1959, pp. 29 f.).

The role of the father. By speaking of the *parent* in concurrent treatment we have glossed over an issue which plagues many child guidance clinics: the role of the father in the treatment plan. In the vast majority of cases, the parent in concurrent treatment is the mother and this more often represents a compromise with expediency than the result of rational conclusions drawn on the basis of an exploration of family dynamics.

Because of the biological and physical closeness of mother and child, particularly during the early years, the mother is often seen as the basic parent. Theories of child development and therapists working on the emotional problems of childhood thus often tend to stress the mother's role more heavily than that of the father, ignoring the fact that the father plays an important and often crucial role in the parent-child complex. He not only affects the interaction by the part he plays in the husband-wife system and through which he may support or disturb the mother's relation to the child, but he also contributes directly in either positive or negative fashion to the development of the child's personality.

Only in recent years has more attention begun to be paid to the role of fathers whose attitudes are now seen as "at least as intimately related as the attitudes of mothers to maladjustive tendencies among children" (Peterson *et al.*, 1961, p. 161). Child guidance clinics are also beginning to shift their focus from an almost exclusive concern with mother-child relationships to an orientation which sees the family as the patient.

For a long time child guidance workers expressed the belief that fathers would not come for treatment, even if given the opportunity, because their interest was not great enough or because their work responsibilities did not leave sufficient "psychic energy" for treatment to make the experience meaningful and constructive. Plotsky and Shereshefsky (1960) question these assumptions and, working in a clinic which includes the father in all cases under treatment, found only two instances where fathers excluded themselves after treatment had begun.

> What has been striking in these instances is that the father did not independently and stubbornly refuse to go on in treatment. We found that in these and in similar situations the father's failure to engage himself in treatment did not arise from his lack of interest or the demands of his outside responsibilities. Rather, he seemed to have been driven out, forced into an isolation pattern that was characteristic of the interaction between him and the rest of the family. This interaction often took the form of a kind of unconscious collusion between husband and wife (Plotsky & Shereshefsky, 1960, p. 781).

The isolation pattern of which these writers speak appears to be a part of the psychopathologic picture in many families with an emotionally disturbed child. Where this is the case, failure to include the father in the treatment plan plays into and thus supports the pathology, making therapeutic success difficult if not unlikely.

> The pattern of isolation in these fathers can best be understood by realizing that they are not merely manipulated by their wives. Rather, by their withdrawal they are actively reacting to her pressures. Thus, there is an interaction betwen husband and wife that affects children and the family so that we have a neurotic child or children too closely tied to their mother and essentially unidentified with the father. Through our investigation we have attained greater awareness that, in the treatment process, parents will act out a pattern of maneuvering and isolating which graphically illustrates what is going on at home. The therapist as a new force may interrupt a process which has been repeated in a sterotyped fashion year after year. With a father able to participate as parent and husband and with a mother less dependent and consequently less in need of narcissistic gratification, the family can become a more fully supporting medium for the child's growth (*ibid.*, p. 787).

Guilt and shame. The emotions of guilt and shame, so frequently encountered in parents of exceptional children whose disability is in the physical area, are shared by parents of emotionally disturbed children but the implications are different. When a child has a physical defect or is mentally retarded the parents' guilt is irrational and has its basis in the parent's own personality dynamics. Realistically, the parent has done nothing to damage his child and since he cannot be blamed the defect is nothing to be guilty or ashamed of. The professional counselor can work on the unrealistic reactions and help the parent overcome them.

In the case of the emotionally disturbed child, on the other hand, the very insistence that the parent enter into concurrent treatment gives recognition to the theoretical assumption that the parent has contributed to the child's problem. *Contributing* to the development of a problem and doing so unwittingly and out of one's own unconscious conflicts is, however, not the same as *causing* the problem but this distinction is a difficult one to interpret to the anxious and guilt-ridden parent. If he wants to be constructive the counselor must neither overtly or covertly blame the parent for the child's condition but unless the counselor is himself clear on the distinction between contributing and causative factors he will be unable to help the parents.

A given mother may have been raised in a family where her younger brother was overtly favored and preferred so that she grew up with repressed hostility toward little boys. This repressed hostility may later enter into her relations to her own male child in a variety of ways. The mechanism of reaction formation may cause her to infantilize the boy, who may develop the well-known syndrome of the overprotected child (Levy, 1943). Her best conscious intentions to be a good mother can thus lead to the development of an emotionally disturbed youngster and it is just as senseless to blame her for the child's condition as it would be futile to exhort her to be less infantilizing. Only therapeutic work designed to help her recognize her basic hostility and its true object can free the mother to raise the child constructively and to accept his increasing independence and maturity.

The example of the overprotective mother can also serve to reiterate the importance of concurrent treatment of mother and child. Therapy of the child would have as its aim to help the boy gain increasing confidence in his own ability to look after his needs and to free him from repressed resentment against his infantilizing mother. With reduced ambivalence and increased confidence, the child will, as therapy progresses, insist on more independence. If the mother is not in concurrent treatment this insistence will threaten to upset her own psychic economy since she needs to over-protect in order to ward off her repressed hostility against the boy child. The threat will arouse anxiety which may lead to even more infantilization and the decision to terminate the child's treatment which she sees as the cause of the boy's threatening behavior. With concurrent and coordinated treatment of mother and child, however, she will hopefully be ready to accept the child's improvement because she has learned to deal with her unacceptable impulses in a more constructive fashion.

A recognition of the motivational dynamics of mothers of emotionally disturbed children helps in understanding why these mothers readily experience guilt about having a child who needs professional help around his emotional problems. Again using the infantilizing mother as the model of the parent whose own unconscious conflicts and defenses against them create an environment in which the child's emotional difficulties arise, we can recall that this mother's conflicts date from her own childhood experiences and her hostile feeling about her little brother. These unacceptable feelings were repressed and later manifested themselves in overprotection of the woman's own male child. One of the major motivational sources of the original repression was guilt which thus became an important aspect of the mother's personality dynamics. Though the reaction formation serves to reduce guilt, this emotion continues to be present in the motivational structure, making the mother easily subject to experiencing guilt around anything having to do with her relationship to the child. When he becomes emotionally disturbed, the mother may vaguely sense her contribution to his condition, experience guilt—and redouble her defensive efforts by increased overprotection. At the same time, the child's disturbed, clinging, and immature behavior tends to be disturbing to the mother who may react with anger toward the child, anger which is again guilt-arousing, and which again calls forth her defensive overprotection. Unless these dynamics are understood and therapeutically handled, any attempt to reassure the mother that she has nothing to be guilty about will fail to be of help to either mother or child.

The related emotion of shame is also often encountered in parents of emotionally disturbed children. While guilt is an internalized super-ego reaction to unacceptable impulses, shame is an interpersonal response vis à vis the social environment (Ausubel, 1955). Once the super-ego is developed, a person can experience guilt in social isolation and in the privacy of his own mental processes, while shame requires at least the potential presence of an external other whose reactions to one's behavior are being anticipated. Shame is essentially an ego function, responsive to the thought, "What will people think of me?"

This or similar thoughts are involved in parents who experience shame around having an emotionally disturbed child and it often takes the form of their trying to hide or disguise the fact that they are seeking professional help with their problem. Child guidance clinics and others who treat emotionally disturbed children often encounter parents who desire that their visits be kept a secret. The child may be exhorted not to tell anyone about his treatment and intricate cover stories may be invented in an attempt to disguise and hide the "shameful" fact. Extensive dental work or a long series of repeated "allergy shots" are somehow seen as more acceptable reasons for leaving school at the same time each week than an admission that the child is receiving psychotherapy.

Since one of the basic principles of psychotherapy is complete frankness and honesty it is readily apparent that the child cannot be helped as long as treatment is conducted on the premise of secrecy and dissimulation. If the child is under the impression that whatever it is that troubles him is something to be ashamed of, he is not going to be able to make use of the therapist's potential help. Nor can the therapist hope to accomplish very much if he becomes a partner to the conspiracy of secrecy. One of the first things the person working with the parents must thus aim for is an acceptance of the fact that coming for help with emotional problems is nothing to be ashamed of. Since shame is a conscious ego reaction it is far more readily dealt with by direct discussion than guilt with its unconscious motivational basis.

Unfortunately, the shame-evoking anticipation of "what people will think" is not always based on distorted perceptions of the social reality. One still encounters people—in-laws, neighbors, and even teachers—whose attitude toward emotional problems and mental illness leads them to react with fear, disdain, disgust, or censure to the discovery that someone is in need of psychotherapy. When the patient is a child, neighbors may not want him to associate with their children (and sometimes his disturbed behavior may give them good grounds for rationalizing this), teachers may view him as "impossible to teach" and "not worth the effort," while relatives reproach the parents for having "spoiled" the child. It is not difficult to understand a parent who wishes to forestall these reactions by the ruse of presenting a socially more acceptable reason for the regular therapeutic appointments. Yet despite the fact that the parent's behavior may have some basis in social reality the therapist cannot accept untruth as a condition of treatment.

The shame of parents of a physically handicapped child is also frequently based on the reality of social prejudices or superstitions, yet the counselor would be amiss if he encouraged or even endorsed the parent's desire to hide their epileptic child from view in order to avoid having some people react to him as if he were dangerous. Just as these parents would have to be helped to cope with social reactions as part of the reality of having an exceptional child, so must the parents of the emotionally disturbed child be helped to face their problem constructively. At times it may be possible for the counselor, with the consent of the parents, to help particularly significant individuals in the child's environment to a more favorable acceptance of his condition and the treatment necessary to alleviate it. A grandparent who lives in the home may need to be involved in the treatment plan for the family and visits to the school may be necessary to give teachers the support they need in order to maintain the disturbed child in the class. Such collateral contacts are rarely initiated in psychotherapy with adults, but when working with children they are often essential if treatment is to get under way and be successful.

The requirement that parents not disguise the fact that their child is receiving treatment does not mean of course that they should advertise the fact to people whom it can not possibly concern. The social reality frequently makes discretion in these matters the most adaptive response and a healthy, reality-oriented parent will be able to differentiate between the child's teacher, who should know the truth about where the child is going every week, and a talkative neighbor, for whom this knowledge would merely be a satisfaction of idle curiosity.

The parent who is unable to make a differentiation on this need-to-know basis is manifesting his own conflicts in the matter and needs help in resolving them. We would disagree with Mayer and Hoover (1961) who, in an otherwise excellent pamphlet for parents on the question of treatment for childhood emotional problems, suggest that the fact that a child is in treatment can be kept as private a matter as how one votes. How one votes can be a secret, just as what one tells one's therapist is confidential; but if one feels that the fact of going to vote must be kept a secret, something is surely wrong with one's attitude toward voting. Following this analogy, one should be able to tell the employer the reason for taking time off to go and vote (he has need to know) while one would not announce to a stranger on the bus where one is going (he has no need to know). Yet some parents, compulsively overreacting to their unresolved feelings about therapy, indiscriminately announce that their child is in treatment to almost anyone they encounter. This irrational behavior becomes just as much a subject to be taken up in the parent's own treatment contacts as does its behavioral opposite of secrecy and dissimulation.

WORK WITH PARENTS OF THE MENTALLY ILL CHILD

In some respects work with parents of mentally ill children is similar to work with parents of emotionally disturbed children, in others it differs considerably. This difference is not only due to the fact that the disorder of the mentally ill child is of far more severe proportions than that of the emotionaly disturbed youngster and that less is known about how to treat him. The difference also follows from the fact that mental illness and emotional disturbance may represent different etiologic entities.

The term *mentally ill child* is here used to subsume severely disturbed children variously called psychotic, schizophrenic, atypical, autistic, or symbiotic. The classificatory scheme is not well worked out and the bases of the various disturbances remain poorly understood. As discussed earlier, there are indications that at least some of these children are biologically impaired, while for others a strictly psychogenic explanation is thought to be appropriate. Then again, there appear to be many children who are said to have one or the other of these forms of childhood mental illness but who are later found to have been misdiagnosed cases of brain injury, deafness, aphasia, or mental retardation. This rather chaotic state of affairs greatly complicates the lot of parents who will encounter a variety of professional opinion and advice—all of which usually has in common only the theme that the child's condition is extremely serious and the prognosis for improvement quite guarded.

The help for parents of mentally ill children must, in view of our present state of ignorance, be based on long-range plans and it is thus similar to the counseling needed by a parent of a child with any other chronic disability. Not only questions relative to treatment but also those involving the education and possible institutionalization of the mentally ill child call for counseling over a long period of time. At different stages of the child's development and illness, different problems will arise which cannot possibly be dealt with in any one-shot counseling session. Living with a mentally ill child is exceedingly wearing and demanding on the parent because the core of the child's problem involves his communication and interaction with others in his environment. He is unable to form satisfying interpersonal relationships and thus denies his parents the usual gratifications of parenthood. He may be oblivious to them, treat them as an object to be manipulated, and refuse to be held and cuddled. One must have lived with one of these youngsters to appreciate the intensity of the emotional reactions which they can produce. No other type of sick child elicits such varied and contrasting feelings so continuously. Little wonder that these parents often themselves display emotional problems which, because they obscure cause and effect relationship, contribute to the further confusion of scientists trying to investigate childhood mental illness.

For the professional counselor this means that parents of mentally ill children need advice on how to deal with and plan for their child as well as help and support so that they can weather the emotional onslaught their child's behavior represents. At times, it may be possible to give the family a respite by arranging for temporary foster home or institutional placement of the ill child. In other instances day-care centers may provide the mother with a period during the day when she can permit herself to look after her own interests without having to be the constant protector, guard, and companion to a child who does not reciprocate. Any placement, however temporary, must be carefully planned and worked through so that the mother will not feel that she has failed her child, is rejecting and exposing him to untold dangers when she is not there to look after him. Again, there is guilt related to this; guilt which must be handled much in the same way in which one handles it with parents who are placing a mentally retarded child in an institution.

Another unfortunate reality, unique to parents of mentally ill children, is the dearth of adequate facilities for treatment, day care or institutionalization for their child. Because of the excessive cost of most private institutions, placement in a state hospital may need to be considered, even though most of these are poorly equipped to accept the mentally ill child for more than custodial care. The decision for placement thus becomes an agonizing step which no parent should be expected to take without professional support. The decision must be based not only on considerations of the child's condition and prognosis, but also on the recognition that other family members, both parents and siblings, are entitled to lead as normal a life as possible. If the ill child so disrupts the home that the health of others suffers, siblings have no parental attention, and parents no peaceful moment, removal of the sick child becomes imperative.

The counselor must, in all cases, be thoroughly familiar with available resources but where institutionalization in a state hospital is involved, he must also know the legal requirements and implications. The need for commitment and the consequences of this step differ from state to state but inasmuch as it may affect the child's and parents' future legal rights, the implications should be carefully explored and clarified with the parents. With the possible exception of the mental defective, the mentally ill child is unique among exceptional children in that his problem not only has psychological, medical, and educational, but also legal involvements.

VII.

The Gifted Child in the Family

THE EXCEPTIONAL STATE OF THE GIFTED CHILD

PARENTS WHOSE child is mentally deficient may look with envy on the parents whose child has exceptionally high intellectual endowment; and to someone whose experience with exceptional children has been primarily with those whose difficulties center around a handicap or deficiency, a discussion of problems faced by parents of gifted children may come as a surprise. Yet when intellectual endowment is exceptionally high, the exceptional condition does present potential problems to the parents and to the child with which the professional person must be prepared to help.

Child-rearing behavior of parents is largely based on expectations derived from their image of the "normal" or average child, because this is the model most widely encountered and the condition the parents themselves passed through during their childhood. When the child does not conform to this image the parents often need help in adapting their behavior to the reality—they must learn to cope with the dissonance between their image of "a child" and the reality of "their child." Where the parents themselves have exceptionally high intellectual endowment this dissonance and the potential problem is reduced and such parents may in fact have a greater problem if they have a child who is "only" of average intelligence.

THE SOCIAL REALITY

The handicapped child is born into a society whose institutions and technology are geared to the average unimpaired person. Society must make special provisions for the handicapped in order to permit him to make optimal use of his capacities, and the parents of the handicapped child must be helped to locate these special provisions and to accept the fact that their child needs them. This principle also holds for the gifted child, but our society has in the past been more ready to provide special facilities for the impaired and handicapped than for the overendowed and gifted. Thus, while nearly all school systems make provisions to train or educate the mentally deficient or retarded, special facilities for gifted children are relatively rare and opinions are

157

divided on whether special facilities for gifted children should indeed exist.

The special educational needs of the gifted child have only relatively recently become recognized and educators and educational administrators are still debating such issues as homogenous grouping, "enriched" programs, acceleration, skipping of grades, and other modifications of the curriculum. While parents of retarded children are rarely given a choice whether they want their child in a special class, the decision of special placement of the gifted child is often left up to the parents. It is around this decision that the professional counselor is most often asked for advice, but it is by no means the only issue around which parents of a gifted child can use professional help.

The reason why our society seems singularly unprepared, if not unwilling, to make special provisions for the gifted child can in part be traced to a socio-cultural ethos which puts a premium on equality and tends to look with distrust or disfavor upon those individuals who do not meet the norm. Humanitarian trends have gradually reduced the social rejection of handicapped and defective individuals, who, until relatively recently, had been isolated in remote institutions or hidden in attics. A similar motivation has not been operating in improving the facilities and enhancing the recognition of the gifted child. Because of his giftedness this child has generally been expected to shift for himself in the educational setting and only a technological competition on the international scene led to a reëvaluation of our approaches to the gifted child. As Barbe (1958) has pointed out, we have generally distrusted the gifted child because of his not too clearly understood uniqueness; we have largely overemphasized the average in our society and maintained that the gifted child requires no help from others because he is sufficiently talented to guide himself. The fallacy of these attitudes was underscored by Laycock (1951–52) who writes that "a gifted child is often not understood. His needs for emotional security, independence, achievement, recognition, and a sense of worth may be frustrated even more greatly than are those of the handicapped child" (p. 132). In our distrust of those who are different we have tended to neglect the gifted child and teachers and even parents have felt threatened by him to the point where Laycock (loc. cit.) believes that gifted children are often rejected.

Because the uniqueness of the gifted child is often not clearly understood certain stereotypes have arisen which tend to contribute to the anxieties and confusions of the parents. Gifted children are often expected to be seen as strange and different by their peers, to be physically clumsy and athletically inept, to become social outcasts or isolates, and to maintain poor emotional adjustment. While in specific cases some or all of these characteristics might apply, studies have shown that this is not necessarily nor generally the case (Abraham, 1957; Grace & Booth, 1958). Indeed it would seem that the gifted child's psycho-social adjustment is largely a function of how his parents react to his exceptional condition.

Gifted children, as Dunlap (1958) has so aptly stressed, are first of all *children*. As such they share with other children needs for love, security, companionship, acceptance, motivation, challenge, opportunity for self-expression, guidance, appreciation and other basic support which fosters the effective development of all children. If their home and neighborhood environment has similar interests and abilities, these needs are generally satisfied, but as the gifted child moves out into the larger, less congenial world, his adjustment may become complicated. To quote Dunlap (1958),

> The activities of their associates often take place at a different tempo and level from those which bright youngsters require to give them satisfactions. Schoolwork in particular is commonly geared to pupils of just above average ability and the school setting usually does not take into account the personal qualities accompanying high intelligence which frequently result in unique requirements. Should the bright child also come from a home or a neighborhood at odds with his exceptional ability, his problems are further multiplied. In consequence, bright children have unusual needs, not so much because they are bright but because they are *different* from the majority of their contemporaries for whom most school programs are planned. Differences in intellectual ability need consideration in education as much as other differences need special planning (p. 148).

THE GIFTED CHILD AND FAMILY INTERACTION

The effect of a gifted child on family interaction and the degree to which his superior endowment represents a problem to him and his parents is largely a function of the size of the discrepancy between the intellectual capacity of the gifted child and other members of his family. The larger this discrepancy the greater the potential problem and the more important the need for professional counseling. Morrow and Wilson (1961) report a study of family relations in which they compared 48 high school boys of superior intelligence who were achieving high grades in school with a similar number of boys of matched intelligence who were making mediocre or poor grades. On the assumption that the underachieving gifted boys were manifesting adjustment difficulties in their school performance, one can interpret the findings of this study to indicate that parents who are able to share confidences, ideas and decisions with their children and encourage their development without pressuring, tend to have children who are able to utilize their high endowment in school performance. In general it would seem that healthy family relations and parent-child interaction contribute to the positive adjustment of the gifted child just as they do to the adjustment of any other child.

Practices which will help a gifted child develop his creative potential are no different from practices which will permit the average or even the retarded child to maximize his capacities. Torrance (1962) suggests that parents encourage a child's questions by giving him frank and simple answers and by asking him questions of their own. When the parents do not know the answer to a child's questions, a frank statement to this effect and help in finding the answer is the constructive step, while ignoring the question, avoiding the answer, or making fun of the child will eventually stifle the creative interests. All children must learn to cope with failure and to respond to challenge; the gifted child is no exception. Parents who try to arrange his environment in such a way that the child always meets success are no more contributing to his intellectual growth than if they saw to it that he could never succeed.

The discrepancy between the intellectual and social-emotional development of the gifted child often creates stress for child and parents alike. His interests are far advanced and on a different level from those of his less endowed peers or siblings so that he may prefer the company of older children or adults to that of children his own age. He may tend to isolate himself in preoccupation with his particular interests and many parents find it difficult to accept a child's preference of intellectual pursuits over activities generally thought to be more age appropriate. Parents often need help in permitting a gifted child to develop his individuality and to follow his own interests; in teaching him to differentiate between popularity and friendship; and in supporting him to withstand the often powerful pressures to conformity for the sake of which all too many gifted children have sacrificed their creative talents.

Sibling relations are another source of stress for the parents of a gifted child. How to provide the gifted child with the necessary opportunities without making his siblings feel neglected; how to avoid having the gifted child monopolize dinner conversation to the exclusion of his brothers and sisters; how to keep an older, less highly endowed sibling, from feeling frustrated and inferior when the younger, gifted child surpasses his achievements, all are problems with which such parents may need professional help. Meeting the individual needs of each child in the family in such a way that each feels accepted and finding a unique role for everyone so that all feel that they have a valuable contribution to make is a challenge to parental ingenuity and imagination. An uninvolved professional counselor is often in a position to point out reality factors in family interaction which the parents in their own involvement are unable to recognize.

WORK WITH PARENTS OF THE GIFTED CHILD

The approach to parents of a gifted child is essentially no different from the approach to parents of children with other exceptional states. Local conditions, parental resources, family constellation, and the specific nature of the gifted child's special endowment make it impossible to outline a plan which would be suitable for all children under all situations. As always, the aim of counseling is to help the parents to a clear and accurate perception of reality so that their relationship to the child can be free of distorted perceptions and disrupting conflicts. In order to be able to do his work the counselor must be fully acquainted with the local situations and resources. He must, through interview and testing, explore the needs of the specific family with whom he is dealing so that his counsel can indeed be oriented to reality. Finally, the counselor must have explored his own attitudes toward gifted children. Professionals, no less so than the general public, are likely to react to a gifted child with hostile envy and the beginning counselor must be able to recognize and deal with his own feelings before he can hope to help.

Parents of gifted children often hesitate to seek professional help because they feel that, compared to parents of defective of handicapped children, they have nothing to complain about. This attitude frequently leads them to postpone seeking help until the child, responding to conflicts and tensions, becomes shyly withdrawn and indifferent or develops learning difficulties and other emotional problems. Early prophylactic help is just as important here as in cases of other exceptional children, and the professional who first gives the parents confirmation that they have a gifted child has the responsibility of doing more for them than to suggest educational facilities.

The educational question is only one of many which parents of a gifted child must face. In addition, they often have many conflicted feelings with which they can use help. Parents of gifted children may feel guilty about their inability to provide the child with what they see as necessary intellectual stimulation or educational opportunities. They may feel guilty about giving more attention to the gifted child than to their other children -and conflicted about his not participating in the usual social or athletic activities. They may feel threatened by their gifted child who is more and more frequently demonstrating that he is becoming much brighter than they and who, in increasingly frequent situations, can find answers to problems the parents themselves are unable to solve. Helping parents accept their child's difference and supporting them to accommodate family life and sibling relations to the presence of a gifted youngster can be as difficult a task as helping other parents adjust to having a defective child and it requires and deserves no less time and effort.

In the context of a perspicacious discussion of the educational needs of gifted children Dunlap (1958) stresses the need for counseling for parents of exceptionally gifted children and points out that while parents often sense that their child is bright they are usually unable to arrive at an accurate appreciation of their child's special abilities. They thus cannot be expected to give him intelligent guidance without professional help. Because the exact numerical value of a child's I.Q. may not be a good index of creative potential and usually has little meaning to the layman, parents gain little by being told his intelligence quotient. This point holds true regardless whether the child is in the average range, retarded or gifted. More general descriptive statements of the child's abilities combined with illustrations of his educational and vocational potential are far more meaningful and constructive than an easily-misinterpreted numerical statement.

Finding the proper balance between encouragement without pressuring, on the one hand, and understimulation, on the other, is often a difficult task for parents who are frequently tempted to abdicate this responsibility to the school only to find that the school more often than not is unprepared to present the gifted child with a suitable program. Where the school system can provide special educational offerings to gifted children parents should be helped to recognize that these opportunities are neither an honor nor a special privilege. Dunlap (1958) stresses that adaptations of the curriculum for gifted children are simply the school's way of recognizing individual differences by helping each child to function optimally. This is the frame of reference within which special educational facilities should be interpreted to parents and child alike. Where parents and child do not recognize this the resulting attitudes of superiority over other children can easily disrupt peer relations to the detriment of the child's social development.

Since the mentally retarded and the intellectually gifted child share an exceptional mental endowment, some of their problems are remarkably similar. In both cases the major environmental modification must be in the area of education. This places the educator at the focus because it is he who has been charged with providing special education for these exceptional children.

Educators all too often feel that helping parents of exceptional children is largely an educational process. They sometimes write guide-books for parents containing concrete advice on "How to be a Gifted Parent" but unless such advice takes cognizance of the parent's emotional readiness to use the advice, exhortational *do's* and *dont's* are likely to be more confusing than helpful.

While the educator is among all professions best prepared to deal with the reality of educational requirements, the feelings parents have about the exceptional condition of their child are best handled by a professional counselor with special training in the area of emotional and other psychological processes. Counselor and educator should work in a collaborative team relationship, and if each recognizes and respects the other's specialized knowledge their joint efforts are more likely to meet with success.

VIII.

The Adopted Child in the Family

THE EXCEPTIONAL STATE OF THE ADOPTIVE FAMILY

ADOPTIVE PARENTS and workers in the mental health professions like to maintain that the only difference between adopted and biological children lies in how they came to live with their present parents; that in no other respect is there or should there be a differentiation, and that the parent-child relationship should in no way be affected by how the child came to be in the family. This would, indeed, be an ideal state of affairs, but recent reports from several sources (Kirk, 1959, Schechter, 1960) strongly suggest that in all too many cases this ideal remains far from realized. It does, in fact, appear that the state of adoption is an exceptional state for both parents and child and that many more adoptive parents than are currently reached could benefit from professional help for longer periods than is presently made available. For this reason a discussion of the adopted child finds inclusion in a book on exceptional children and their families.

The psychologic hazards. Reports from child psychiatric facilities in various parts of the country reflect an increasing concern on the part of people in the mental health professions "that children who have been adopted have potentially a more fertile soil for development of neurotic and psychotic states" (Schechter, 1960, p. 31) than do children who are being raised by their natural parents. This concern is based on the observation that a disproportionately high number of the emotionally disturbed children who are brought for psychotherapy are children who had been adopted. This seems to be true whether the adoption had been carefully arranged through a responsible social agency or carried out in the more haphazard fashion still possible in many states. Schechter (1960) reports that during five years of private psychiatric practice 13.3 per cent of his child patients were adopted, while children under twenty-one years of age who have petitions for adoptions filed for them represent only a fraction of one per cent (.134%) of the general population. Similarly disproportionate ratios are reported by child guidance clinics (Sweeny, Gasbarro, & Gluck, 1963) and Schechter (ibid.) cites information to the effect that the outpatient service of one of the largest and

164

best-known psychiatric facilities in the country finds that one-third of all their patients are adopted.

Figures on the incidence of adoptions in the general population are difficult to obtain because court statistics, on which they are based, usually do not report children according to age at which they were adopted, nor do they differentiate between adoptions by unrelated strangers and adoptions by relatives in whose home the children may have lived since birth or by step-parents coming into the child's home through marrying the child's natural parent. If these intra-family adoptions were excluded from the statistics, the disproportion reported by psychiatric facilities would be even more striking.

If adopted children are found with significantly greater relative frequency among child psychiatric patients than among the general population, the question as to what this might mean is inescapable, yet all the incidence figures tell us is that there is a correlation between being adopted and coming for psychiatric treatment. One can only speculate about the causal relations. Are adopted children more prone to emotional disturbance and mental illness? Are parents who adopt more likely to create emotional difficulties for their children? Do adopted children and the parents who raise them have more difficulty adapting to one another than do biological parent-child units? Are adopting parents more sensitive to emotional problems and thus more likely to seek professional help than parents in general?

What are the factors adoption introduces into parent-child relations? Are people who adopt psychologically different from men and women who produce their own offspring? Does the fact of adoption introduce a feature into the child-parent relationship with which the parents are often unable to cope? Does our society have attitudes toward adopted children which complicate the lives of parents and child alike? Do adoptive parents try to deal with the stresses of child rearing in ways which are in some essential manner different from the stress adaptations of most biological families?

There are, at present, no answers to these questions. Answers must await painstaking and well-controlled research but, as usual, the practitioner cannot sit idly by until he has all the answers when human beings are obviously in need of help. Meanwhile, an exploration, albeit largely theoretical, of the psychological relationship between adoptive parents and their adopted child may further the improvement of counseling services for families with an adopted child. Regardless of what research may eventually find to be the reason for the emotional vulnerability of adopted children, improved parent counseling cannot fail to contribute something to the alleviation of the problem.

Child welfare workers generally view adoption as desirable when a child needs a family and when an acceptable adoptive home is available for him. In states where the thinking of social workers has succeeded in becoming reflected in enlightened legislation, adoptions can be carried out only if a social agency has made a detailed study of the child and the adopting family. Every attempt is made to match parents and child in terms of physical characteristics and intellectual potential. The biological mother is helped to work through the emotional implications of releasing the child, and steps are taken to assure that the natural and adoptive parents do not know each other's identity. In most instances the social agency involved in the placement continues to offer casework services to the adoptive parents after the child is placed in the home.

Despite these elaborate and at times cumbersome safeguards which child welfare workers consider progressive and desirable, we find the alarming figures previously described. What is wrong? One thing which may play a role is the fact that casework for the adoptive parents continues for only a relatively short time after the child is placed, usually until the adoption becomes final. Feelings of anxiety and insecurity which the adoptive parents may experience around having a new child can be worked through during that period but if adoption is viewed as a life-long exceptional state, it becomes clear that counseling should be available for as long as the child continues to live in the home. Caseworkers frequently discuss with the parents how to tell the child that he is adopted but this discussion usually takes place when the infant is first placed with the family. This abstract discussion does little to help a parent cope with his anxieties when telling the child about his origin several years later. As with any other chronic condition, different stages in the child's development and the family's life cycle bring different problems which call for supportive help at the time they occur.

Schechter (1960) believes that emotional vulnerability of adopted children is related to the child's reaction to learning about the fact of being adopted and the fantasies of rejection and abandonment which this disclosure may arouse.

> The knowledge of their adoptive status, so often coming in at the time of the Oedipal conflict, can seem to prolong and actually prevent the resolution of this particular area of personality development. There is a lack of boundaries constituting a self; rather, what can be seen is a diffuseness in poorly integrated identifications.
>
> The anxiety these children manifest often refers to the possibility of returning to their original parents or, having been given up once for undetermined reasons, they may be given up again at some future time—

also for undetermined, fantasied reasons. These concepts enhance the feeling of lack of closeness, and we again raise the question as to the timing of the knowledge of adoption prior to the resolving of the Oedipal phase.

The material presented suggests that the immature ego cannot cope with the knowledge of the rejection by its original parents, representing a severe narcissistic injury. The child tends to react to this information by character change or symptom formation. It is, therefore, recommended that a thorough investigation of the child and his environment should be accomplished to determine the method and timing of giving the information of his adopted status (*ibid.*, p. 31).

Schechter's explanation of his findings represents an oversimplification which neglects the fact that the child grows up in a family environment of which his adoptive parents, their role perceptions and their emotions form an integral part. Clothier (1939, 1943) who wrote on the psychology of the adopted child many years ago, also focused on the child's reactions, ignoring the part the psychology of his parents might play in contributing to the child's difficulties. To Clothier (1939) the central problem revolved around the "family romance," the child's fantasies about who his *real* parents were. These fantasies may play a role but if one wishes to understand the family it is well to explore possible contributing factors on the part of the adoptive parents, particularly since better understanding of their psychology may contribute to better counseling.

THE PSYCHOLOGY OF COUPLES WHO ADOPT

A group of people who have only the fact of adoption in common are psychologically as diverse as any other collection of people who are grouped together because they share one feature. A discussion of the psychology of adoptive couples is therefore a somewhat artificial generalization. To make this generalization more meaningful we shall limit this discussion to the psychology of married couples without children of their own who adopt an unrelated child.

Adoption agencies by and large try to place children with couples who for biological reasons are unable to produce children of their own. This policy is based on several considerations, including that, among the white population, there are far more couples willing to adopt than there are children available for adoption. It is also held to be psychologically undesirable to mix adopted and biological children, especially where the adopted child is the first to come into the family. Since a couple able to conceive might produce a child of their own after adopting, biologically sterile couples are generally given preference by adoption agencies.

This policy has the effect of forcing couples wishing to adopt to bring proof that they are unable to have children of their own; proof, that is, of reproductive incapacity, which to many is proof of personal inadequacy. In our child-oriented culture, having children carries tremendous value, a value in which the adopting couple shares, for otherwise they would not wish to adopt.

To understand the psychological state of such a couple at the point of adoption one must go back to the years of marriage before the decision to adopt was made. These are years of wishing, of hoping, of planning, and finally of trying to produce a child. As month after month passes without signs of impregnation, the couple becomes more and more tense and apprehensive; there results an emotional condition which may, in itself, be antagonistic to reproduction. Sometimes the wife does become pregnant only to lose the fetus in miscarriage. In such cases there is a sequence of raised expectations and dashed hopes which may repeat itself several times before the eventual application for adoption.

With feelings of inadequacy or failure only too close to consciousness, adoptive parents, once given a child, tend to react to the ordinary crises of child rearing in extraordinary fashion. Minor feeding problems, refusal to go to sleep, negativism, toilet mishaps, temper outbursts or fights with neighbor children, generally accepted by biological parents as part of parenthood, can to the adoptive parents come to be stress situations which test their security. Insecure to begin with, incidents such as these may be viewed as further proof of the dreaded inadequacy with which they embarked on parenthood by adoption. Fear of failure can become one of the basic motivations which make adoptive parents tense and selfconsciously artificial in their relationships with the child. It is as if the parent were saying, "I failed in producing a child of my own—now that this child has been given to me I must not fail again by being an inadequate parent."

We know that in child rearing self-conscious tension is antithetical to emotionally healthy parent-child relations. The mother who cannot relax and spontaneously act in the way which is most comfortable to her—who is too unsure of herself to "do what comes naturally"—communicates her tension to the child in numerous subtle ways. When the child responds to this tension with colic, allergy, nightmares or bedwetting and the mother, in turn, responds to this with increased insecurity and tension, a vicious cycle of negative emotional interaction is begun which may lead to eventual referral to a child psychiatric clinic.

The way in which a given parent deals with tension, insecurity and anxiety is, as we have said earlier, a function of the parent's individual personality. When self-esteem is threatened by the awareness of inadequacy as a parent, some adoptive parents tend to turn to rationalizations which in their case are all too readily available. Since the child does not share the heredity of his adopted parents his genetic background may explicitly or implicitly come to be blamed for the behavior which is puzzling or disconcerting to his parents. When biological parents encounter problematic child behavior they are forced to examine themselves as contributing factors regardless of whether they favor a genetic or an environmental theory for the explanation of such behavior. Adoptive parents, on the other hand, can protect themselves from thus examining their own contribution by blaming the child's "bad blood" when things go wrong. Thus, instead of seeking constructive solutions to the problem they may write the child off as destined to be a problem and matters can then go from bad to worse.

Eiduson and Livermore (1953), in discussing the complications they encountered in therapy with adopted children, point to the potential for neurotic interaction between mother and child when the reality factor of adoption meets the neurotic conflict halfway and reinforces certain types of defenses against the conflict.

> A repressed mother perceives in the child's acting out behavior the instinctual impulses which she has found so unacceptable. Her knowledge that the child was 'conceived in sin' adds to her tendency to regard him as 'bad,' just as are those impulses within her. In order to maintain her defenses, she must reject the child. This is facilitated by the reality that the child is not her own (ibid., p. 800).

It is generally thought desirable to inform the adopted child of his adoptive status. Social agencies work toward this and try to help the adopting parents communicate this in as constructive a manner as possible. With the best of intentions, however, attempts at telling the child that he is adopted can become complicated by the parents' own unconscious conflicts. Anxiety over how the child will react to this information is confounded by anxiety over having to admit to what they may still perceive as their original inadequacy. In addition the parents' own archaic fantasies about not being the real child of their own parents tend to become reawakened at this point and may further contribute to tension in their discussions with the child. It seems that almost all children go through periods when, for some reason angry at their parents, they have fantasies that these parents are not their own. As children grow into adults these fantasies tend to become forgotten but when one adopts a child and comes face to face with the reality of a youngster who is brought up by parents other than his own, these old childhood fantasies tend to be reawakened and may serve to disrupt the relationship, particularly at the point when the fact of adoption must be discussed with the child.

THE PSYCHOLOGY OF THE ADOPTED CHILD

So far we have assumed that the child enters the adoptive family with an emotional *tabula rasa*. This, unfortunately, is only rarely the case. The older the child at the time he enters the adoptive home the greater the likelihood that he has experienced traumatic separation from his biological or foster mother or been exposed to emotionally crippling institutionalization. His mother may have vacillated in her decision to give him up and delayed signing the necessary documents releasing the child for adoption. Practices of adoption agencies and courts sometimes contribute to a delay between the infant's birth and his placement in the adoptive family. Such delays all too often lead to infants remaining in institutions which, even under the best circumstances, provide poor substitutes for the stimulation of a devoted adoptive mother. The somewhat more fortunate infant who was placed in a foster home instead of an institution is not exposed to the same deprivation but does encounter, when the adoption placement is made, a usually abrupt separation from the woman to whom he has formed an attachment. The later placement with the adoptive parents occurs, the greater will be the potential trauma of separation from the intermediate foster mother. The infant who is placed with his adoptive parents immediately after release from the newborn nursery is a rarity and usually represents one of the unofficial, non-agency adoptions so frowned upon by child welfare workers.

In all too many cases a child with possible emotional impairment joins adoptive parents whose own emotional adjustment has undergone considerable strain. As the adopted child grows older and is informed of his status he must be able to integrate this information in his psychological development. We have already pointed out that when children are angry at their parents, as they sometimes are, they tend to have fantasies about who their "good" parents might be since these "bad" parents could not possibly be their own. For the child living with his biological parents this largely remains a fantasy, but for the adopted child this fantasy has some basis in fact and he may begin an imaginary or actual search for his "lost" parents. While the biological child must learn to cope with the ambiguity of parents who are both giving and withholding, the adopted child may become diverted from constructively coming to terms with reality and have his emotional development further complicated.

Another area in which the adopted child encounters reality not faced

by the biological child is that involving fears and fantasies of rejection
by the parents. Fears of being deserted or rejected by a parent are probably very common phenomena among children. The vast majority deals
with these fears constructively in the process of growing up. The reality
complicating this process for the adopted child is that he feels that his
biological mother has indeed rejected and deserted him; for no matter
what euphemism might have been used in explaining why his mother
placed him for adoption, the fact that she did not keep him remains
forever starkly in the child's psychological background. From this it is
not far to the fantasy, "If I was rejected by my real mother why could I
not also be rejected by my adoptive parents?" This logic may well contribute to an increased insecurity and anxiety of the adopted child, particularly at times of conflict with the adoptive parents.

Related to this fantasy is the essentially synthetic nature of parenthood by adoption. Biological birth is an irrevocable fact. In contrast,
adoption is a man-made, a statutory arrangement. A court decreed that
the child belong to the adoptive parents. It does not take much childish
imagination to fantasy that if a judge was able to give you to your parents
a judge might also take you away, or that, conversely, parents who went
to court to get you might return to court to give you back. The fact that
this is legally impossible does, of course, not negate the threat represented by such a fantasy. Marriages, leases or contracts are backed by
court decrees, if they can be broken and undone, why not adoption? The
fantasies and reactions on the part of the child may interact with the
anxieties and conflicts of his adoptive parents and lead to emotional
difficulties which seem reflected in the incidence figures cited at the
beginning of this chapter. As Eiduson and Livermore (1953) point out,
the mother may reject the child because she must reject his behavior in
which she unconsciously senses her own unacceptable impulses, while
the adopted child experiences conflict between his impulses and his
need to be loved and approved. This conflict he shares with all children
but for him the conflict is

> heightened because he is unconsciously aware of the gratification to his
> mother of his impulsive behavior, and on the other hand finds her repres-
> sive demands too much for him. Again, in common with all children, he
> tends, upon feeling rejected, to resort to the fantasy of the family ro-
> mance, but for him there is the reality of another, *unknown* set of parents.
> Upon these he can conveniently project the fantasy that they are all-
> loving, all-permissive. Therefore the neuroses of mother and child are
> complementary, and the defenses of each are magnified by those of the
> other. . . . Like other types of cases in which the neuroses are fed by
> reality factors, these cases are extremely difficult in treatment (*ibid.*, p.
> 800).

The intractable nature of emotional problems thus created lends further emphasis to the need for early and ongoing preventive counseling.

THE ATTITUDE OF SOCIETY

One of the questions we asked at the beginning of this discussion was whether the attitudes of our society towards adoptions might be complicating the lives of parents and their adopted child. While we cannot document this contention it does seem that public opinion values producing one's own child more highly than obtaining a child through adoption. Motherhood is idealized and inability to become a mother is at best viewed with tolerant compassion, and couples who adopt are all too aware of this social bias.

Paradoxically, while we idealize motherhood we condemn pregnancy when it occurs outside wedlock. The majority of children who come up for adoption are the offspring of unmarried mothers and our society's puritanical attitude tends to make it difficult for an adopted child to be accepted into the community without comment. There remains something special, something exceptional, about a child who was adopted. When the information is available and the family comes to public attention, newspapers frequently publish the fact that a filial relationship was based on adoption.

Despite our attempts to be sophisticated and enlightened about it, adoption continues to carry a mild implicit stigma and this stigma is another factor which complicates the relationship of adoptive parents with their adoptive child. Some of these parents seem to over-react to the felt stigma and to mention that their child was adopted on occasions when this information is totally uncalled for. They flaunt the fact of adoption as if they dared the world to make a negative comment about it; others try to keep it a secret, giving the child the impression that there is something bad about his origin.

Neither over-reaction nor secretive behavior on the parents' part is conducive to healthy emotional development and both reactions call for professional help. In fact, if our speculations are correct and both the adopted child and the adoptive parents labor under an emotional handicap from the moment of adoption, it would appear important to make counseling services available to adoptive parents for as long as the child lives in the home.

IX

The Case of Bobby Bolczek and his Family

INTRODUCTION

THIS CASE was selected from the files of a parent counseling center in a large mid-western city in order to illustrate some of the aspects of work with parents of an exceptional child. It is meant to exemplify the complex reality factors which often enter this type of counseling, frequently to frustrate even the best of efforts.

When the varieties of exceptional children are discussed under separate chapter headings one of the facts which tend to become obscured by the need for topical organization is that many exceptional children have more than one disability or disorder. Mental deficiency is often accompanied by such physical disabilities as cardiac impairment, defective hearing, or sensory-motor disturbances. The cerebral palsied child may have speech disorders or impairment in vision or hearing, and many physical handicaps may be complicated by secondary emotional disturbances. Bobby Bolczek is such a child. He has a number of defects, all of which at one time or another entered into the work with his parents.

This is not an ideal case in which everything went smoothly, where no one made mistakes, and where, at the end, all problems were resolved. Published case histories all too often end on a positive note because authors have the understandable tendency to select those cases for publication in which their work was faultless and successful. This bias may lead the student to expect that he too should be able to work successfully with most, if not all, of his cases, contributing to a sense of frustration and disappointment when in his later professional life he encounters the reality that most of his cases fall far short of the ideal described in the textbook. The case of Bobby Bolczek then, is far from ideal and is meant to communicate the often frustrating reality the counselor must be prepared to encounter in his professional life.

Except for the disguising of identifying information and some necessary condensation, this material is presented just as it was found in the case record. Comments, retrospective speculations, and critical remarks

173

have been kept to a minimum to permit the reader to draw his own conclusions by relating the case material to the discussions in earlier parts of this book. There are a number of different and better ways in which aspects of this case might have been handled. The reader is invited to explore these alternatives.

THE FAMILY HISTORY

Bobby was five years old when his 36-year-old parents were referred to the counseling center. Bobby was the youngest of three children; his sister Barbara was nine; his brother Bernie was seven. The family rented a small house in a working class neighborhood where they lived on a marginal income earned by the father, who was an elevator operator in a department store. The house was in a run-down condition, poorly heated and insulated, it had no yard or other area where the children might play without going into the street.

Mrs. Bolczek has three brothers and two sisters. Her parents had come to the United States from Czechoslovakia ten years before she was born. Mrs. B views her mother as a very lonely woman who worked hard and carried all the responsibility for the six children. Her mother died from a cerebral hemorrhage when Bobby was three years old. Mrs. B told her worker that her father, who operated a small lunch counter, never had time for his family and her memory of her childhood is an unhappy one.

Bobby's maternal grandfather is still living and in retirement. Mrs. B cannot visit him because he and one of her sisters, with whom he lives, cannot tolerate or accept Bobby. When the grandfather makes one of his rare visits to the Bolczek home he stays for only a short time and mother attributes this to her father's feelings about Bobby.

An important aspect of mother's background which figures prominently in her attitude toward having an exceptional child is her experience with her older sister, Carol. As a child, Carol had been at Mark State School as a mute mental defective. As is true of nearly all state institutions for the mentally defective or mentally ill, in the communities which the school serves the name "Mark" carries with it a highly aversive connotation, a mixture of shame, revulsion and fear. In the public eye, being sent to this institution is viewed with horror and morose jokes about the place only thinly disguise the general anxiety its mention arouses. This was the attitude the community held about Mark State School although, objectively it is one of the better institutions of its kind.

Mrs. Bolczek's grandmother did not feel that Carol was properly cared for at the instiution, took her out and brought her to live in her house. The child's parents did not object and the arrangement worked out all right until the grandmother died. At that point Carol returned home to live with her own parents and siblings. When Carol was an adolescent the family could no longer cope with her and she now was committed to a state mental institution because her condition had deteriorated to the point where she was no longer considered merely defective but also psychotic.

Mrs. Bolczek's other sister graduated from high school but as an adult spent a few months in a psychiatric hospital with the diagnosis of schizophrenia. She was discharged as cured and now works as a typist in a local mail order house. One of Mrs. B's brothers graduated from college and works as a pharmacist. The other two boys are high school graduates, married and employed.

Mr. Bolczek also come from a large immigrant family. He has six sisters and one brother and both of his parents are still living. They have a limited knowledge of English and Mr. B's mother can neither read nor write. His father still works in a factory as a crane operator. All of Mr. B's siblings have graduated from high school; three sisters are married and employed, one lives at home and keeps house for the parents. One of the sisters had spent some time in a psychiatric hospital with an undiagnosed mental disorder but she was pronounced cured upon discharge. The Bolczeks and their children frequently visit Bobby's paternal grandparents and there is a fairly close relationship among these family members.

Mr. Bolczek attended a local college for two years on a football scholarship but during the depression financial difficulties forced him to go to work and for awhile he had a good position as an office worker in New York. Mr. and Mrs. Bolczek had been married shortly before he left college. The first two children had been born while they lived in New York. Mrs. B soon became homesick and they returned to their home town. Since then father had difficulty holding jobs until he found his present occupation as elevator operator.

THE CHILD'S HISTORY

Mother became pregnant with Bobby seven years after marriage. Just before pregnancy she had not felt well and during pregnancy she complained of nausea and vomiting. Bobby was a full-term baby but mother remembers nothing of the delivery because she was under heavy sedation from the time she entered the hospital.

Bobby is described as having been a beautiful baby who was perhaps "too good." He did not cry much compared to the other children and because mother was very busy with the new home to which they had just moved on their return from New York, he was left alone a great deal. Mother had wanted to breast-feed Bobby but she did not have enough milk and he was bottle-fed without difficulty.

When Bobby was three months old mother noticed that his eyes were beginning to cross. She took him to a physician who recommended that the child be hospitalized for corrective eye surgery. Before this could be done, however, and when Bobby was five months old, mother became pregnant again. Three months later she was hospitalized because of a miscarriage. While mother was in the hospital Bobby was cared for by the paternal grandparents who, mother felt were very good with him. The same grandparents took care of Bobby during several later hospitalizations of mother and during one of these periods grandmother noticed that Bobby was not urinating. He was taken to the hospital and catheterized, though physicians who saw him later on thought that the urine retention might have been of psychological origin caused by the trauma of being separated from both parents.

Bobby was weaned without reported difficulty when he was nine months old. At this time he had no trouble sleeping and he ate well, although mother noticed that the child always drooled.

At one year of age Bobby was hospitalized for the corrective eye surgery recommended earlier. Mother felt at the time that the operation was a success but, as we shall see later, the boy continued to have considerable difficulty with his eyes.

Bobby stood without support when he was eighteen months old and mother remembers that it was around this time that he started head banging. To correct this mother padded the wall, but it did not help and Bobby was still banging his head when, at age five, he was seen at the counseling center.

Mother could not recall when Bobby started to crawl nor was she sure whether the child ever had convulsions. She did remember that on three occasions during his first two years Bobby had wakened during the night with a loud scream and that when she went to him she had found him rigid and sobbing. He had quieted down after an enema and gone back to sleep without difficulty. Why she had decided to give him an enema mother could not say, but this is a fairly common home remedy among people of her social background, thought to be effective in a great variety of ailments.

Before his eye operation Bobby's motor coordination had been poor, but after surgery this had improved. It was not until the child was nearly two years old that mother became concerned about his development. Not only did she again notice a lack of coordination but she also felt that he was not getting along with others, that he bit and kicked and was generally difficult. Though she felt that he was not learning as a normal child should, mother rationalized this by thinking that he might just be slow. Around this time her own mother commented that "something is wrong with Bobby" and when a friend made a similar remark Mrs. Bolczek decided to take the child to her family physician. This physician was unable to determine whether Bobby's condition had anything to do with the scarlet fever accompanied by high temperatures which the child had a few months earlier. He made a referral to a neurologist who examined Bobby and, according to Mrs. Bolczek, made the following statement: "He is definitely a mental defective and should be committed to Mark State School right away." When mother could not accept this diagnosis, the physician warned her that if she did not follow his advice she would be back a year later, realizing that he had been right. He prescribed a daily dose of glutamic acid on which Bobby was continued for the next three years.

We do, of course, not know whether this physician's diagnosis and recommendation were really put in as blunt and brutal a fashion as mother reports but the fact that she was unable to accept it indicates that the mother was neither prepared for this recommendation nor helped to accept it.

Unable to accept the diagnosis, mother consulted a psychiatrist two weeks later. Though Bobby had not been given a psychological evaluation, this physician also advised mother to make immediate application to have him committed to Mark State School. Mrs. Bolczek had somewhat more faith in the psychiatrist's diagnosis, not only because it confirmed the earlier one, but also because he had treated her older sister during her hospitalization for schizophrenia. Though the parents were greatly upset by this discovery they decided to make application to the state school because they wanted to do the best thing for their child and hoped that the training program at the school would help him. Bobby remained at home for the next two years awaiting admission to the state institution.

Bobby's development continued to be slow. He did not get his first tooth until he was two years old and he had difficulty learning to walk. He would place his toes down first and then bang down hard on his heels, stumbled a great deal, and did not seem able to see too well. Around two years of age he began to say simple words.

When he was two Bobby was hospitalized for tonsillectomy and short-

ly afterwards was sick with mumps and chickenpox. Around this time
mother was once again in the hospital, this time for three weeks, for
removal of a Fallopian tube and an appendectomy.

A year and a half later mother was again hospitalized in connection
with a tubal pregnancy. By this time Bobby was dry at night but would
still wet himself during the day and bowel control was not yet established.

Bobby was three and one half years old when Mark State School
was ready to admit him and a social worker from the state school made
a home visit which she described as follows:

> Bobby is a slightly-built child who except for slightly crossed eyes is nor-
> mal in appearance. Worker observed him throughout the interview and
> noticed that he was extremely hyperactive and restless. Because of the
> information that had come with the application worker was surprised
> when she listened to the child talk, for he used short sentences very well
> and made his wants known very clearly. Worker gained the impression
> that this child, besides the possible mental retardation, may also be
> severely emotionally disturbed. He is hyperactive and has a habit of
> biting, kicking, and striking his head. The mother was questioned con-
> cerning this behavior. She replied that Bobby began head-banging before
> he was able to walk, and when old enough to crawl he started banging
> his head against the panel of his crib; at the present time he still bangs
> his head against the bed or wall. The mother explained that she had
> padded the wall, thinking it would break him of the habit, but though
> this was not effective it has been continued to this day.
>
> On the day of the interview the mother took Bobby upstairs for his
> nap. Worker heard a noise to which the mother called her attention, ex-
> plaining that this was Bobby banging his head against the crib. According
> to the mother, he sleeps well at the present time.
>
> Bobby is unable to play cooperatively for any length of time with
> either brother or sister. When he is frustrated he will bite, pinch, or
> scratch, and because of this and his constant screaming it is necessary
> for his brother and sister to allow him to have his way. Worker observed
> that on one occasion when the mother picked him up and turned him
> over her lap to spank, he bit his mother's leg in retaliation.
>
> Worker questioned mother concerning the incident mentioned in the
> application that Bobby put his hands in the fire. She explained this by
> saying that the child never actually puts his hand in the flame but that
> he was attracted by the bright color and reached toward it. Since he
> often reaches for hot objects he must be constantly supervised. Bobby is
> also reported to turn on the gas stove if he has an opportunity to do so.
>
> The worker observed that Bobby's brother and sister have been trained
> to give in to Bobby and that he is certainly very hyperactive and unpre-
> dictable. During the interview he tipped the furniture over, climbed on
> the gas stove, and attempted to turn on the gas jets. The child's behavior
> made the mother so tense and nervous that she spanked him on several

occasions. Mrs. Bolczek's nervous reactions to her son are undoubtedly caused not only by his behavior but also by the fact that she has herself been in poor health and upset about family financial and health problems.

At that time Bobby was also given his first psychological test. The psychometrician wrote in her report: "Because the mother found it necessary to discipline Bobby due to his hyperactivity he had become extremely negativistic during testing. The examiner therefore feels that the test score may be depressed. The fact that Bobby has suffered a series of traumatic experiences ever since he was eight months old should also be taken into consideration." These considerations notwithstanding, she reported an intelligence quotient of 64 from the Stanford-Binet and a social quotient of 76 from the Vineland Social Maturity Scale and on the basis of these scores Bobby was admitted to the institution for mental defectives.

Shortly after admission Bobby was described as subject to temper tantrums, stubborn, wanting his own way and stomping his feet when angry. He would not use a spoon and wanted to mess in the food with his hands. He paid no attention to toilet needs and would wet and soil both day and night. He was seclusive and showed some fear of the other patients.

Except for the home visit which was made as part of the preadmission study and which consisted primarily of information-gathering, the parents had no contact with anyone from the state school who might have helped them with their feelings either before or during his stay there.

The parents visited Bobby at Mark State School and took him out to eat in nearby restaurants. They thought that the child was quieter than he had been, that he seemed withdrawn and afraid to do things or to move despite the parents' assurance that it would be all right. The parents were troubled by this but there was no one to whom they could talk. To add to their confusion they had a visit from Bobby's cottage parents who told them how well the child was doing and who added that he was not mentally defective and should therefore not be at Mark.

Three weeks after admission Bobby had been seen by the physician in charge of the institution who made the following observation for the institutional records: "He has some visual defect but on the surface does not appear to be mentally defective even to the degree shown by the test data so far. His behavior also does not seem to indicate mental deficiency. In all probability this boy's defect stems from an emotional problem very probably due to the family and also his and his mother's hospitalizations. After adjustment and further study this boy possibly should be considered for removal from the institution."

After Bobby had been at the state school for six months he seemed much less nervous and excitable, fed himself fairly well, his temper tantrums had disappeared and he would inform his attendants of his bathroom needs. He had gained weight and though he remained seclusive in the cottage he had become quite affectionate toward the cottage parents. At this point and without any preparation, the parents received a letter from the superintendent advising them that they should take Bobby out of the institution because he considered the child's difficulty an emotional one rather than mental deficiency. The parents were overjoyed to receive this news and immediately removed Bobby from the school. Several months later they were still maintaining a relationship with some of the cottage parents who had visited them. One of these told them that they should never consider returning Bobby to Mark School because he was different from the children there and not mentally defective.

The parents were happy to have their child at home and thought that he had shown great improvement. His toilet habits continued to be good, his eating behavior adequate, and he seemed to get along better with his brother and sister. Mother reported that Barbara and Bernie liked and accepted their little brother. Before his admission to Mark they had been taught to give him his way at all times because he was not well. They seemed to do so willingly and are reported to have missed him a great deal while he was away. Both brother and sister were pleased to have him back and mother felt that Barbara often behaved like a little mother toward him. Bernie too played with the child and tried to teach him how to use new toys.

It took Bobby a few weeks to adjust to being home again and once he had done so much of his old puzzling and unusual behavior returned. The parents were quite upset by this and six months after the child had returned from the state school they applied to the counseling center for help. When they were seen there for the first time Bobby was five years old and manifested hyperactivity and an inability to focus on an activity for any length of time. The parents described him as "real nice" on some days but then again moody, listless, and difficult to manage. They noticed that his walk was not well coordinated and that in order to recognize play objects he had to hold them very close to his eyes. By now his play with his siblings was more often than not disrupted by fighting and scratching.

Bobby had a number of peculiarities which puzzled the parents. He was fascinated by streetcars and displayed a remarkable knowledge of their route numbers and destinations. He seemed overly concerned about cleanliness and insisted on immediate change of clothes when they became dirty. When outside playing he would constantly run into the house to have his hands washed and he was also very preoccupied with mechanical household appliances and insisted on being near his mother whenever she used one of them.

This then was the picture at the time the family came to the counseling center. They had been through five years of puzzlement, anxiety and discouragement, still did not know what was wrong with their child and had made the painful discovery that professional opinion and advice can be highly unreliable and inaccurate. The staff of the counseling center was surprised at the lack of anger they found in the parents toward the professional people who had misguided them. The intake worker saw them as a solid, closely-knit family group which, though it had been through many diffiicult experiences, seemed to have strength to adjust and accept their reality situation. To what extent the absence of reactive anger at those who had hurt them was a reflection of underlying guilt will need to kept in mind as we trace the further developments of this case.

WORK WITH THE FAMILY

When Bobby was being discharged from the state school the superintendent told his parents that he considered the child to be emotionally disturbed and not mentally defective. The mother later quoted him as saying, "Your child has an emotional block, but he'll grow out of it in time." Beyond this the parents received no help or advice. They were not referred to a more appropriate facility, but since Bobby was technically on parole from the school, space was held open for him in case he had to be returned. All this had left the Bolczeks quite confused. They vaguely understood that there was "something mental" troubling their child but the difference between mental retardation and emotional disturbance was more than they could comprehend without help. Since Bobby's behavior continued to puzzle and upset her, Mrs. B tried to find help from a variety of sources. Once she wrote to a well-known syndicated newspaper column on child rearing and received an answer which spoke of maturational readiness and individual differences. This failed to reassure her. Six months after Bobby had returned home she happened to attend a public meeting at which a physician discussed mentally retarded children. At the end of the meeting Mrs. Bolczek approached the speaker and told him about her child. It was only then and in this unplanned and almost accidental manner that Mrs. Bolczek was told about the parent counseling center and urged to contact it for help with her problem.

First thing next morning Mrs. Bolczek called the center and described her concern about Bobby, his hyperactivity and tendency to get into mischief and danger. Over the telephone mother did not sound greatly concerned about her child, to whom she referred as her "baby," though when she was told that she might have to wait two or three months before she could be seen at the center she stressed Bobby's probationary status with the state school and hoped that she could be seen before this period of probation expired. The worker told her that the center would get in touch with the superintendent of the school and ask that action on Bobby's case be held in abeyance until the center had had an opportunity to study the case. Mother greeted this information with considerable relief and her "Oh, thank you very much" seemed to express her gratitude at finally having found a professional person who seemed willing to take an interest in her problem.

Although Mrs. B had not sounded greatly concerned about her child when she made the first phone call, she expressed her anxiety when she called the center again two months later and wondered why she had not yet been contacted. She told the worker on the phone about what the superintendent at the state school had said about an emotional block. Mrs. B was willing to keep Bobby at home until he had "grown out of it" but was finding it increasingly difficult to contain him, particularly since he interfered with the play and activities of his older siblings. She described fluctuations in Bobby's behavior which she somehow related to the weather, claiming that he was "real nice" on sunny days but would become upset and scream when it rained. The worker assured Mrs. B that the center had not forgotten her and sympathized with the difficulty she had around Bobby's problem.

Intake interviews. A month later, in March 1958, the center was able to pick up with the Bolczeks. The worker assigned to the family phoned mother who was very pleased and glad to hear from the center. Mother admitted that she had been very impatient and had been about to call the center again, having hesitated only because she did not want to make a nuisance of herself. Mrs. B's eagerness for help was again apparent when she arrived quite early for her first appointment. The intake worker described her as a neatly dressed but rather plain-looking woman who seemed tense and anxious throughout most of the interview. Mrs. B appeared at pains to convince the worker that Bobby was not mentally defective by describing all sorts of things he could do which reflected what she saw as his "good mind."

Some of what the intake worker recorded after this first interview reads as follows:

> Because of mother's quite apparent anxiety I explained our procedures to her and told her that I thought if she knew the way we did things here she might feel more comfortable about coming. Mrs. B seemed interested in the explanation and was able to admit how hard it was for her to come to a new place. She went on to tell how hard it had been for her to send Bobby to Mark State School. The only way she had been able to do it was by convincing herself that it was for the child's own good and that he could be helped most by being at that school. Mother described how she had been panicky and very much afraid at the time she applied for admission to Mark because the physicians she had seen had made her feel that it was a great emergency and that the child should be rushed to the state school as soon as possible. Mrs. B said that she did not think she could send Bobby to 'that place' again even though he was only on parole and they still had a place for him. The worker did not follow this up because she felt Mrs. B had raised re-commitment mostly out of her own anxiety about coming to the center and that it reflected her fear about what the outcome of her contact with the center might be. Later on in the interview as Mrs. B felt somewhat reassured and less anxious, she spontaneously said that she would be willing to send Bobby to an institution again if she was sure that it was for the child's own good. She added, however, that her husband would not be able to take this step.

Mrs. B then spoke about the difficulties Bobby presented at home. Though she stressed that he was not as hard to manage as he had been before he went to Mark, he still seemed to stumble when he walks. "It is as if he were stumbling over himself," she said. Mother told how when Bobby had first come home from Mark it had taken him a long time to adjust to the family household. She said that he would sit still and seem afraid to do things. Mrs. B said that she had been patient with him and that she had constantly reassured him that he did not just have to sit still and that he could play without being punished. Again she reassured the worker that she really did not think that Bobby was mentally defective and that, although he was shy around people, he could talk very well on the phone. It was just that he would not talk to strangers outside. "Bobby can also dress himself, he can recognize and identify various makes of cars; he is learning to play with blocks and to build things." All of this mother thought was a good sign.

As if to illustrate her confusion, Mrs. B followed these protestations with the revelation that she and her husband had joined a club of parents of mentally retarded children and that they had recently taken

Bobby to a children's party sponsored by that club. At that party Mrs. B had felt that Bobby did not look like the other children, that he seemed brighter and faster than they. She said, "He just does not have the same look about him," but after a pause added, "They tell me that's what all the mothers think but I am really convinced that it is true in Bobby's case." This was again followed by more evidence of Bobby's intelligence. She said that he knows the stores she goes to for shopping and that if she had been to a store once Bobby could find the way back there the next time. He also runs little errands at home such as bringing father's slippers.

The worker pointed out that mother must be quite confused about what is wrong with Bobby. Mother readily agreed to this and seemed glad when she was told that the center would try to help her understand Bobby's condition.

Mrs. B then told how the superintendent at Mark State School had told her that he did not think that Bobby was a mentally defective child and how the letter from the newspaper columnist had warned her not to compare him with other children his age, that instead she should take note of the progress he makes by himself. Though she recognized that this was good advice, Mrs. B said that it was almost impossible to carry out. Even though she realized that Bobby is an individual and not as fast as other children, she said that there were other children among her relatives almost the same age as Bobby and that she could not help but compare Bobby with them. The worker told Mrs. B that she realized how hard it was for her not to make invidious comparisons and lauded her for understanding that Bobby was an individual with a personality of his own who ought to be evaluated in terms of his own individual rate of progress.

Mrs. B then told of the visits Bobby's cottage parents had made after he had been discharged and how she had appreciated their saying that Bobby did not belong in the state school. The worker said how reassuring it must have been to mother to hear this from people who had watched the child closely and that this must have confirmed her own belief that Bobby was not mentally defective. Mrs. B now said that she hoped the center would be able to tell her whether or not Bobby would ever become dangerous to himself or to the community. She said that she did not feel disgrace or shame if he was not too bright, in that case she was willing to keep him at home and to care for him. If, however, it was found that he might be dangerous and could harm someone she would want to put him in some sort of an institution.

Having given expression to her fear that Bobby might be dangerous and uncontrollable, mother immediately turned to a discussion of her childhood and present family. She compared her own father with her husband and pointed out the two were not at all alike. She stated that her husband is much more of a family man, that he does not drink, and that she never has to worry about him. Mrs. B felt that she is very fortunate and that she is very happy in her married life. When the worker said that it must have been hard for Mrs. B to grow up in an unhappy family she answered that it was hard but that she now feels compensated for it because her family life is so secure and because she does not have to worry about her husband's affection, knowing that she is more important to him than anything else.

The worker now asked how Mr. Bolczek felt about Bobby's difficulty. Mrs. B reported that it is very hard on him and that he had missed Bobby a great deal when he was at state school. She added that Barbara and Bernie had also missed Bobby and that Barbara in particular had often cried and asked them to please bring Bobby home again. Mr. B now spends a great deal of time with Bobby to whom he is very close. The worker pointed out that she would also like to talk to Mr. Bolczek and since he worked it was agreed that a Saturday interview would be scheduled.

Some of the feelings Mrs. Bolczek had about physicians and other professional people came out when, at the end of the interview, the worker raised the question of fees. Based on the center's sliding scale the fee for the Bolczek family came to 50c per visit. The worker dictated the following:

> Mother was very surprised that she would have to pay so little and said she did not think that this was right. I showed her how we moved back one step for each child in the family and she could hardly believe this. She said that she had brought $10.00 today to pay for her appointment and asked if she could not at least give me $5.00 in payment for the interview. I told Mrs. B that I thought we had better stay with the fee schedule and assured her that the service would be just the same no matter how much she paid. To this Mrs. B answered that this was the most wonderful thing that had happened to her for a long time. She said that when she went to see the other doctor, who saw her for only a few minutes and told her very little, it had cost her a lot of money. Mrs. B said that she was willing to pay any amount to take care of Bobby but that they really needed the money for other things too. I told Mrs. B that I knew this and that our fee schedule was based on the consideration that a family had many needs. Mrs. B asked if she had talked too much during this interview and said that she was afraid she had talked more about herself and her family than about Bobby. I told her that this was perfectly all right, that this was a chance for her to talk and to tell me how she

felt about things. Mrs. B said that it made her feel better just to be able to talk and that some people she knew had asked her why she would want to go and talk about Bobby and the problems she was having. She said that she just could not keep all her concerns bottled up inside, that she did not think it was healthy. I agreed with mother and assured her of the confidentiality of things she told me and said that I would be looking forward to seeing her next week and that we would talk more then.

Following this first interview with Mrs. Bolczek the center wrote the superintendent of Mark State School asking whether it might be possible for him to hold the space for Bobby until the center's study had been completed and requesting a report of the school's findings and a statement of the child's response to the institution. In reply the center received a statement of the dates of admission and discharge, one sentence which confirmed the mother's statement that the school had thought Bobby to be emotionally disturbed and a request that the center send a summary of its study, diagnosis and recommendations to the state school.

Finding this information of little help in their own planning, the center arranged for Bobby to be given a series of psychological tests. The psychologist described Bobby in the following terms:

> This is a sturdily-built, stocky boy who appears somewhat short for his age. He has a round, full face, closely cropped dark red hair. The child's speech is markedly infantile. On the day of testing he wore his Sunday clothes, complete with white shirt, bowtie, jacket, and long pants. Though proud of it, he did not seem particularly comfortable in this attire. The most noticeable thing about this child is the way he looks at everything out of the corner of his pale, almost lifeless-appearing eyes. There is a strong suspicion that he has a visual defect which should be checked out as soon as possible. Bobby has a very short attention span and throughout the testing session was extremely distractible.

Bobby's tests responses were quite erratic and occasionally interspersed with bizarre verbalizations and meaningless chatter. He obtained an I.Q. score of 80 on the Stanford-Binet but the psychologist was not sure to what extent both emotional and visual difficulties had interfered with his performace. (A year and a half earlier the child was supposed to have had an I.Q. of 64.)

Mrs. Bolczek, returning for her second interview, seemed much more relaxed and better able to talk about Bobby and to ask questions about things which had been bothering her. She was particularly concerned about the fluctuations in the boy's behavior when on some days she saw him as easily managed and controlled while on others he was "just plain ornery." The worker asked Mrs. Bolczek to explain what she meant by "ornery," saying that she did not quite understand what mother meant by that. Thus questioned, Mrs. Bolczek gave a fairly detailed description of Bobby's impulsive and changeable behavior. At times he seemed listless and disinterested and the next minute he would try to run away from her when she had him out on the street. She described his intense head banging, episodes in which he tried to scratch his brother Bernie and a recent recurrence of bed wetting.

Asked how she handled this behavior Mrs. Bolczek told that she knew she ought to discipline him since he must learn to listen like any other child, but that she hestitated to hit him because she felt sorry for the boy. To a direct question about discipline Mrs. Bolczek explained that she would usually put him to bed early, but then added with an embarrassed smile, that she would occasionally "crack him one on his behind," quickly adding that this isn't really hitting him since it was just meant to remind him that he had to behave.

At this point the mother suddenly changed the topic and after seeking permission to ask a question, inquired about the children's ward in the local psychiatric hospital. She wanted to know what sort of children were sent there and asked whether Bobby might conceivably be admitted. The worker explained that the children on that ward were emotionally disturbed, that they were patients for whom hospital care was thought more effective than outpatient treatment and that she could not tell whether this was the place for Bobby until a more extensive study of the child had been completed.

Since mother had raised this question and though it had not previously been discussed, the worker asked how Mrs. Bolczek would feel if admission to a psychiatric inpatient service were to be a recommendation. Mother initially evaded an answer by focusing on the financial situation, saying that she and her husband had not even thought of the hospital as a place for Bobby because they viewed it as much too expensive for them. When told that fees were set in relation to the family's ability to pay, mother said that in that case she would like it if Bobby could be admitted there "because it would be nearer." She continued that she thought that the sooner something could be done for Bobby the better and that she did not want his case to drag on the way her sister's had when she was sick. Mrs. B now mentioned the story of her sister who had at first been at Mark State School until her grandmother had taken her out and who eventually had to be admitted to a state mental hospital because the family could not cope with her. It was obvious that Mrs. Bolczek was relating this history to Bobby's situation for she added that she would like something done for Bobby rather than let a similar development take place with him.

Somewhat later in this hour when discussing Bobby's early development Mrs. Bolczek spoke of his second year of life which was the time she first noticed that he was different from other children. She spoke of the illnesses Bobby had had and of her own repeated hospitalizations. She thought that all of this had been very upsetting to the child and that it probably had a great deal to do with his current condition.

From this Mrs. Bolczek again turned to an enumeration of all the things Bobby could do, how fond he was of books and what great pride he took in his personal appearance. From this she briefly turned to a discussion of the other two children, focusing on their achievements and stressing what normal children they were.

At the end of the hour an appointment was made for father to come in the following week. Mrs. Bolczek thought that her husband would be glad to come and that she only hoped that he would be able to talk freely since he did not do much talking at home. Mrs. B again assured the worker how very, very glad she was that she had come to the center and that she really felt that she had come to the right place.

Interview with the father. When Bobby's father came for his interview he seemed quite depressed, both when talking about Bobby and in discussing his life situation in general. He spoke in a slow, hesitant way, sometimes searching for the right word to describe Bobby. He related the many things he did with the boy, such as trying to teach him to play with toys and taking him out for walks, but when the worker commented on the great deal of time he was spending with Bobby Mr. Bolczek immediately became unsure of himself and wondered if this was the right thing for him to do. In fact, he now tried to deny that he spent a great deal of time with his boy and only after the worker assured him that this was all right was he able to say that he liked Bobby a great deal, felt a little sorry for him and wanted to give him as much time as he possibly could.

In talking about Bobby, Mr. Bolczek tried to convince the worker of the many things this boy could do and how he had improved since coming back from the state school. Many of these accomplishments seemed exaggerated, however, and when the worker asked for details Mr. B would usually admit that Bobby's achievements were really quite limited. For example, father told that Bobby knew the days of the week but when asked in what way he knew them he said that he could give the correct answer when asked what the family usually did on a certain day.

The worker asked Mr. B when he had noticed that Bobby was different and father too placed it at about eighteen months of age. Asked if anything special had happened around this time, Mr. B said that the family had moved several times and that it had really been a hard period for them. Bobby had been sick, father and mother had been busy fixing up the house, and father had been under great pressure in his new job. Mr. Bolczek said that he was afraid that at that time they had not given Bobby as much attention as they should have and he too seemed to relate this to the child's current problems.

Mr. B thought that maybe their biggest mistake had been moving back to the city after having had a home in New York. "Maybe," he said, "it would have been better if we had not come back at all." Asked to elaborate, Mr. B told of his wife's homesickness, of the good job he had to give up in order to make the move, and of the fact that since that time things had not gone at all well for them. He spoke with some depression of the many moves they had made since that time and of the disappointment with their present house. In a somewhat fatalistic way Mr. B said that one never knew how things were going to work out.

In talking of his having had to drop out of college after two years for economic reasons, Mr. B denied that this had been a difficult step for him, explained that it had been the only thing he could have done, and again appeared very depressed and discouraged. Mr. B then said that people were not the same any more, that they had changed. The worker asked what he meant by this and Mr. B added that people were not as friendly as they used to be. "You never can count on them, one day they are nice and the next day you really don't know what they are going to do."

Toward the end of the hour the worker tried to explain the operations of the center but did not make another appointment with Mr. Bolczek. Instead they discussed the next visit which was scheduled for mother, and father expressed the hope that they and the center would soon come to some definite plan for Bobby, about whom he was quite anxious and for whom he wanted to do the right thing.

The last intake interview. At her next interview Mrs. Bolczek expressed more concern about Bobby. He had been fussy all week and one night had cried a great deal. Though he would usually not permit his mother to look into his mouth or throat he had finally let her inspect and she had discovered a bad tooth which seemed to be giving him trouble. Mrs. B had taken Bobby to a dentist who had advised immediate extraction.

Mrs. Bolczek had not let the dentist pull the tooth but wanted to wait until she had had a chance to talk with the worker at the center about this. She didn't know whether this would be all right and how Bobby would react to it. The worker discussed with the mother what the dentist had said. Mrs. B reported that he had described it as a relatively easy job and that he had pictured the alternative as considerable pain and suffering. When the worker suggested that it sounded as though the extraction had to be made mother quickly agreed and now wondered whether she should tell the dentist anything about Bobby and his problems. The worker suggested that this might be a good idea since it would help the dentist cope with Bobby, and Mrs. B thought that this was what she would do.

In seeking a more detailed history of Bobby's earlier years the worker obtained additional information about the child's vision. Mrs. B had begun to wonder about Bobby's eyes when he was about four months old and later when he started to walk she had noticed his bumping into things and wondered whether he could see all right. His eyes had been examined and when he was about twenty months old he was hospitalized for corrective eye surgery. At the time she had been told that the operation had been a success but now mother was again wondering whether the child could really see all right because he held objects very close to his eyes in order to study them and looked at things in a strange fashion.

The worker asked how mother felt about Bobby and was told that theirs was a very close family. Mother liked all of her children but when she thought about Bobby she thought she felt closest to him. If anything should happen to him, she said, she would really not know how she could go on. She spoke of having recently watched a television show about crippled and spastic children and that she had been so thankful that Bobby's condition was not that bad. Mrs. B thought that at this point she could still control Bobby and care for him quite well but she was anxious about what might happen in the future.

After speaking briefly and with much praise of her in-laws who were so friendly and giving, Mr. Bolczek expressed some of her concern about her husband. She felt that he was depressed and moody and that she could not understand his almost fanatic need to be neat and clean, a trait which she thought Bobby had picked up from his father, since the child always wanted his hands wiped and frequently insisted on sweeping the floor.

Asked why she thought her husband was depressed, Mrs. B expressed the belief that it was because he had promised her so many things before they were married but really could not give them to her now. She maintained that she really did not care about these things, immediately adding that all of her brothers and sisters had nicer homes and more things than she, and then again pointing out that she realized how hard her husband was working, how good he was to her and how this was all she wanted. The trouble, she said, was her inability to convince her husband that she was satisfied and happy.

There was some more discussion of the family's financial situation, their relationship to the in-laws and Mr. B's early college experience, and then Mrs. Bolczek stopped suddenly and said to the worker, "You are a wonderful listener." The worker answered that she was interested in Mr. and Mrs. Bolczek and in Bobby and that the more Mrs. B could tell about the family the better the center might be able to help. Mrs. B now spoke briefly about the other two children and admitted that she was sometimes worried about Barbara, who seemed to be like her husband, quiet, not one to argue, but tending to keep things inside. The girl too was described as moody and rather unfriendly and in this Mrs. B again saw traits she recognized in her husband. The older boy, Bernie, was also described like father, retiring and not willing to stick up for himself. Having likened the other children to her husband, she now said that Bobby was very much like herself, "very nervous, yet friendly with everyone."

At the end of the hour Mrs. B spoke of the difference between her own parents and her husband's parents. She said that her own father had always insisted that his children be busy all of the time. When he had seen them sitting around doing nothing he would think up jobs for them, while her husband's family had been quite different. They had been able to relax, and Mrs. B felt that life was more enjoyable in that family. It was only when she had married her husband that she learned how to relax, for when she was first married she had the need to be busy with something every single minute of the day.

The worker now explained the next steps in the center's procedures, including a psychiatric evaluation for Bobby and a staff conference, after which Mrs. B and her husband would be invited to return for a discussion of future plans.

PLANNING FOR THE FAMILY

In preparation for their staff discussion the center wrote another letter to the superintendent of the state school asking for more detailed information on Bobby's behavior and adjustment while at that institution. In reply they received a communication which mentioned the child's behavior on admission and his condition at discharge, giving the center staff the impression that the school had no other record on the child.

When the worker called in order to make an appointment for Bobby's psychiatric evaluation Mrs. B asked whether worker could advise her on something. Over the telephone she explained that they had visited Mrs. B's brother over the week end. This brother lives in the country and Bobby seemed to enjoy the freedom of playing outdoors and running around. When the uncle noticed this he suggested that he might be able to persuade the child's maternal grandfather to advance enough money so that the Bolczeks could buy a home in the country. Mrs. B thought that this would be very nice for the whole family but that the move would be made mainly for Bobby's sake. The worker explained that she could not make a recommendation at that stage but assured Mrs. B that this was information the staff would keep in mind in their forthcoming discussion. At this Mrs. B expressed her thanks and said that she knew the worker would take care of matters but that she wanted the worker to know that this step was something they thought they could take if the center wanted them to.

The child psychiatrist who examined Bobby the following week saw him as a hyperactive child who had some difficulty concentrating on any one activity for more than a short period of time. He noted the boy's tendency to order his world in a compulsive manner which was reflected in his need for cleanliness and in his play activities. The child's visual difficulty was quite apparent to the psychiatrist and when he later spoke with Mrs. Bolczek he urged her to have an eye examination as soon as possible. The psychiatrist spoke with Mrs. Bolczek for some time, got her to express some of her concerns of which she had previously spoken, and then asked whether the parents would be interested in an ongoing contact with the center which would be designed to help them with some of the day-to-day management problems which he knew would arise because of Bobby's physical and emotional problems. Mrs. Bolczek seemed very relieved that no mention was made of further institutionalization, but she was quite surprised when the psychiatrist told her that ongoing contact would be with someone other than the worker whom she had seen up to then because that worker was leaving the center.

Mrs. Bolczek telephoned her worker early next day ostensibly to ask for the name of an ophthalmologist to whom she might take Bobby.

She had a number of questions which she had not felt free to ask the psychiatrist. She wanted to know whether the center would recommend a pediatrician to whom she could take Bobby for regular checkups and inquired whether the psychiatrist would want to see Bobby again at some later time.

Mrs. Bolczek exclaimed how much better she felt since she had talked to the child psychiatrist whom she praised for his skill and patience. When worker replied that she was pleased mother had come to the center for help Mrs. B rather casually remarked that the psychiatrist had told her that the worker would be leaving in a few months. The worker had not been aware that this had been told to Mrs. B but confirmed this fact and assured mother that she would make arrangements for a transfer to someone else and promised to be in touch with mother in order to tell her the details.

Promptly following the psychiatrist's recommendation, Mrs. Bolczek took Bobby to the ophthalmologist who had been recommended by the center. A rather thorough examination revealed that Bobby had a severe visual defect which was probably of a progressive nature. In a letter he was later to write to the center, the ophthalmologist reported that he had found indications of a fair amount of optic atrophy and that he considered it problematical how much vision this child would develop within the next few years. He suggested that special schooling be considered, at least in the form of sight-saving class, and added that the boy might eventually be a candidate for the regional school for the blind. In the meantime he had prescribed glasses designed to give Bobby some correction, though he doubted that they would markedly improve his vision.

A few days later, but before the ophthalmologist's report was available to them, the members of the center's professional staff who had been involved with this family met for a conference. They recorded the impression that Bobby was a child with possible brain damage whose history gave evidence of developmental lag in both physical and emotional areas. Because Bobby had recently shown a spurt in development it was felt that the prognosis for the future was good. The staff felt that Bobby's emotional disturbance stemmed from his many traumatic experiences and was not the result of pathology in the family relationships. Mrs. Bolczek was seen as a well-integrated, capable woman who, though she appeared to be the dominant member of the family, seemed to handle relationships quite well. It was felt that Mr. Bolczek was less decisive and more apt to give up easily but that he, with his wife's support, seemed to function quite adequately. In order to assure an ongoing contact the case was assigned to a new staff member who was to see the mother on a monthly basis.

HOPES AND DISAPPOINTMENTS

The new staff member assigned to the Bolczek family was a man, who saw mother for the first time a month after the staff conference. Mrs. B was friendly and readily able to relate to him. She told him about the visit to the ophthalmologist and asked whether he would get in touch with that physician and get the details of the examination. She reported that she had been told that Bobby had astigmatism and "pale eye muscles" and then mentioned the glasses which had been prescribed. Mrs. B wondered whether the visual difficulty might have been the whole problem all the time, but then was able to answer her own question by saying that she knew that there were many factors which needed to be explored and understood. (It must here be pointed out that the ophthalmologist's letter was by now in the case record but it is not know whether Mrs. B's worker was aware of this.)

Mrs. Bolczek recapitulated for her new worker some of the descriptive material about the child's behavior, stressing both the negative and positive aspects of Bobby. She was able to say that he was often a nuisance around the house, that he was hard to handle and frequently disobedient, adding for the first time that she believed in strict discipline and obedience. She said that she had been brought up in that fashion and felt that it was the right way to bring up children. She seemed to seek approval for this point of view and the worker commented that children appreciate loving firmness. To this Mrs. B replied that Bobby was always appreciative and cooperative, adding that "in many ways he's my most satisfactory child."

Mrs. Bolczek now wanted to know whether she should enroll Bobby in kindergarten and the worker suggested that she go ahead and register him so that he would not lose his place and that the decision whether to send him could then be made later on.

Following this first visit the worker recorded that mother seemed to have enjoyed her interview and appeared appreciative of the opportunity to talk over her problems. He added that the family appeared to have many strengths.

The worker now had a telephone conversation with the ophthalmologist who had seen Bobby. They discussed the possibility of referring the child to the School for the Blind and the ophthalmologist suggested that the Association for the Blind might be of help in this. A further telephone call confirmed that the School for the Blind had a class for children of Bobby's age, though it was felt that he should be enrolled as a day student because residence at the school was inadvisable due to Bobby's emotional difficulties and traumatic history. These telephone calls were the first of a long series of collateral contacts in which the center had to engage in order to work with the Bolczek family.

When Mrs. Bolczek came for her interview the following month she immediately referred to her earlier discussion with the psychiatrist who had seen Bobby and who, she said, had mentioned the possibility of therapy for Bobby at some later time. Her new worker agreed that this might be something to consider at a later date but Mrs. Bolczek exclaimed, "He needs treatment. I don't know what, but he needs something." She seemed quite distraught at some of the child's most recent behavior but the worker was impressed by the innocuous nature of the things she described. For example, she told how when Bobby drew streetcars, which he did continually and untiringly, he insisted on drawing them as ovals. The worker suggested that there must be something else which was upsetting Mrs. B and after much hesitation and embarrassment she told about the boy's unusual interest in the bare feet of women. "Wherever he finds a woman with her shoes off Bobby will go and fondle her feet and this is very embarrassing to me." It seemed that mother saw some sexual implications in this activity for she spontaneously pointed out that Bobby was a "good boy who never played with himself."

The worker had the impression that Mrs. Bolczek was looking for support in prohibiting Bobby this activity. She claimed never to have said anything to Bobby about this and accepted the worker's suggestion that she place some verbal limits on him to see whether he could obey this prohibition.

Mrs. Bolczek now began to enumerate some of Bobby's difficulties, spoke of his temper tantrums and screaming spells and mentioned his inability to get along with his siblings for any length of time. She also mentioned that he frequently stumbled, had poor coordination, and bumped into things. Then she discussed his dental condition and that he had had two teeth pulled the week before.

The interviewer pointed out that Mrs. Bolczek seemed to be wondering just what was wrong with Bobby. He said that the child certainly had a variety of difficulties, some of which might be related while others had no connection. He now mentioned the center's contact with the ophthalmologist and said that at this point Bobby's intellectual and emotional state could not be definitely determined but that his visual difficulties were an important factor and that for the time being it would be well if he and Mrs. Bolczek could focus on this problem and discuss plans for the child in terms of his being a visually handicapped youngster. This led to a discussion of school and the interviewer and Mrs. Bolczek agreed that at least for the present Bobby should have a chance in a regular kindergarten placement though sight saving classes might need to be considered at a later time.

Mrs. Bolczek seemed relieved to have the question of visual handicap as a focus and entered with apparent investment into the plans for Bobby's schooling. The rest of the hour was spent in some discussion of Mrs. Bolczek's feelings about her family and in-laws, complaints about her brother, who ignored and avoided them because of Bobby's condition, and an admission of how lonely she felt because the neighbors would not have much to do with her. When she said that she could not visit friends because it was difficult to take Bobby along, the interviewer remarked how angry she must feel at Bobby for keeping her from her friends and family, but Mrs. Bolczek denied any such feelings and assured the worker of her great love and devotion to the child, pointing out that she bought only the very best of everything for him. This was followed with the declaration that she had such a wonderful husband and that it was he who helped her keep going. She also said how much better she had been feeling since receiving help at the counseling center, adding, "I don't feel guilty about anything I have done. Before I sent Bobby to the state school on the doctor's advice I talked it all over with my priest."

Following this Mrs. Bolczek talked more about plans for kindergarten for Bobby and wondered if she should tell the teacher about Bobby's condition. The counselor suggested that they might talk about this question some more before a decision needed to be made and assured Mrs. B that the center would help her in getting Bobby into the school.

During the summer months with the older children not in school, Mrs. Bolczek brought Bobby and his siblings to the center and when the counselor wondered whether Mrs. B had to show him that she was capable of producing healthy children, she protested that the only reason she brought them was that there was no one with whom to leave them. With all three children at home Mrs. B had difficulty maintaining peace and order. She told the counselor how distraught she was and how much she wished that school would begin. She told of Bobby's impulsivity and difficulty in getting along with his brother Bernie and said, "I wonder if I am spoiling him because I let him get away with so much. He gets into things and makes an awful mess." Immediately following this she said, "But he does know all the cars by sight and the number of the streetcars and where they go." The counselor reflected that Mrs. B was still quite confused about whether Bobby was or was not mentally retarded.

One day Bernie and Bobby had fought so much that Mrs. Bolczek had taken the older boy aside and asked him if he wanted her to send Bobby away again. To this Bernie had answered with a decided "No," assuring her that he would try harder to get along with Bobby, but on the following day they were fighting just as much as before. The counselor tried to point out how Bernie too must find it difficult to have Bobby constantly annoying him and that the fact that Mrs. B sometimes asked Bernie to stay in the house to play with Bobby instead of going out and joining children his age was not helping Bernie to feel more kindly toward his younger brother. The counselor explained how the older children might feel resentful. He stressed that putting it up to Bernie whether or not Bobby should be sent away again was not a fair question because Bernie undoubtedly had very mixed feelings toward Bobby, feelings of both fondness and anger, which probably everyone in the family shared to some extent.

Mrs. Bolczek responded to this by saying that she was afraid she was ruining Bernie's childhood, and then she added, "Maybe I am disturbed. My father is very sick with liver trouble and I have been upset and guess I feel things more than otherwise." She talked about her father's condition and that she could not get to see him because it was impossible to take the children along since they bothered him. The counselor offered reassurance about Mrs. B's own responsibilities and wondered whether there was realistically anything she could do for her father. This seemed to relax Mrs. Bolczek a little and she began talking about Bobby again.

Mrs. B's sister had told her that she thought Bobby should go to a private residential school for visually handicapped children. Mrs. B had answered that the people at the counseling center thought that it would be best for Bobby to be with his mother. There seemed considerable pride in her voice as she told of this. Then she said all of a sudden, "Is there any way we can get help if coming to the center does no good? Are there any hospitals?" The counselor reassured Mrs. Bolczek, saying that he knew how confusing things must be for her but that it was necessary that they work one step at a time, that the first thing they needed to do was to plan for Bobby's schooling in the fall. This led Mrs. Bolczek to talk about school and she again wondered what she should tell Bobby's teacher. The interviewer suggested she tell that the center felt most of Bobby's difficulties at this time to be with his eyes. Mrs. B wondered what she should say about the fact that Bobby had been away to the state school, and the counselor said that there was no need to mention this unless the school people asked her, which was unlikely. He stressed that the current reality was that she was getting help at the center and that Bobby was a patient of the ophthalmologist and that the center and the eye doctor were working on the case together. Mrs. B now related that she would leave Bobby with a local baby-sitting nursery while she went shopping and that there he did very well. Because of this she felt that he would also do well in school, but the counselor reminded her that when Bobby went for more than a brief period and every day she would undoubtedly encounter different problems.

At the end of this hour the counselor discussed plans for the months to come which were to be based on treating the situation as a family matter so that father too should come in for interviews. Once a month the center wanted to re-evaluate Bobby to assess his progress and possibly help in obtaining a better understanding of his problems. In addition the center was going to contact the school and to offer the school personnel any help they could give. Mrs. Bolczek seemed pleased with this plan.

When school opened the counselor at the center contacted Bobby's teacher and described Bobby as a child with visual difficulties who also manifested some behavior problems. The teacher appeared very understanding and welcomed the center's offer to be available for consultation. The counselor brought out the fact that Bobby would probably not be a problem in terms of disrupting the class, though he might well behave somewhat differently than most of the other children.

After Bobby had been in school for one week Mrs. Bolczek came to the center and told the counselor that the teacher had called her to say that she could not handle Bobby in her class. Bobby had done fairly well for the first few days but had then become disruptive, aggressive, and disobedient. Mrs. B vacillated between criticizing the teacher and her inability to cope with the child and sympathizing with her, knowing how difficult Bobby could be. Again she would jump from talking about Bobby's difficulties to how bright he was, then expressing some doubts about his visual difficulties since he was able to see streetcar numbers quite well.

Because of the teacher's complaint Mrs. Bolczek had kept Bobby home from school, though this had not been one of the school's requests. Mrs.

Bolczek thought she would keep Bobby home and send him to parochial school in the following year where, she thought, they could handle him better. She expressed her conviction that teachers should hit children if they deserved it, that she was not one of those parents who disapproved of teachers hitting children. She then told the counselor for the first time that on several occasions when Bobby had become very exasperating she had hit him very hard, but quickly added that she wondered whether this was the right thing to do.

The counselor tried to reassure her about hitting Bobby because he did not see Mrs. Bolczek as a particularly punitive mother who would hurt the child. He offered to call Bobby's teacher, but Mrs. Bolczek protested and said that she did not think this was necessary because she was planning to keep Bobby at home. The counselor wondered whether mother was really ready to let Bobby go to school, and Mrs. Bolczek was able to admit that she had mixed feelings about this. Counselor now stressed how important it was for Bobby to attend school as long as they were willing to keep him, even though it was difficult.

Because this seemed a crucial period, another appointment was made for the following week at which time Mrs. Bolczek seemed very distraught. She had been talking to some friends and relatives who had given her mixed and contradictory advice, each one remembering a child with "similar problems" and talking of the treatment which had been given to him. One child had been put on a tranquilizer while another had had a "brain waves test." Mrs. Bolczek wondered whether any of these things might do some good for Bobby, who had been "impossible" over the week end.

The counselor tried to stress that what Bobby needed was a good and understanding mother and a pleasant home, both of which he had. He pointed out that the doctors who were taking care of Bobby were trying to do what was best for him and that treatments or tests which were used on other children with different problems were not necessarily indicated for her child. Though Mrs. Bolczek accepted this she seemed disappointed and when the counselor again suggested a meeting for the following week she said that she could not come in that frequently and an appointment for two weeks hence was agreed upon.

Instead of coming for her appointment Mrs. Bolczek called the center by telephone to cancel, saying that Bobby was back in school, the teacher having called her to ask that he be sent back. Mrs. Bolczek's counselor now called Bobby's teacher who told him that Bobby had a very short attention span, that she was worried because other children in class tended to laugh at him. He engaged in impulsive and sometimes irresponsible activities and the counselor tried to give the teacher support in setting firm limits and enforcing them consistently.

With the previous appointment cancelled by Mrs. Bolczek, the counselor called her to arrange for a new appointment. For a week things had gone fairly smoothly and mother seemed somewhat reassured to have Bobby back in school. She wondered, however, whether the teacher "doesn't really suspect that Bobby is more than just a visual problem." She said, "We are fooling her and she is fooling us," to which the counselor replied that the teacher knew Bobby was a behavior problem and difficult to handle and that the only thing the teacher did not know was that he had been away at state school. An appointment was then arranged for the counselor to see Bobby's father, who came in the following week.

Mr. Bolczek seemed relaxed and communicated quite freely with the counselor. He spoke of the improvements he had seen in Bobby during the last few months and now that he was in school he was even getting along better with his siblings. Mr. Bolczek spoke warmly of his wife and then related how in the past when they had seen various physicians about Bobby's condition they had never received any help, adding how much they thought they got out of their contact with the center.

Since Mr. Bolczek painted such a rosy picture the counselor stated that things must have been very hard for them in the past but wondered whether there were not still many difficulties which they had to face right now. Mr. B denied this, saying that the progress he saw made up for all past difficulties. The counselor now pointed out that Bobby's vision was very much of a problem and that it was unlikely to become better in the near future, but again Mr. Bolczek insisted that Bobby's glasses made a lot of difference, that he was less clumsy and stumbled less frequently. The counselor wondered whether father would like to become more involved in the family's work with the center but Mr. Bolczek replied that he himself really had no questions and that he thought his wife was getting all the help they needed. He said that he would agree to come in occasionally if the center thought this was necessary but then stressed how difficult it was for him to get away from work, leaving the counselor with the impression that this man was really quite resistive to receiving help.

When Mrs. Bolczek came for her interview two weeks later she was obviously upset and said that things were going very badly with Bobby. In a rapid and excited manner she told that Bobby was no longer in school. She first gave the impression that he had been expelled because he had not behaved, but when the counselor asked mother to explain just what happened it turned out that one day Mrs. Bolczek had picked Bobby up after school and he had had his jacket on upside down. She said, "Poor kid, he just looked terrible and the other children laughed at him. They were talking about him. I don't know what they were saying but I know they were talking about him!" At that moment Mrs. Bolczek had decided not to send Bobby back to school. The day before the interview the teacher had called her to ask why Bobby was not in school and Mrs. B had told her that she thought he was too much for teacher to handle. Mrs. B went on to blame the teacher, saying to the counselor that she had done a poor job and should have been able to help Bobby more than she did.

During all this Mrs. Bolczek appeared very anxious, spoke in a rapid fashion and wrung her hands continuously. She complained about the condition of their house and then returned to talking about Bobby, complaining how difficult he was to handle and that spanking did no good at all. She commented that when she hit the child he always tried to shield his head and added, "Why do children like this always shield their head?" The counselor wondered what she meant by "children like this" and Mrs. Bolczek somewhat sheepishly said that she had noticed children at Mark State School behaving in this fashion. The counselor commented that Mrs. Bolczek still was not sure whether Bobby did or did not belong in the state school but she did not pick this up and continued to tell about her disciplinary problems with him. She reported that the week before she had tied Bobby in a chair because there had been something she just had to get done. He had managed to escape from this confinement and though she had started out to report this in connection with her complaint about how hard he was to manage, she now switched and used it as an example of how clever and bright Bobby can be.

Mrs. Bolczek then complained about how difficult it was to get Bobby into bed at night and then she suddenly said, "I don't want to send him back to Mark. I want to keep him with us. We were so unhappy when he was away." Since Mrs. Bolczek was becoming progressively more anxious, the counselor interrupted the flow of her almost constant talk and reminded her of the plan for counseling on which they had agreed. He reminded her that they had talked of the fact that difficult periods had to be anticipated and stressed that trying to understand and help Bobby was a matter of many years. He turned to some explanations of the need for activity and exploration of children Bobby's age and of how excessive spanking and restraint would only have the effect opposite to that which mother desired.

Mrs. Bolczek responded to all this by again raising the question whether there was not some medicine which would help Bobby and the counselor repeated that they had to rely on the medical opinion of the people who had examined Bobby.

Returning to a period of complaining about the teacher, who should have been able to help Bobby more with his getting dressed, Mrs. Bolczek brought up the possibility of enrolling Bobby in a church-connected school for deaf children where, she had been told, they also accepted a few children who were blind or mentally retarded. The counselor pointed out that Mrs. B was again unsure of just what was wrong with Bobby and stated that he did not believe that this particular school was suitable for Bobby's needs. Mrs. Bolczek, however, was ready with an alternative and wondered whether the Catholic Association for the Blind might be able to provide a school experience for Bobby. Not being familiar with this agency, the counselor promised to look into the possibility. He then added that he thought it was important that he saw Mrs. Bolczek more frequently and she readily accepted the idea of coming in every other week from now on.

Local elections were held on the day of Mrs. Bolczek's next appointment. She came in and immediately began to talk about the election until the counselor interrupted her to wonder whether she had really come to talk about that. After a moment's hesitation Mrs. Bolczek again began talking quite rapidly, relating that Bobby was doing all sorts of things now that he used to do but hadn't for some time. He stumbled a lot, refused to wear shoes, bumped his head against the bed at night, broke things, messed with water, and got into everything. She said, "He has started to mess up all my pots and pans again and that's why we had sent him away in the first place."

Immediately following this Mrs. Bolczek changed the subject and mentioned how Bobby was getting along so much better with his brother and sister and then asked whether the counselor did not think she should be changing physicians since Bobby was due a physical checkup, but before the counselor could respond to this she talked about the physicians whom they had seen and who had recommended that Bobby be sent to the state school. She spoke of an eighteen-year-old boy about whom she had recently heard and who was said to be mentally retarded and unable to keep a job. She wondered whether Bobby would be like this, and at this point the counselor went over the diagnostic impression of the center staff, repeating much of what had been gone over several times during earlier visits. He told her that Bobby was seen as a child with a very mild type of cerebral palsy whose main difficulties were in vision, co-ordination, and developmental retardation.

The counselor pointed out that he knew how difficult it was to take care of Bobby and to live with some of his behavior, much of which seemed appropriate for a child much younger than he. Mrs. B again complained about the destructive aspects of Bobby's behavior which were rapidly ruining the house until she hardly cared about it any more. The counselor tried to have Mrs. B talk more about her own feelings and she mentioned how much she had done in taking care of her invalid mother and then added that she knew that the way she felt affected the way she handled the children. The counselor wondered whether water play and activities involving the pots and pans was really such a problem, but Mrs. Bolczek could only reply that the counselor could not possibly understand since he did not have to live with Bobby twenty-four hours a day.

When the counselor discussed this case with his supervisor following this interview both agreed that they had been overly optimistic about this mother and the family situation. They thought that their own initial anger at the way the child had been sent to the state school on the basis of a mis-diagnosis had blinded them to the essential rigidity of this mother so that they had not taken the parent-child relationship fully enough into account, ignoring how much it must have contributed to the whole picture. It had taken almost a year for the center staff to recognize that Mrs. Bolczek was really quite punitive with Bobby and that some of her handling had many irrational aspects. Both counselor and his supervisor were concerned about Mrs. Bolczek's recent admission of hitting the child and tying him to a chair. It was decided that Mrs. Bolczek needed more help than she was presently receiving with bi-monthly interviews and it was decided to increase the frequency of her visits.

Mrs. Bolczek did not accept the offer for increasing the frequency of her visits and her relationship to the center was further complicated by the fact that the counselor who had seen her for the past six months was leaving so that the case had to be transferred to someone else. Though she claimed not to mind being transferred and assured her old worker how much she was getting out of coming to the center, she never seemed to be able to form a relationship to her new counselor who continued to see her on a monthly basis for another year. In reviewing the record from here on one is struck by the repetition of the same complaints, met by attempts at giving her reassurance and support, occasional periods of apparent improvement followed by sessions in which Mrs. Bolczek was thoroughly discouraged. We shall not attempt to follow the details of these interviews but will instead focus on the center's collateral activities designed to help the Bolczek family find a suitable school placement for Bobby.

Work with the community. The agency for blind children about which Mrs. Bolczek had inquired turned out to be a branch of the school for the deaf which the center could not see as a suitable placement for Bobby. Mrs. Bolczek very much wanted her boy in a private school largely because of her resentment toward the experience she had had with the public school. Before the first appointment with her new counselor and without direct help from the center, the Bolczeks had replied to an inquiry from Mark State School to the effect that they wanted Bobby dropped from the parole list since they did not ever intend to send Bobby back. The fact that the state school had kept a bed available for Bobby had apparently complicated things for the Bolczeks ever since the child had come home and Mrs. Bolczek reported that once they had made the decision to give the place up they had felt so much better.

The center contacted the local branch of the State Association for the Blind in order to get help in finding a kindergarten situation for Bobby which would be satisfactory. Two kindergartens run by local churches were recommended but when this was transmitted to Mrs. Bolczek she decided to contact a parochial school which, though it did not have an official kindergarten, had an ungraded class into which Bobby might fit. Her priest had encouraged her to try that school and assured her that there Bobby would be well taken care of. Without discussing this with the center, Mrs. Bolczek enrolled Bobby in that setting, where he was in the same room with children one and two years older than he, a situation which the center did not consider ideal. However, the fact that Mrs. Bolczek had been able to take this step on her own was taken as a positive sign and the center did not intervene.

It soon developed that the kindergarten placement did not work out. Bobby was disruptive and because he could not be controlled he had to be withdrawn from this class. After some vacillation over whether or not to send Bobby to another private school of her own choosing Mrs. Bolczek thought it would be best to keep him at home for another year before trying to enroll him in first grade. The counselor tried to help her accept a plan involving special class in public school and Mrs. Bolczek finally agreed to explore this. The center contacted the special education branch of the local board of education and with the mother's permission sent them a summary of the center's contact and impressions involving Bobby.

With her counselor's help Mrs. Bolczek was able to abandon her earlier plan and to agree to have Bobby entered in public school kindergarten preparatory to his starting in special class at the beginning of the next school year. Both the counselor at the center and the head of the division of special education in the public school system were in frequent contact with the child's teacher and the principal of the school and with this help the school was able to maintain Bobby in the kindergarten although he frequently presented considerable management problems.

During the summer months while Bobby was out of school the Bolczeks managed to find a new home in a neighborhood which gave the children more play space but which also meant that he would no longer be living in the area served by the school into which he was supposed to go. Again Mrs. Bolczek faced the center staff with a *fait accompli,* having decided to enroll Bobby in the local parochial school even though a different special class placement in a public school could have been arranged. Just before admission, however, she had to take Bobby to that school for an evaluation at which point the school decided that he was not suitable for their program. Mrs. Bolczek now came to the center somewhat panicky and last-minute efforts made it possible for Bobby to begin school in a special class of the public school system as had been originally planned.

Because of the last-minute arrangements, the teacher into whose class Bobby was placed had not been informed about his difficulties and she became quite upset when she discovered that instead of a handicapped or defective child she was faced with a boy who also had some major behavior problems. As a result the teacher became quite hostile toward the center, feeling that they had been instrumental in "putting something over on her." Some of this hostility was vented against Bobby's parents, who reacted with confusion and anxiety. Two weeks later Mrs. Bolczek received a letter from the principal of the school advising her that they could no longer handle Bobby and recommending that she withdraw him. This time the school system recommended a reading readiness class in a different public school and several members of the center staff attended a conference at that school prior to Bobby's admission there. This conference had been arranged by the head of the special education department in an attempt to help the personnel at the school to accept Bobby. They were fully informed of Bobby's condition and behavior as well as of his previous school history. A plan was worked out according to which Bobby would attend kindergarten for one hour in the afternoon while his mother would remain in the school building so that she could be on hand in case he had to be removed from class before the hour was up.

Mrs. Bolczek agreed to this plan but a month later reported that she had withdrawn Bobby from the school because she had found it too difficult to go back and forth with him every day.

Bobby was now at home and Mrs. Bolczek reported that his behavior had improved so that she saw no particular need for continuing her contacts with the center. Before terminating the contact, and at her insistence, Bobby was evaluated for conceivable admission to a psychiatric in-patient unit at the local mental hospital. In the course of this study another intelligence test was administered on which Bobby attained an I.Q. rating of 80 but inasmuch as the boy was clearly not psychotic he was not considered suitable for treatment in that hospital setting.

Mrs. Bolczek was informed that the center would be glad to have her reopen the contact at any time she wanted more help, particularly in what was viewed to be another critical period a year later when Bobby's admission to school would again become topical.

The center never heard from the Bolczek family again, but two years after the last visit a request for information was received from another psychiatric hospital and after still another two years, a school for blind children wanted to have a report on the center's contact with the family. We do not know what became of Bobby Bolczek and his family.

X

An Annotated Bibliography of Selected Guides for Parents

THE MANY QUESTIONS, anxieties and doubts of parents of exceptional children and their need for support, advice and help is reflected in the plethora of books which aim to fill this need. Some of these books are popularizations written by professional people, others are accounts written by people who are themselves parents of an exceptional child and who hope that by sharing their experience they might be helpful to other parents in similar situations.

The professional person engaged in counseling parents of exceptional children will need to know something about these books for two reasons. One is that many of the parents he sees will have read one or the other of these books whose real or distorted message may be brought into the counseling session, sometimes constructively at others as as an expression of hostility or resistance. The other reason which makes it desirable for the counselor to be familiar with these guides for parents is that some of them can be used constructively with some parents if they are selected wisely and brought into the helping relationship at the proper time.

A book which discusses reality factors and gives straightforward, practical suggestions, while keeping the feelings of the parents and the emotional development of the child clearly in mind, can do much to further the aim of counseling. Parents who have read a guide or parts of a guide between counseling sessions can react to the suggestions, permitting the counselor to explore which aspects of the discussion they found helpful and which objectionable, and why. A well-written book which faces issues and problems frankly and realistically may help parents look at their own problems since reading about them in print may take them out of the realm of the secretive and embarrassing.

Few people can get the help they need merely by reading a book. Unconscious conflicts and the defenses against them cannot be handled by the do-it-yourself approach on which some of these guides are based. An unacceptable suggestion does not become palatable merely because it is found in a book; a child toward whom a parent has strongly ambivalent feelings does not become completely accepted and loved as

207

the result of a written exhortation. For this reason books can be thought of only as an adjunct to, not as a substitute for professional counseling.

In preparing the following annotated bibliography of selected books addressed to parents of exceptional children, each work was evaluated in the light of three questions: Are the practical suggestions reasonable? Are the emotional feelings and reactions of the parents taken into account? Are the child's emotional reactions considered and discussed? Only for a few of the books reviewed can all three of these questions be answered in the affirmative. Some are good from the point of view of practical, "how-to" advice but ignore emotional aspects; others are overly sentimental and gloss over the difficult realities parents of exceptional children must face in their daily lives.

Before recommending any one book to parents, the professional counselor would do well to obtain first-hand knowledge of how the author handles various questions. It is not as important that the book recommended agree in every detail with the counselor's own orientation as it is that the counselor know what it is he asks the parents to read so he can handle their reactions in terms of the reality presented by the book.

MENTALLY RETARDED CHILDREN

Abraham, W. *Barbara, a Prologue.* New York, London: Rinehart & Company, Inc., 1958.

This case history of a Mongoloid child is written as a letter to her from her father. Often sentimental, it nevertheless does deal with the parents' feelings and could be of some help to a parent of a retarded child.

The question of whether the child should be kept at home or placed in an institution is discussed, and general information about this condition is given. However, the book is descriptive rather than instructive. The emotional problems of the mother, for example, are discussed rather than resolved.

In all, though this first-person account may be of some comfort to parents in a similar situation, it cannot be considered a very valuable source of practical help for them.

Buck, Pearl S. *The Child Who Never Grew.* New York: The John Day Company, 1950.

This is a beautifully written account of the author's experience with her mentally retarded daughter. Its outlook is optimistic, for the book was written to make people realize how unnecessary much of the tragedy is in cases of mentally retarded children. The fact that these children need not be useless members of society is emphasized.

Definitely not a handbook, *The Child Who Never Grew* provides comfort rather than practical information for parents of these exceptional children. The more mature parent might benefit from reading it.

Dittman, Laura. *The Mentally Retarded Child at Home:* A Manual for Parents. United States Department of Health, Education, and Welfare, Social Security Administration, Children's Bureau, 1959.

The author writes: "Undoubtedly, many parents share the satisfaction that so much research and practical program effort is being directed toward improving and understanding the problems and needs of the mentally retarded child. But parents have long been seeking more practical information about day-to-day care."

This pamphlet is meant to provide an end to this search. Information about day-to-day care of the mentally retarded child is given in a direct, yet understanding manner, and should be very helpful to a parent whose child is at home. Problems such as feeding, dressing, and toilet training the child are discussed clearly and realistically, and specific suggestions are offered. Emphasis is placed upon helping the child gain more independence. Emotional problems are discussed to some extent.

The pamphlet is not concerned with such topics as the education of the child. Limited in its scope, it is nevertheless a very valuable source of information about the child at home.

French, E. L., & Scott, J. C. *Child in the Shadows:* A Manual for Parents of Retarded Children. Philadelphia: J. B. Lippincott Company, 1960.

This book begins with a case history, and often uses this device in discussing the problems of the parents of mentally retarded children. A summary after each chapter is often too brief to provide meaningful help for these problems.

Often vague in its discussions and explanations, this book's value as a guide is limited. It examines the child's social maturity in a textbook fashion, and is sometimes confusing in dealing with specific topics like various parental reactions. Little is said about the child's emotional needs.

The section containing questions and answers is often quite good, but its scope is not very wide. Several other books are available on this subject which would be much more helpful to parents of mentally retarded children.

Kirk, S. A., Karnes, Merle, B., & Kirk, Winifred: *You and Your Retarded Child:* A Manual for Parents of Retarded Children. New York: The Macmillan Company, 1955.

This book begins with a chapter on the levels of retardation and a discussion to help parents answer the question, "How retarded is my child?" An extensive checklist of normal child development is included, and parents can compare their children's development to this. The roles of the psychologist and social worker are explained and parents are encouraged to seek professional help if they suspect retardation.

Much of the book is concerned with teaching the parent to help the child help himself. Such topics as eating habits, play, talking, and cleanliness receive much attention. The emotional needs of the child are also considered and specific suggestions are offered.

Several chapters give information and advice about the education of the child, and a listing of public and private schools with special facilities for the mentally retarded is included. The major shortcoming of this book is that it says little about parents' feelings toward the child. Except for that, it should be a useful guide for parents.

Levinson, A. *The Mentally Retarded Child:* A Guide for Parents. New York: The John Day Company, 1952.

The author tries to be both sympathetic and frank in his discussion of attitudes a parent might have toward his mentally retarded child. He does not, however, quite succeed in this attempt, and his advice on the topic is too specific and too brief. His list of *do's* and *dont's* is not sufficient to provide a useful solution to such problems as the parents' shame, bitterness, etc. The emotional needs of the child are dealt with in a similar fashion.

Much of the book is a technical discussion of the many causes of retardation and the anatomy of the brain. These explanations would be of little interest or value to parents concerned with more personal aspects of the problem of mental retardation.

Levinson quickly divides mentally retarded children into the educable and the non-educable by referring to the I.Q. score. He then discusses problems involved in education, but his presentation of these problems seems to be directed more to school administrators than to parents. He doesn't really deal with available resources other than to criticize them.

The section of questions and answers at the end of the book is probably its most valuable chapter. In all, this text would not seem to be very helpful to parents of mentally retarded children.

Loewy, Herta. *The Retarded Child:* A Guide for Parents and Teachers. New York: Staples Press, 1949.

The author of this book feels strongly that parents should begin very early to help the mentally retarded child, and stresses the need for parents to be strong in this matter. She does, however, not give them much advice about how to be "strong," and devotes much of her book to a discussion of practical problems.

Feeding is considered at some length and the quantity and quality of foods receive much attention. The problems involved in play activity and social behavior are treated fairly well but much more extensive information is given about education. This material seems written primarily for teachers, and the author spends much of her time in explaining her method of teaching by using games. Various other methods of teaching speech, handwork, etc. are explored.

The emotional needs of the child receive limited coverage, though the chapter on fear is quite good.

Though a competent study, particularly of education, this book is somewhat limited in its usefulness for parents.

BRAIN-DAMAGED AND CEREBRAL PALSIED CHILDREN

Frank, J. P. *My Son's Story.* New York: Alfred A. Knopf, 1952.

This book was written by the father of a child with cortical atrophy, and is often quite sentimental in its account of this condition. It does contain helpful information about symptoms and diagnostic procedures and gives suggestions to other parents of these exceptional children concerning the need for institutionalization, the necessity for parental adjustment, etc.

Since it is a first-person account, this book may help other parents to see more clearly what they can do for their children and for themselves. It is also somewhat encouraging since it ends with details of the child's learning to walk and to talk. While hopeful, it does not imply that all children with this kind of brain damage will make such progress.

Lewis, R., Strauss, A., & Lehtinen, Laura. *The Other Child.* The Brain Injured Child (rev. ed.). A Book for Parents and Laymen. New York, London: Grune & Stratton, 1960.

This book is more difficult to understand than the average manual for "parents and laymen." Its vocabulary is often quite technical and the authors talk about parents rather than to them.

Various topics, such as language, perception, and behavior are discussed in detail. There are also practical suggestions concerning the education and management of the brain-injured child. Institutions are dealt with at some length.

Often, however, the fact that this is not a very readable book limits its usefulness. It is not a manual for parents so much as it is a textbook about brain-damaged children. Because of the difficulty in reading this book one should hesitate to recommend it to every parent of this kind of exceptional child.

Phelps, W., Hopkins, T., & Cousins, R. *The Cerebral Palsied Child:* A Guide for Parents. New York: Simon & Schuster, 1958.

The vocabulary of this book is more difficult than that of the average manual for parents but the information given should be very useful to parents of the cerebral palsied child.

Physical causes of the disease and early signs and symptoms are discussed with a minimum of technical terminology, and basic kinds of treatment are explained.

Handling the child at home is the main topic of discussion and both the physical and emotional needs of the child are interpreted. Advice is given regarding such problems as feeding and dressing the child, and parents are also told, though briefly, how to handle their own attitudes. The chapter dealing with the child's emotional behavior is quite good, and parents are advised how to discipline the child, how to help him get along with other children, etc.

School programs are evaluated and the question of the child's future is discussed very well.

Several appendices give information about various facilities available for the care and education of the cerebral palsied child.

This book should be very valuable to the parents of cerebral palsied children.

BLIND CHILDREN

Lowenfeld, B. *Our Blind Children:* Growing and Learning with Them. Springfield, Ill.: Charles C Thomas, 1956.

This book is somewhat over-simplified but should be a valuable guide for parents of blind children. Emphasis is placed upon helping the child to gain independence, and practical problems in the care of these exceptional children are discussed.

The chapter on the attitudes of parents is quite good, and the emotional growth of the child is also examined in some detail. The parent is told that child guidance clinics are available and equipped to handle the more serious problems of both parent and child.

The section containing answers to questions parents of blind children often ask is of particular value. Advice is given for problems like the following: Should I punish my blind child? How can I explain sex differences? What about my child's future? Should I learn Braille?

Additional reading is suggested and an annotated list of educational facilities is included.

Parents of blind children would probably find this book very helpful.

Van den Broek, Gertrude. *Guide for Parents of a Preschool Blind Child.* New York: Commission for the Blind of the State Department of Social Welfare, 1951.

This little (48-page) guide is written in a straightforward and rational manner. It covers important areas as the parents' attitudes and reactions and the child's physical, emotional, and intellectual needs. A section presenting norms of social maturity, based on a study of 100 "presumably" normal, blind children is meant to give parents some guidelines on what they can expect from their child at various stages during the preschool years. Since these norms may be inapplicable for any one particular child, the counselor may wish to review these with parents before recommending this booklet.

DEAF CHILDREN

Myklebust, H. R. *Your Deaf Child; a Guide for Parents.* Springfield, Ill.: Charles C Thomas, 1950.

Although it is among the oldest of the guides for parents here discussed, this work by an acknowledged authority in the field of speech and hearing disorders undoubtedly remains one of the best. It deals not only with the facts of deafness in children but also with the parents' emotional reactions and the emotional needs of the child, easily earning a rating of "excellent" on all three of the criteria used in evaluating books for this section.

Parental grief reactions upon first learning that their child is deaf receive realistic and sympathetic discussion, followed by a skillfully-worded coverage of such defenses as denial, projection, over-protection, and rejection. Without attempting to set up spurious norms, the author covers various stages of child development showing how deafness complicates such tasks as learning to eat. The child's needs for consistency, success, independence and discipline are discussed in a straightforward manner and reactions such as jealousy, fear, temper tantrums and thumbsucking receive brief but realistic consideration.

While emotional reactions and needs are successfully presented, the book does not neglect to inform the parents about various causes of deafness, the ways in which a deaf child learns and is taught to communicate, and what they may expect from their child in terms of school achievement and eventual economic self-sufficiency. Lists of organizations, publications, and schools for the deaf conclude this helpful guide.

Although this book was written for parents of children with impaired hearing many of its sections, particularly those on parental reactions and children's emotional needs, might profitably be recommended to any parent of a handicapped child.

MENTALLY ILL CHILDREN

Getz, S. B., & Rees, Elizabeth L. *The Mentally Ill Child:* A Guide for Parents. Springfield, Ill.: Charles C. Thomas, 1957.

This is the first book ever written specifically for parents of children diagnosed as schizophrenic, autistic, or severely disturbed. The language is overly-simplified but some of the information, particularly about parents' attitudes, should be helpful.

The book is, however, confusing in its explanations of emotional illness, and there is no adequate definition of mental illness. The importance of professional help is not emphasized and, indeed, is often minimized. Different theories of the causes and treatment of emotional disorders are of limited value and may serve to confuse the layman.

This book is not about the emotionally disturbed child in general, nor is it concerned with treatment to any great extent. Rather, diagnostic procedures and educational facilities are the authors' main concerns here. While parts of the book might be helpful to parents, the professional person should be circumspect in recommending it.

EXCEPTIONAL CHILDREN (GENERAL)

Directory for Exceptional Children. Boston: Porter Sargent.

This well-known and authoritative directory lists educational and training facilities, schools, homes, clinics, hospitals and services for socially maladjusted, mentaly retarded, emotionally disturbed, orthopedically handicapped, cerebral palsied, speech handicapped, brain-injured, epileptic, cardiac, blind, and deaf children. Brought up-to-date in irregularly appearing new editions, it is a valuable reference for parents and counselors alike.

Stern, Edith M. *The Handicapped Child:* A Guide for Parents. New York: A. A. Wyn, Inc., 1950.

This volume contains separate chapters about children who are blind, deaf, crippled, or retarded, those who have cerebral palsy, epilepsy, a speech handicap, or a long physical illness like rheumatic fever. Every chapter is informative and well-written.

The book is exceptionally good in discussing the parents' attitudes and feelings. Advice is given simply, but frankly; sentimentality is avoided. The author does not merely give a list of *do's* and *dont's* but provides a positive approach for parents to follow in dealing with their own emotions.

Practical as well as emotional problems of exceptional children are well handled. Parents, while shown how to help themselves with many problems, are also told where to get help if they need it.

In dealing with the future of the exceptional child, the author is both encouraging and realistic. In all, one can highly recommend this book as a valuable guide for parents.

GIFTED CHILDREN

Abraham, W. *Common Sense about Gifted Children.* New York: Harper & Brothers, 1958.

On the more practical problems parents of gifted children might face, this book is quite helpful. Its section on education is well presented and includes a lengthy discussion of the advantages and disadvantages of special classes, skipping grades, and various educational programs.

There is very little in the book about the mental health of the parents. Some advice is given concerning such topics as the parent who worries about his child mixing in, and the parent who pushes his child. In such cases the author encourages the parent to listen to his child and to have both affection and respect for him.

After reading this book the reader has little doubt that the author's major concern is for the development of the child's giftedness. The emotional needs of the child are relegated to a position of minor importance and emphasis is placed upon the responsibility of the parents and the community to provide the best educational facilities for these exceptional children.

Brumbaugh, Florence N. & Roshco, B. *Your Gifted Child.* New York: Henry Holt & Company, 1959.

According to the authors of this book, the basic responsibility for developing a child's giftedness rests with the parents. The aim of the book, then, is to help the parents meet this responsibility. Unfortunately, however, the book is so overloaded with vague generalizations and unnecessary examples that this aim often becomes obscured.

The authors also often digress from the topic being presented to go into much detail about a subject which is not really relevant to it. Thus, rather than merely mentioning as an illustrative example that some parents force their gifted children into becoming entertainers, the authors devote much time to discusing specific facts about such parents. The example becomes a separate topic, confusing rather than helpful to the reader.

Some attention is given to parents' attitudes toward gifted children, but the treatment of this subject is both brief and general. A sentence or two containing advice is presented and the subject is then dismissed. The child's emotional needs, too, are not discused at any length.

Part of the book is concerned with education for the gifted child, but there is little discussion of the advantages and disadvantages of special classes, private schools, etc. In all, this book does not really reach its goal of helping parents to accept their "responsibility" to their gifted children.

Cutts, Norma & Mosely, N. *Bright Children:* A Guide for Parents. New York: C. G. Putnam's Sons, 1953.

This book was the first ever written for parents of gifted children. Except for a rather biased discussion of private schools, the information it contains is both interesting and helpful.

Much attention is given to the education of the child and such topics as the bright child in a regular class, skipping grades, and special classes are included. No stand is taken in such matters but a criterion for making decisions is given and should be hepful to parents concerned with these problems.

There is also a fairly lengthy discussion about the emotional needs of the gifted child. Parents' attitudes are more briefly considered.

Problems parents might face in disciplining the bright child, handling sibling rivalry, etc. are treated intelligently. Professional help is suggested if needed, and the parent is advised to consult a private psychologist if a school psychologist is not available.

Less concerned with parents than with the gifted child himself, this book should nevertheless prove quite helpful to parents, particularly in answering their more practical questions.

Strang, Ruth. *Helping Your Gifted Child*. New York: E. P. Dutton & Company, Inc., 1961.

This is the best book for parents of exceptionally bright children currently available. Many problems parents might have are frankly and clearly discussed. Generalizations are avoided, and the individuality of the child is stressed. Examples are used for clarification rather than for decoration.

The book follows the child through adolescence, and is at all times directed to the parent. Since this is so, there is much more discussion of the parents' feelings than is usually found in a book about the gifted child. The emotional needs of the child also receive much attention and emphasis is placed upon the ways in which these needs differ from those of the average child. Professional help is suggested if necessary but parents are encouraged to try to help the child themselves.

Educational problems—special classes, special schools, etc.—are dealt with at some length. Sources of additional information about this subject are given.

Appendices include an annotated bibliography of books about gifted children, a bibliography of books for the child to read, and a list of book clubs.

This book can be recommended without hesitation.

ADOPTED CHILDREN

Raymond, Louise. *Adoption—and after*. New York: Harper & Brothers, 1955.

A well-written book which discusses the various aspects of adoption from both the practical and emotional point of view. The feelings of parents and the reactions of the child are taken into consideration and recognition is given to the help which social agencies are able to give.

Realistically written, the book touches upon many of the complications and crises which may arise in the course of raising an adopted child. The author stresses that all parents encounter problems and that adoptive parents are no exception. A slightly out-dated directory of adoption agencies is appended. This guide has been highly recommended by a number of authorities in the field of adoption.

OTHER ARTICLES AND PAMPHLETS

Fuller, C. W. "Your Child, Maturity and You: A Talk to Parents." *Amer. Ann. Deaf.*, 1962, 107 (3), 320-328.

Mayer, Greta & Hoover, Mary. *When Children Need Special Help with Emotional Problems.* New York: Child Study Assoc. of Amer., 1961.

Spock, B. "On Being a Parent . . . of a Handicaped Child." National Society for Crippled Children and Adults, Parent Series No. 8. Chicago, Ill.: 1961.

Wishik, S. M. "How to Help your Handicapped Child." *Public Affairs Pamphlet* No. 219. New York: Public Affairs Committee, 1955.

References

Abraham, W. A hundred gifted children. *Understanding the child,* 1957, 26, 116–120.

Ackerman, N. W. *The psychodynamics of family life.* New York: Basic Books, 1958.

Adorno, T. W., Frenkel-Brunswick, Else, Levinson, D., & Sanford, R. N. *The authoritarian personality.* New York: Harper, 1950.

Auerbach, Aline B. What can parents gain from group experience? In Child Study Association of America, *Helping parents of handicapped children—* Group approaches. New York: Child Study Assoc. of Amer., 1959, pp. 15–24.

Ausubel, D. P. Relationship between shame and guilt in the socializing process. *Psychol. Rev.,* 1955, 62, 378–390.

Baldwin, A. L., Kalhorn, J., & Breese, F. H. Patterns of parent behavior. *Psychol. Monogr.,* 1945, 58, No. 3 (Whole No. 268).

Barbe, W. B. Helping gifted children. *Gifted child Quart.,* 1959, 3, 4–9, 16.

Barsch, R. Explanations offered by parents and siblings of brain-damaged children. *Except. Child.,* 1961, 27, 286–291.

Baum, Marian H. Some dynamic factors affecting family adjustment to the handicapped child. *Except. Child.,* 1962, 28, 387–392.

Beck, Helen L. Counseling parents of retarded children. *Children,* 1959, 6, 225–230.

Begab, M. Factors in counseling parents of retarded children. *Amer. J. ment. Def.,* 1956, 60, 515–525.

Behrens, Marjorie L. Child rearing and the character structure of the mother. *Child Develpm.,* 1954, 25, 225–238.

Bell, N. W., & Vogel, E. F. (Eds.) *A modern introduction to the family.* Glencoe, Ill.: Free Press, 1960.

Bibring, Grete L., Dwyer, T. F., Huntingdon, Dorothy S., & Valenstein, A. F. A study of the psychological processes in pregnancy and the earliest mother-child relationship. *Psychoan. Stud. Child,* 1961, 16, 9–72.

Blanchard, P. Interpreting psychological data to parents. *J. consult. Psychol.,* 1940, 4, 120–123.

Blum, G. S. *Psychoanalytic theories of personality.* New York: McGraw-Hill, 1953.

Boles, G. Personality factors in mothers of cerebral palsied children. *Genet. Psychol. Monogr.,* 1959, 59, 159–218.

Brim, O. G., Jr. The parent-child relation as a social system: I. parent and child roles. *Child Develpm.,* 1957, 28, 343–364.

Brody, Sylvia. *Patterns of mothering: maternal influences during infancy.* New York: Int. Univer. Press, 1956.

Bronfenbrenner, U. Toward a theoretical model for the analysis of parent-child relationships in a social context. In Glidewell, J. C. (Ed.) *Parental attitudes and child behavior.* Springfield, Ill.: Thomas, 1961, pp. 90–109.

Burchinal, L. G., Hawkes, G. R., & Gardner, B. Marriage adjustment, personality characteristics of parents and the personality adjustment of their children. *Marriage Fam. Living,* 1957, 19, 366–372.

Caldwell, Bettye, & Guze, S. A study of adjustment of parents and siblings of institutionalized and non-institutionalized retarded children. *Amer. J. ment. Def.,* 1960, 64, 845–861.

Casler, L. Maternal deprivation: a critical review of the literature. *Monogr. Soc. Res. Child Develpm.*, 1961, 26, No. 2.

Chance, Erika. Measuring pathogenic family relationships. *Int. J. soc. Psychiat.*, 1958, 4, 10–17.

Children's Bureau. U. S. Department of Health, Education, and Welfare. *Emotional problems associated with handicapping conditions in children.* Children's Bureau Publication No. 336. Washington, D. C.: Children's Bureau, 1952.

Clothier, F. Some aspects of the problem of adoption. *Amer. J. Orthopsychiat.*, 1939, 9, 598–615.

Clothier, F. The psychology of the adopted child. *Ment. Hyg.*, 1943, 27, 222–230.

Cohen, Pauline C. The impact of the handicapped child on the family. *Soc. Casewk.*, 1962, 43, 137–142.

Coughlin, E. W. Parental attitudes toward handicapped children. *Child*, 1947, 2, 11.

Crandall, V. J., & Preston, Anne. Patterns and levels of maternal behavior. *Child Develpm.*, 1955, 26, 267–277.

Cruickshank, W. M., & Johnson, G. O. (Eds.) *Education of exceptional children and youth.* Englewood Cliffs, N. J.: Prentice-Hall, 1958.

Cummings, S. T., & Stock, Dorothy. Brief group therapy of mothers of retarded children outside the specialty clinic setting. *Amer. J. ment. Def.*, 1962, 66, 739–748.

Davids, A., DeVault, S., & Talmadge, M. Anxiety, pregnancy, and childbirth abnormalities. *J. consult. Psychol.*, 1961, 25, 74–77.

Deutsch, Helene. *The psychology of women.* (2 vols.) New York: Grune & Stratton, 1944–1945.

Doll, E. A. Counseling parents of severely mentally retarded children. *J. clin. Psychol.*, 1953, 9, 114–117.

Donnelly, E. M. The quantitative analysis of parent behavior toward psychotic children and their siblings. *Genet. Psychol. Monogr.*, 1960, 62, 331–376.

Dunlap, J. M. The education of children with high mental ability. In W. M. Cruickshank and G. O. Johnson (Eds.) *Education of exceptional children and youth.* Englewood Cliffs, N. J.: Prentice-Hall. 1958, pp. 147–188.

Edwards, A. L. *Edwards personal preference schedule, manual.* New York: Psychological Corp., 1954.

Eiduson, Bernice T., & Livermore, Jean B. Complications in therapy with adopted children. *Amer. J. Orthopsychiat.*, 1953, 23, 795–800.

Ericson, Martha C. Child-rearing and social status. *Amer. J. Sociol.*, 1946, 52, 190–192.

Escalona, Sibylle, Leitch, Mary *et al.* Early phases of personality development: a non-normative study of infant behavior. *Monogr. Soc. Res. Child Develpm.*, 1953, 17, 1.

Ewert, Josephine C., & Green, M. W. Conditions associated with the mother's estimate of the ability of her retarded child. *Amer. J. ment. Def.*, 1957–58, 62, 521–533.

Farber, B. Effects of a severely mentally retarded child on family integration. *Monogr. Soc. Res. Child Develm.*, 1959, 24, 2.

Forbes, Lorna M. Some psychiatric problems related to mental retardation. *Amer J. ment. Def.*, 1958, 62, 637–641.

Frankiel, Rita V. *A review of research on parent influences on child personality.*

New York: Family Service Assoc. of Amer., 1959.

Freedman, A. M., Helme, W., Havel, Joan, Eustis, Marjorie J., Riley, C., & Langford, W. S. Psychiatric aspects of familial dysautonomia. *Amer. J. Orthopsychiat.*, 1957, 27, 96–104.

Freud, Anna. *The ego and the mechanisms of defense.* New York: Int. Univer. Press, 1946.

Freud, S. Mourning and melancholia. In *Collected papers*, Vol. IV. London: Hogarth Press, 1949, pp. 152–170.

Fries, Margaret E., & Woolf, P. J. Some hypotheses on the role of the congenital activity type in personality development. In Eissler, Ruth S. *et al.* (Eds.) *The psychoanalytic study of the child:* Vol. 8. New York: Int. Univer. Press, 1953, 48–62.

Gardner, W. I., & Nisonger, H. W. A manual on program development in mental retardation. *Amer. J. ment. Def. Monogr. Suppl.*, 1962, 66, 4.

Garrett, Annette. *Interviewing; its principles and methods.* New York: Family Service Assoc., 1942.

Gildea, Margaret C. L., Glidewell, J. C., & Kantor, Mildred B. Maternal attitudes and general adjustment in school children. In Glidewell, J. C. (Ed.) *Parental attitudes and child behavior,* Springfield, Ill.: Thomas, 1961, pp. 42–89.

Goldfarb, W. The mutual impact of mother and child in childhood schizophrenia. *Amer. J. Orthopsychiat.*, 1961, 31, 738–747.

Gordon, J. E. The validity of Shoben's parent attitude survey. *J. clin. Psychol.*, 1957, 13, 154–156.

Grace, H. A., & Booth, Nancy L. Is the "gifted" child a social isolate? *Peabody J. Educ.*, 1958, 35, 195–196.

Graliker, Betty V., Fishler, Karol, & Koch, R. Teenage reaction to a mentally retarded sibling. *Amer. J. ment. Def.*, 1962, 66 (6), 838–843.

Green, R. Treatment of parent-child relationships. *Amer. J. Orthopsychiat.*, 1948, 18, 442–446.

Guertin, W. H. Are differences in schizophrenic symptoms related to the mother's avowed attitudes toward child rearing? *J. abnorm. soc. Psychol.*, 1961, 63, 440–442.

Hamilton, Gordon. *Theory and practice of social case work.* (2nd Ed., rev.) New York: Columbia Univer. Press, 1951.

Hess, R. D., & Handel, G. Patterns of aggression: parents and their children. *J. genet. Psychol.*, 1956, 89, 199–212.

Holt, K. S. The home care of severely retarded children. *Pediatrics*, 1958, 22, 746–755.

Hunt, J. McV. *Intelligence and experience.* New York: Ronald Press, 1961.

Irwin, O. C. The amount and nature of activities of newborn infants under constant external stimulating conditions during the first ten days of life. *Genet. Psychol. Monogr.*, 1930, 8, 1–92.

Jensen, R. A. Counseling with parents at time of first knowledge of retardation. In Woods Schools for Exceptional Children, *Counseling parents of children with mental handicaps.* (Proceedings of the 33rd Spring Conference). Langhorne, Pa.: Woods Schools, 1958.

Kanner, L. Parents' feelings about retarded children. *Amer. J. ment. Def.*, 1953, 57, 375–383.

Katz, A. H. *Parents of the handicapped.* Springfield, Ill.: Thomas, 1961.

Kirk, H. D. A dilemma of adoptive parenthood: incongruous role obligations.

Marriage fam. Liv., 1959, 21, 316–328.

Klatskin, Ethelyn H. Shifts in child care practices in three social classes under an infant care program of flexible methodology. *Amer. J. Orthopsychiat.*, 1952, 22, 52–61.

Klebanoff, L. B. Parents of schizophrenic children: I. Parental attitudes of mothers of schizophrenic, brain-injured and retarded, and normal children. *Amer. J. Orthopsychiat.*, 1959, 29, 445–454.

Lakin, M. Assessment of significant role attitudes in primiparous mothers by means of a modification of the TAT. *Psychosom. Med.*, 1957, 19, 50–60.

Laycock, S. R. Helping parents to accept their exceptional children. *Except. Child.*, 1951–52, 18, 129–132, 160.

Leton, D. A. A study of the validity of parent attitude measurement. *Child Develpm.*, 1958, 29, 515–520.

Levy, D. M. *Maternal overprotection.* New York: Columbia University Press, 1943.

Lewin, K. Psychology and the process of group living. *J. soc. Psychol.* 1943, 17, 113–131.

Lidz, T., Fleck, S., Cornelison, Alice, & Terry, Dorothy. The intrafamilial environment of the schizophrenic patient: IV. Parental personalities and family interaction. *Amer J. Orthopsychiat.*, 1958, 28, 764–776.

Macauley, E. Portrait studies of some exceptional children. *Forum Educ.*, 1927, 5, 27–36.

Madoff, J. M. The attitudes of mothers of juvenile delinquents toward child rearing. *J. consult. Psychol.*, 1959, 23, 518–520.

Mahoney, S. C. Observations concerning counseling with parents of mentally retarded children. *Amer. J. ment. Def.*, 1958, 63, 81–86.

Margolies, Jeannette A., & Wortis, Helen Z. Parents of children with cerebral palsy. *J. Child Psychiat.*, 1956, 3, 105–114.

Margolis, M. The mother-child relationship in bronchial asthma. *J. abnorm. soc. Psychol.*, 1961, 63, 360–367.

Martin, W. E. Effects of early training on personality. *Marriage Fam. Liv.*, 1957, 19, 39–45.

Masland, R. L., Sarason, S. B., & Gladwin, T. *Mental subnormality;* biological, psychological, and cultural factors. New York: Basic Books, 1958.

Mayer, Greta, & Hoover, Mary. *When children need special help with emotional problems.* New York: Child Study Association of America, 1961.

Mednick, S. A., & Shaffer, J. B. P. Mothers' retrospective reports in child-rearing research. *Amer. J. Orthopsychiat.*, 1963, 33, 457–461.

Merrill, Barbara A. A measurement of mother-child interaction. *J. abnorm. soc. Psychol.*, 1946, 41, 37–49.

Michaels, J., & Schucman, Helen. Observations on the psychodynamics of parents of retarded children. *Amer. J. ment. Def.*, 1962, 66, 568–573.

Michal-Smith, H., & Kastein, S. *The special child, diagnosis, treatment, habilitation.* Seattle: New school for the special child, 1962.

Miller, Elsa A. Cerebral palsied children and their parents. *Except. Child.*, 1958, 24, 298–302, 305.

Morrow, W. R., & Wilson, R. C. Family relations of bright high-achieving and under-achieving high schools boys. *Child Develpm.*, 1961, 32, 501–510.

Munroe, Ruth L. *Schools of psychoanalytic thought.* New York: Dryden, 1955.

Murray, (Mrs.) Max. Needs of parents of mentally retarded children. *Amer. J. ment. Def.*, 1959, 63, 1078–1088.

Mussen, P. H., Conger, J. J., & Kagan, J. *Child development and personality.* New York: Harper & Row, 1963.

McCandless, B. R. *Children and adolescents.* New York: Holt, Rinehart & Winston, 1961.

Norris, Miriam, Spaulding, Patricia J., & Brodie, Fern H. *Blindness in children.* Chicago: Univer. of Chicago Press, 1957.

Orlansky, H. Infant care and personality. *Psychol. Bull.,* 1949, 46, 1–48.

Parsons, T., & Bales, R. F. *Family, socialization and interaction process.* Glencoe, Ill.: Free Press, 1955.

Parsons, T., & Fox, Renee C. Illness, therapy, and the modern urban American family. In Bell, N. W., & Vogel, E. F. (Eds) *A modern introduction to the family.* Glencoe, Ill.: Free Press, 1960, pp. 347–360.

Patterson, Letha L. Some pointers for professionals. *Children,* 1956, 3, 13–17.

Peterson, D. R., Becker, W. C., Shoemaker, D. J., & Hunter, L. A. Child behavior problems and parental attitudes. *Child Develpm.,* 1961, 1, 151–162.

Plotsky, H., & Shereshefsky, Pauline M. An isolation pattern in fathers of emotionally disturbed children. *Amer. J. Orthopsychiat.,* 1960, 30, 780–787.

Radke, M. J. The relation of parental authority to children's behavior and attitudes. *Univ. of Minnesota Institute of Child Welfare Monograph,* 1946, Series No. 22.

Reid, Eleanor S. Helping parents of handicapped children. *Children,* 1958, 5, 15–19.

Ricketts, Betty M. *Child placement and its effects on the family.* Unpublished thesis, Smith Coll. School for Social Work, 1958.

Rogers, C. R. The characteristics of a helping relationship. *Personnel Guid. J.,* 1958, 37, 6–16.

Rose, J. A. Factors in the development of mentally handicapped children. In Woods Schools for Exceptional Children, *Counseling parents of children with mental handicaps.* (Proceedings of the 33rd Spring Conference). Langhorne, Pa.: Woods Schools, 1958.

Rosenthal, M. J., Finkelstein, M., Ni, E., & Robertson, R. E. A study of mother-child relationships in the emotional disorders of children. *Genet. Psychol. Monogr.,* 1959, 60, 65–116.

Ross, A. O. A schizophrenic child and his mother. *J. abnorm. soc. Psychol.,* 1955, 51, 133–139.

Ross, A. O. *The practice of clinical child psychology.* New York: Grune & Stratton, 1959.

Roucek, J. S. (Ed.) *The unusual child.* New York: Philosophical Library, 1962.

Sarason, S. B. The psychology of the exceptional child. In Woods Schools, *Helping parents understand the exceptional child.* (Proceedings of the Annual Spring Conference). Langhorne, Pa.: Woods Schools, 1952.

Sarason, S. B. *Psychological problems in mental deficiency* (2nd ed.). New York: Harper, 1953.

Schaefer, E. S. A circumplex model for maternal behavior. *J. abnorm. soc. Psychol.,* 1959, 59, 226–235.

Schaefer, E. S. Converging conceptual models for maternal behavior and for child behavior. In Glidewell, J. C. (Ed.) *Parental attitudes and child behavior.* Springfield, Ill.: Thomas, 1961.

Schaefer, E. S., & Bell, R. Q. Patterns of attitudes toward child rearing and the family. *J. abnorm. soc. Psychol.,* 1957, 54, 391–395.

Schaefer, E. S., & Bell, R. Q. Development of a parental attitude research instrument. *Child Develpm.*, 1958, 29, 339–361.

Schechter, M. D. Observations on adopted children. *Arch. gen. Psychiat.*, 1960, 3, 21–32.

Scheidemann, Norma V. *The psychology of exceptional children.* Vol I. Boston: Houghton Mifflin, 1931.

Schmideberg, Melitta. Multiple origins and functions of guilt. *Psychiat. quart.*, 1956, 30, 1–7.

Schulman, J. L., & Stern, Shiela. Parents' estimate of the intelligence of retarded children. *Amer. J. ment. Def.*, 1959, 63, 696–698.

Sears, R. R., Maccoby, Eleanor E., & Levin, H. *Patterns of child rearing.* Evanston, Ill.: Row, Peterson, 1957.

Sewel, W. H., & Mussen, P. H. The effects of feeding, weaning, and scheduling procedures on childhood adjustment and the formation of oral symptoms. *Child Develpm.*, 1952, 23, 185–191.

Sheimo, S. L. Problems in helping parents of mentally defective and handicapped children. *Amer. J. ment. Def.*, 1951, 56, 42–47.

Shere, Marie O. Socio-emotional factors in families of the twin with cerebral palsy. *Except. Child*, 1956, 22, 197–199; 206–208.

Shirley, M. M. The first two years, a study of twenty-five babies: Vol. III. Personality manifestations. *Inst. Child Welfare Monogr. Ser.* No. 8. Minneapolis: Univer.. Minnesota Press, 1933.

Shirley, M. M. A behavior syndrome characterizing prematurely-born children. *Child Develpm.*, 1939, 10, 115–128.

Shoben, E. J., Jr. The assessment of parental attitudes in relation to child adjustment. *Genet. Psychol. Monogr.*, 1949, 39, 101–148.

Smith, Emily A., Ricketts, Betty M., & Smith, Sarah H. The recommendation for child placement by a psychiatric clinic. *Amer. J. Orthopsychiat.*, 1962, 32, 42–50.

Solnit, A. J., & Stark, Mary H. Mourning and the birth of a defective child. *Psychoanal. Stud. Child*, 1961, 16, 523–537.

Spiegel, J. P. The resolution of role conflict within the family. *Psychiatry*, 1957, 20, 1–16.

Spock, B. *On being a parent—of a handicapped child.* Chicago: Natl. Soc. Crippled Child. & Adults, 1961.

Stoddard, Hilda M. The relation of parental attitudes and achievements of severely mentally retarded children. *Amer. J. ment. Def.*, 1959, 63, 575–598.

Stone, Marguerite M. Parental attitudes to retardation. *Amer. J. ment. Def.*, 1948, 53, 363–372.

Sweeny, Dolores M., Gasbarro, Diana T., & Gluck, M. R. A descriptive study of adopted children seen in a child guidance center. *Child Welfare*, 1963, 42, 345–349.

Symonds, P. M. *The psychology of parent-child relationships.* New York: Appleton-Century, 1939.

Thorne, F. C., & Andrews, J. S. Unworthy parental attitudes toward mental defectives. *Amer. J. ment. Def.*, 1946, 50, 411–418.

Tindall, R. H., & Robinson, F. P. The use of silence as a technique in counseling. *J. clin. Psychol.*, 1947, 3, 136–141.

Tisza, Veronica B. Management of the parents of the chronically ill child. *Amer. J. Orthopsychiat.*, 1962, 32, 53–59.

Torrance, E. P. *Guiding creative talent*. Englewood-Cliffs, N. J : Prentice-Hall, 1962.

Vogel, E. F., & Bell, N. W. The emotionally disturbed child as the family scapegoat. In Bell, N. W., & Vogel, E. F. (Eds.) *A modern introduction to the family*. Glencoe, Ill.: Free Press, 1960, pp. 382–397.

Wall, B. D. Rapport: an outmoded concept. *Ment. Hyg.*, 1958, 42, 340–342.

Wardell, Winifred. Case work with parents of mentally deficient children. *Amer. J. ment. Def.*, 1947, 52, 91–97.

Watson, R. I. *Psychology of the child*. New York: Wiley, 1959.

Weingold, J. T., & Hormuth, R. P. Group guidance of parents of mentally retarded children. *J. clin Psychol.*, 1953, 9, 118–124.

Wenar, C. The reliability of mothers' histories. *Child Develpm.*, 1961, 32, 491–500.

White, R. W. Motivation reconsidered: the concept of competence. *Psychol. Rev.*, 1959, 66, 297–333.

White, R. W. Competence and the psychosexual stages of development. In Jones, M. R., (Ed.), *Nebraska symposium on motivation*, 1960. Lincoln, Neb.: Univers. Nebraska Press, 1960.

Whiting, J. W. M., & Child, I. L. *Child training and personality: a cross-cultural study*. New Haven: Yale Univer. Press, 1953.

Wickman, K. M., & Langford, W. S. The parent in the children's psychiatric clinic. *Amer. J. Orthopsychiat.*, 1944, 14, 219–225.

Woods School for Exceptional Children. Symposium *Heuristic hypotheses about the variant child in our culture*. Proceedings of symposium held at Woods School May 17, 1961.

Worchel, Tillie, L., & Worchel, P. The parental concept of the mentally retarded child *Amer. J. ment. Def.*, 1961, 65, 782–788.

Zuckerman, M., Barrett, Beatrice H., & Bragiel, R. M. The parental attitudes of parents of child guidance cases: I. comparisons with normals, investigations of socio-economic and family constellation factors, and relation to parents' reactions to the clinic. *Child Develpm.*, 1960, 31, 401–417.

Zuckerman, M., Norton, J., & Sprague, D. S. Acquiescence and extreme sets and their role in tests of authoritarianism and parental attitudes. *Psychiat. Res. Rep.*, 1958, 10, 28–45.

Zuckerman, M., & Oltean, Mary. Some relationships between maternal attitude factors and authoritarianism, personality needs, psychopathology, and self-acceptance. *Child Develpm.*, 1959, 30, 27–36.

Zuckerman, M., Ribback, Beatrice, Monashkin, I., & Norton, J. Normative data and factor analysis on the parental attitude research instrument. *J. consult. Psychol.*, 1958, 22, 165–171.

Zuk, G. H. The religious factor and the role of guilt in parental acceptance of the retarded child. *Amer. J. ment. Def.*, 1959, 64, 139–147.

Zuk, G. H. The cultural dilemma and spiritual crisis of the family with a handicapped child. *Except Child*, 1962, 28, 405–408.

Zuk, G. H., Miller, R. L., Bartram, J. B., & Kling, F. Maternal acceptance of retarded children: a questionnaire study of attitudes and religious background. *Child Develpm.*, 1961, 32, 525–540.

Zwerling, I. Initial counseling of parents with retarded children. *J. Pediat.*, 1954, 44, 469–479.

Index of Names

Index of Subjects